I0748461

Writing the Afro-Hispanic

Essays on Africa and Africans in the Spanish Caribbean

Published by
Adonis & Abbey Publishers Ltd
P.O. Box 43418
London
SE11 4XZ, United Kingdom
Email: editor@adonis-abbey.com
Website: http://www.adonis-abbey.com

Nigeria:
Adonis & Abbey Publishing Co.
P.O. Box 10546, Abuja
Email: editor@adonis-abbey.com
Website: http://www.adonis-abbey.com

First Edition, January 2012

British Library Cataloguing-in-Publication Data
A catalogue record for this book is available from the British Library

ISBN 978-1-906704-88-9

Cover Design: Asia Ifitkar

Writing the Afro-Hispanic

Essays on Africa and Africans in the Spanish Caribbean

Edited by Conrad James

Table of Contents

Acknowledgements

I would like to thank all the contributors for their knowledge, enthusiasm and, in many cases, their patience. I would also like to thank my colleague and friend Dr Stewart Brown of the Centre of West African Studies of the University of Birmingham for his generous support of this project and for facilitating, over the years, numerous opportunities at Birmingham for students and staff to think through the relationships between Africa and the Caribbean. Finally, I wish to thank Paul Humphrey and Humberto Rafael Campos for their tireless practical support in putting this manuscript together.

Introduction

Conrad James

Emerging in the late 1970s, Afro-Hispanism has now been consolidated as a discipline within the US academy. The political history of the field is complex but two of the most pivotal moments in the initiation of Afro-Hispanic Studies as a serious field of enquiry were the publication of Richard L. Jackson's *The Black Image in Latin American Literature* (1976) and the launching of the *Afro-Hispanic Review* in 1982 by Howard University professor Ian Isidore Smart and the late Stanley Cyrus (1940 – 1997). Jackson has continued to produce and encourage ground-breaking research on Blacks in the Spanish speaking world and the *Afro-Hispanic Review*, now housed at Vanderbilt University, has distinguished itself as one of the leading journals focussed on African diaspora experience and production. The Afro-Romance Institute the University of Missouri Columbia, from where Marvin Lewis and Edward Mullen edited the *Afro-Hispanic Review* before it was transferred to Vanderbilt, continues to guarantee the growth of the discipline through the publication of seminal scholarly work on the Afro-Hispanic world and through the preparation and training of a new generation of Afro-Hispanist scholars some of whom have contributed to this collection of essays.

That the field has come of age there is no doubt. Today in historically black colleges as well as in Ivy League institutions it is possible to encounter black Latin American topics in both undergraduate and graduate courses. Troublingly though, Afro-Hispanism is still perceived, rightly or wrongly, as a North American discipline. While the study of Black Latin American cultures is pursued in Europe and the United Kingdom, for example, there is very little sense of the Afro-Hispanic as constituting an existing or viable field here. Clearly the implication and, indeed, the desirability of this involve the discussion of a range of demographic, socio-political and institutional imperatives that are beyond the scope of this introduction. However this volume sets out to contribute to the conversation on the stories of Black Latin Americans in essays engaging with their lives in Cuba, The Dominican Republic, Puerto Rico, Colombia and Mexico. Acknowledging, celebrating, extending, questioning and critiquing the views of earlier scholars these essays address a variety of concerns with which the field has grappled since its inception.

Claudette Williams's essay addresses one of the most significant aspects of the body of writing on Africa and Africans produced in the Spanish Caribbean, nineteenth-century Cuban antislavery fiction. A well plumbed field, antislavery fiction has been a site to which many Afro-Hispanist scholars have turned in order to explore and expose the ideological duplicity of the white creole literati in nineteenth-century Cuban slave society. Despite their proclaimed liberal position on slavery, the producers of antislavery fiction have remained rather suspect for most critics. Coming as they did from the very bosom of the slave owning classes, neither their motive nor their message has generally been trusted by the largely black affirmative scholarly enterprises which have explored their texts. Thus the criticism on this body of work invariably points to the persistent 'negative image' of blacks which they encode and the political disingenuousness which this discourse constitutes.

Williams acknowledges the 'intractable Eurocentric racism in their perceptions of Africa' which dogs the imagination of these authors and their narrative discourse. However, applying a postmodern sensibility, she distances herself from the prevailing dismissive critical approach to these texts and produces a reading which accommodates equally the pitfalls as well as the achievements of landmark antislavery efforts such as Anselmo Suárez y Romero's *Francisco* (1839), Gertrudis Gómez de Avellaneda's *Sab* (1841), Francisco Calgano's *Romualdo: uno de tantos* (1869) and Antonio Zambrana's *El negro Francisco* (1875). Through close reading of the narratives Williams unearths key textual evidence to show convincingly that embedded in them are details which, when viewed in diachronic perspective, might be understood as precursors to contemporary themes in postcolonial discourse on slavery. Accordingly, by charting Zambrana's exposé of the capacity for and mechanisms of slave sabotage and Calgano's understanding of the maroons as agents of cultural change, in addition to the multiple nuances explored in the fiction of Suárez y Romero and Avellaneda, this essay ascribes new meaning to the way these authors imagined Africa in antislavery narrative.

If the Cuban antislavery fiction discussed by Williams was written exclusively by whites, Miguel Barnet's The *Autobiography of a Runaway Slave* (*Biografía de un cimarrón*) (1968) claims to present the phenomena of slavery, marronage, the Cuban War of Independence against Spain and the triumph of that process from the perspective of the formerly enslaved African, Esteban Montejo. Published in the heyday of revolutionary zeal, this piece of testimonial fiction fulfilled the revisionist criterion of rewriting the history of the nation from the perspective of the formerly marginalised (in this case black slave) while at the same time remaining within the established parameters of permissible cultural production established by the Castro regime. Not surprisingly, much of the criticism of *The Autobiography of a Runaway Slave* has centred on the tension between its supposed claims of authenticity and the necessity to create an ideologically correct product. A related concern of many commentators has been the paradoxical superseding of aspects of Montejo's story by Barnet's intellectual/political agenda in a project which purports to give voice to the subaltern subject.

Both Miguel Arnedo and Mario Chandler offer fresh perspectives on the Barnet/Montejo narrative. Arnedo takes up the discussion on the authenticity and reliability of the text that has been the abiding preoccupation of many critics. Aided by an engagement with previous work on the subject by Beverly and Zimmerman (1990) Sklodowska (1992), Lienhard (1994, 1996) and Denegri (2003) among others, he too concludes that Barnet's unacknowledged mediating role coupled with the ideological contradictions of producing such a text within revolutionary Cuba of the 1960s seriously undermines any claims to total authenticity. But Arnedo's essay goes beyond this problematic to expand his reading of the text by exploring it as an occasion of what Angel Rama refers to as narrative transculturation. Not previously considered as such, for Arnedo, *Autobiography of a Runaway Slave* is a transcultural text par excellence. While it is true that the informant's voice is at times censored due to a range of political exigencies, the relationship between the two is not as completely linear as most commentaries suggest. Sometimes Montejo's voice is shown to be in conflict with Barnet's and at other times they fuse harmoniously. Similarly to García Márquez's use of the magico-religious elements from Colombian popular culture to inform the narrative point of view in *Cien años de soledad* (*One Hundred Years of Solitude*), Arnedo argues, Barnet has 'consciously used Afro-Cuban popular culture as a guiding formal principle in the narration'.

One of the misgivings Arnedo has concerns Barnet's claim that Esteban Montejo's story might be seen as representative of a class of people who have experienced key moments in Cuban history. For him Montejo is an odd choice to represent Cuban blacks or Cuban slaves. Chandler's engagement with the text also has implications for the question of representativeness. What is clear from his discussion is that, whether consciously or unconsciously, *Autobiography of a Runaway Slave* dispels concepts of African cultural homogeneity through Esteban Montejo's own differentiation between the lucumí (Cuban Yorubas) and the Congolese blacks who for him lack courage and the requisite rebellious nature. Chandler's main interest in the text, however, lies in Montejo's revelation of a tenacious hold on his African roots and his simultaneous observance of a series of diasporan taboos. Esteban Montejo depicts what has come to be seen as a commonplace in postcolonial identity politics, the psychological journey of the fractured and disempowered new world subject to the source of origin in order to reconstitute a sense of self. Barnet's informant demonstrates this, according to Chandler, through the careful provision of details concerning his paternal (African) ancestry and Chandler contends that the speaker's identification with Africa informs his spirit and practice of rebellion in Caribbean plantation society.

Among the diasporan taboos that Chandler's essay discusses is the question of homosexuality in Cuba. Homoeroticism, acts of homosexuality and the assumption of homosexual identities form part of the range of non-normative male-male psycho-sexual interaction to which Montejo refers in his testimonial. The informant's attitude to the subject might best be described as uneven; a putative liberal disposition is ultimately undermined by his careful narrative distancing of himself and more seriously his cultural distancing of Africa from the subject matter. Sodomy is a non-African new world condition he seems to suggest. Esteban Montejo equates homosexuality with effeminate weakness and Chandler concludes that precisely because of this association with femininity the taboo of homosexuality comes to signify the antithesis of the 'rugged, independent *cimarrón*' that he presents himself as in this story of his life.

Issues of masculinity and femininity are integral to the terrain which Conrad James's essay on the poetry of Nicolás Guillén explores. Race and national identity have been and continue to be the major focal points of most critical attention to Guillén's poetry. Within the Afro-Hispanist interpretative tradition in particular, very scant attention has been paid to the multiplicity of other concerns that might be gleaned from Guillén's literary legacy. Of course, as with all fields of cultural enquiry, scholarship on Guillén over the last couple of decades has increasingly paid attention to questions of gender. James's essay addresses the need for further interrogation of his poetry along these lines. Revisiting poems from some of Guillén's early collections *Motivos de son* (1930) and *Sóngoro cosongo* (1931) James's reading highlights some of the contradictory attitudes towards black and mulatto women which feature in his poetry at this stage. Women, he argues, are both liberated and constrained by Guillén's poetic practice. Perhaps more significantly, key poems from *Motivos de son* are interpreted here as essentially essays on black male psychosis. James's essay also points up what he sees as a crisis in the early critical practice that developed around the poetry of Guillén. Black Nationalist priorities override all other forms of identity politics in the work of many of the early commentators. But their elision of gender or apologies for Guillén's undermines their own agenda James argues. The essay concludes by pointing to some of Guillén's later poetry, much of it written for private consumption and as yet unexplored in these terms, as being the most complex in terms of their construction of women and by implication their understanding of wider dynamics of gender.

In some of Guillén's early poetry the voiceless black female body appears as a metaphor for a celebrated pristine African culture. This image is complicated in later collections as the admired black woman is presented as a composite of mind and body in which the invested voice is used for self representation and communal empowerment. The significance of the speaking black female subject is germane to the thesis which Emily Maguire presents on the Cuban declaimer and actress Eusebia Cosme (1911 – 1976). Between 1930 and 1957 Eusebia Cosme performed a one woman show interpreting a range of poetry which featured a central theme of a black racialized identity. Cosme's performances, which eventually took place internationally in Europe, Latin America and the United States, were significant, Maguire argues, because they brought together 'the work of poets whose ideologies and aesthetic approaches to blackness did not always coincide'. One clear strand that runs through some of the *negrista* poetry from which she drew her repertoire is the objectification of the often exoticized black or mulatto woman who invariably is conjured as body parts rather than a whole being. Maguire's argument is that the vocal presence of the declaimer, rather than consolidating stereotypes, visibly contested the objectification of the female in these texts. But despite her vocalized agency as a black Cuban woman developed and perfected over a long career, it would seem that the anxieties of some of the male authors of Cuban national discourse propelled them to either relegate her to invisibility despite her public presence (Fernando Ortiz) or use her as an example simply to further their preferred ideological constructs of Cuba as a site of transcultural harmony (Nicolás Guillén). Despite this, contends Maguire, Eusebia Cosme's career as declaimer and cultural translator becomes an instance which disrupts the homosociality of the national discourse inscribed in some of the very poems she performed.

The politics of race and nation are major concerns for Lourdes Martínez-Echazábal whose essay revisits the development of black consciousness and its associated intellectual production that emerged in the 1960s. The socio-political events of this period, which for her begins as early as 1952, have had profound repercussions, she reminds us, and were to become seminal in the redefinition of key ideologies and social institutions in the west. Martínez-Echazábal highlights the fact that despite its global reach it would be a mistake to conceive of the 1960s in monolithic terms. The largely progressive leftist struggles which have come to define the period occurred in parallel with reactionary tyranny in some places. She thus revisits the Cuban 1960s and their attendant racial/cultural politics within their own 'local specifications and instantiations'. This helps Martínez to explore something of the paradox of the race question in the Cuban 1960s. Throughout the decade and beyond, the Castro regime's symbolic capital had been enhanced significantly by its effectively 'playing the race card' in international affairs. Two examples which are cited are the famous decision Fidel Castro made in 1960 to stay at the Hotel Theresa in Harlem where he met Malcolm X and the sending of a battalion of Black Cubans to fight in Zaire in 1965. Such gestures, Martínez contends have less to do with race than with *realpolitik* and with the Revolution's relentless anti-imperialist attempts to rescue the oppressed. The Cuban 1960s began in political euphoria and ended in Soviet inspired authoritarian dogma widely referred to as 'el quinquenio gris' ('the grey five years'). Even as it established solidarity with black causes internationally Black Cubans at home remained effaced, ostracized and marginalized as domestic policies prioritized class struggles at the expense of race. Building on the longstanding denial of racial prejudice ingrained in Cuban nationalist rhetoric since the 19th century, the Cuban government encroached on Afro-Cuban politics, religion and social practices effectively 'disavowing black civil society' and preventing black political development. The essay poses piercing questions concerning the extent to which these socio-political contradictions regarding race impinged on the first generation of black writers and artists to emerge from the Revolution and concludes that within the Revolution as in previous regimes the Cuban discourse of equality has prevented Black Cubans from attaining full citizenship.

Perhaps the best known and most widely read writer to have emerged out of the first generation of black writers in the Cuban Revolution to which Lourdes Martínez-Echazábal refers is Nancy Morejón (1944 -). In 'Cultural Transnationalism and Contemporary Afro-Caribbean Poetry' Antonio Tillis interrogates Morejón's poetry and that of her Dominican counterpart Blas Jiménez (1949 – 2009) in order to demonstrate the poets' thematization of culture as commodity and the manner in which it might be exchanged, imported or exported. Mindful of the highly contested terrain that constitutes transnationalism and the contingent dangers associated with the appropriations and (mis)appropriations of identity, Tillis suggests that Morejón and Jiménez reflect 'bartered identities' that are an amalgam of a range of contested ideologies which depict the challenges of 'space, time, language and place'. The poets are discussed as global African-descended subjects whose Caribbean creativity bears witness to the multiply contested and reconfigured links between Africa, the Americas and beyond. Reading Morejón's 'Mujer negra' ('Black Woman') and 'Negro' (Black Man') alongside texts from Jiménez's *Caribe africano en despertar* (*Caribbean African Upon Awakening*), Tillis proves that for these writers poetry becomes a creative opportunity to reconcile the national and the transnational; it becomes a key conduit through which they participate in ongoing dialogues concerning human capital, cultural transactions and the complexity of Spanish Caribbean blackness.

Tillis correctly alludes to Blas Jiménez's pioneering role in using poetry as a means of contesting official Dominican racial and cultural categorizations through his relentless writing of the Black Dominican subject. What his work points to is a cultural landscape whose endemic racism is marked by relentless denial of connections with Africa. Of course, Jiménez's poetry also indicates the longstanding presence of an alternative discourse on Africa in the Dominican Republic and the poems thus stage a productive dialectic between denial and affirmation. One aspect of racial prejudice which continues to be under explored in the Dominican Republic concerns the society's attitude towards the descendants of black migrant workers from the Anglophone Caribbean. This is the subject of Lance Cowie's essay 'Cocolos, Emigration and Dominican Narrative'.

The development of the sugar industry in the Dominican Republic in the early nineteenth century required increased manpower in the cutting and harvesting of sugar cane in the factories. The difficulty in obtaining workers resulted in the contracting of migrants from the English speaking Caribbean islands Anguilla, St. Kitts, Antigua, Nevis, Tortola, Barbados and Jamaica where massive unemployment, caused by burgeoning industrialization, facilitated the movement of islanders to the sugar cane fields of the Dominican Republic. The workers settled principally in San Pedro de Macorís and were pejoratively described as 'Cocolos'. Cowie analyzes the history and portrayal of these migrant workers in a number of Dominican texts published between the mid 1930s and the end of the twentieth century. In the process he presents a range of perspectives on their way of life, customs, gastronomy, religious beliefs, education and their impact on the host country. The works discussed by Cowie all communicate the racism, cultural rejection and exploitation of the Cocolos on the Dominican sugar plantations. However the concluding section of the essay which focuses on Avelino Stanley's *Tiempo muerto* (1999) also points to a clear discourse of vindication, an investment in the erasure of reductive stereotypes and a celebration and preservation of the wealth of Cocolo cultural heritage.

The literary vindication of a historically abused and maligned populace is also a feature of the Puerto Rican narratives which Victor Simpson examines in his essay in this volume. *Terrazo* (1947), a collection of short stories by Abelardo Díaz Alfaro (1916 – 1999), is widely discussed in terms of its trenchant resistance to the imposition of North American values on a colonized Puerto Rican society and the resultant clash of cultures which an enforced language (English) and an enforced identity (US) engenders on the island. The thematic corollary to this rejection, a strong defence of the 'jíbaro' (Puerto Rican peasant) and strident outcry at the exploitation he suffers also feature highly in the compendium of critical material on *Terrazo*. Less explored are the stories in the collection which point specifically to Díaz Alfaro's exposure, questioning and denouncement of the exploitation of Puerto Rican blacks which, clearly, predates the North American re-colonization of the island. Simpson centres his discussion on two stories 'Bagazo' and 'El cuento del baquiné' in which the author foregrounds these concerns. The pernicious ubiquity of the sugar cane plantation, the racialization of poverty and power, multiple rituals of conflict and a whole raft of human violations punctuate the narratives. But Simpson's discussion also points to Díaz Alfaro's incorporation of Black Puerto Rican strategies of resistance and rituals of liberation. In giving voice to the experiences of Black Puerto Ricans in these stories, Simpson suggests, this now canonical literary figure was engraving their presence and their validity into the history of a nation out of which they had consistently been excluded.

The last two essays in this volume shift the focus of the discussion from race matters in the Spanish Caribbean islands to engage with related concerns in the Circum-Caribbean region. Alain Lawo-Sukam investigates Afro-Colombian poetry and Marco Polo Hernández-Cuevas discusses the Africanness of Mexican traditional medicine. Despite the so called boom in Latin American literature of the mid twentieth century and the subsequent global interest in authors from the region, many black Latin American writers continued to languish in relative obscurity. Nowhere is this more acutely the case than with writers producing in Colombia where the stratospheric fame of authors such as Gabriel García Márquez and (less so) Álvaro Mutis seems to have blinded critics to the existence of numerous other (mainly black) voices which have been articulating the nation's story from their particular perspective. Lawo-Sukam's essay is an attempt to build on the pioneering work done by Richard Jackson, Marvin Lewis and Laurence Prescott, among others, to bring to light the rich and complex literary production of Colombians of African descent. After providing a brief introduction to the background of Afro-Colombian literature the essay delves into a discussion of some of the main preoccupations of the poets Helcías Martán Góngora (1920-1984) and Guillermo Payán Archer (1921 -). Lawo-Sukam shows that much of their poetry is politically engaged drawing on both secular and sacred Afro-Colombian rituals to reveal an essential dignity and cultural vitality as a means of repairing the distorted images of the community that the dominant society propagates. Beyond politics their work demonstrates keen and moving interest in various aspects of the physical environment and constitutes an example of a neglected Latin American eco poetry.

The fear of blackness, the implementation of both overt and covert strategies of whitening, and a forked tongue discourse on the centrality of racial mixing to the composition of the nation have characterised official attitudes, practices and rhetoric concerning race in Latin America and the Caribbean for centuries. In Mexico, the argument of the disappearance of blacks was forged by *criollos* (American born offspring of Spanish parents), Hernández-Cuevas contends, in order that they might misappropriate patrimonies and obscure the fundamental investment of African cultural capital in the making of what is considered Mexican national identity. It is against this background that he outlines the African characteristics of what is known as traditional medicine in Mexico. Mexican healing practices are not a recent invention. Conducted from the first half of the sixteenth century, they are drawn from holistic African and African diasporic traditions which were 'disfigured through a European discourse which seeks to make them unrecognizable and invalid'. Far from being politically marginal, African healing practices along with song and dance may be placed at the centre of the anti-Spanish discourse that fuelled the initiation of the armed phase of the Mexican War of Independence and led to the birth of the new nation. Not only are Mexican belief systems similar to Cuban *santería* or Brazilian *candomblé* but it is impossible, maintains Hernández-Cuevas, to understand the phenomenon that is Mexico without taking the African components into account.

Together these essays provide a glimpse of both the complexity of the African experience in the Spanish speaking Caribbean and the vital imagined worlds it has spawned. More importantly they point to the serious political issues at stake in conceptualising, reading and writing the Afro-Hispanic.

Chapter 1

Imag(in)ing Africa in Cuban Antislavery Narrative

Claudette Rosegreen-Williams

Antislavery narratives form part of the core of Cuba's nineteenth-century literary tradition. The authors, members of the white Creole intelligentsia for the most part, prided themselves on their liberal views. Their subversive messages run the gamut of literary expression and are communicated through overt means and unobtrusive detail. Yet, not infrequently, an intractable Eurocentric racism in their perceptions of Africa bedevils their attempts at positive self-presentation. This paradox has led many critics to discredit their antislavery efforts. Postmodern thinking, however, allows us to view such a dilemma differently. Where traditional analysis worships at the altar of consistency, unity and coherence, the postmodern sensibility tolerates inconsistency, tension and dispersion; it takes account of shortcoming and positive achievement alike without allowing the one to benefit at the expense of the other. The picture of Africa and Africans presented or implied by the writers under review in the following pages is intelligible in these postmodern terms. Invisibly or explicitly, proslavery discourse is a reference point in their antislavery consciousness. This duality determines their representation of Africa as a fluid space that can conform to different ideological agendas. Evoked by the proslavery imagination as the place to locate savagery and paganism, the likeness of Africa is referenced by antislavery authors as a challenge to the notion of the superiority of European-derived culture.

Anselmo Suárez y Romero's *Francisco* (1839) was the first of Cuba's full-length antislavery novels. Based on his belief that a precedent change in the consciousness of their enslavers would improve the condition of the slaves, Suárez gives his protagonist a profile that implies a make-over of the dominant image of Africa. In slave society, fixing the identity of people of African origin was an almost universal white Creole obsession, born of the Negrophobic desire to establish the supremacy of the white Self over the non-white Other. If one of the effects of this discourse was to normalize the view of the slave as non-human, Suárez responded in his novel by naturalizing his protagonist's humanity, stressing it almost to the point of redundancy. He reverses the 'rigid hierarchy of difference' (Ashcroft et al. 46) by investing civilized values in the 'savage' slave, and this despite the abuse to which he is subjected. With his fine features, proud bearing and innate intelligence, the African-born Francisco stands as a calculated corrective for the equally calculated racist portrait painted by Ricardo the young slave master.

This claim of a common humanity that the slave shares with others notwithstanding, the novelist does not minimize African cultural difference. He offsets the account of the assimilation of the urban house slave into the dominant white Creole culture with the perspective of the unique African cultural retentions in the everyday life of the field slaves. Gordon Lewis (175) includes under the antislavery rubric the ideology immanent in these survivals, which fuelled different types of resistance in the minds and actions of the slaves. In the following anthropological sketch Suárez corrects the misperception of Africa-derived culture as barbarity. The emphasis is on making the unfamiliar intelligible to the uninitiated outsider. It warrants lengthy citation because of the resonances in its rich details:

> Dos negros mozos cogieron los tambores y sin calentarlos siquiera, comenzaron a llamar, como ellos dicen.... La negrada cercó a los tocadores; dos bailan solamente en medio, una negra y un negro; los otros acompañaban palmeando y repitiendo acordes el estribillo.... Los varones iban sacando a las hembras (nosotros diríamos citar); .... y las negras no se esquivaban; jamás desairan a los compañeros, la que se para en el tambor, debe bailar con cualquiera, con el que se le presente, no anda escogiendo como las blancas, no aguarda al novio.... Siempre ajustados los movimientos a los varios compases del tambor, ahora trazaban círculos, la cabeza a un lado, meneando los brazos, la mujer tras el hombre, el hombre tras la mujer, ambos enfrente, pero nunca juntos, nunca cerca .... o poníanse cara a cara, y empezaban a virar, a girar rápidamente, y al volverse abrían los brazos, los extendían, y daban un salto, y sacaban la caja del hacia fuera.... A montones llovían pañuelos y sombreros de los que en torno miraban sobre los diestros bailadores; agotados los pañuelos y sombreros, quien, acaso por congraciarse, tirábales al encuentro un collar ..., a ver cuál lo levantaba

> antes, si el hombre, si la mujer, sin perder el compás (Suárez y Romero 99-101).
>
> Two young Negroes took the drums and without even warming them, began to call, as they say....The Negroes surrounded the drummers. Only two of them dance in the centre, a Negro and a Negress. The others accompanied them by clapping and repeating the chorus.... The men went around taking the women out to dance (we would say asking); .... and the Negresses did not shy away; they never rebuff their male colleagues. The woman who stands up to dance to the drums has to dance with anyone who presents himself; she does not go about choosing like white women do. She doesn't wait for her partner.... The movements always follow the different drum rhythms, sometimes forming circles, heads to one side, arms shaking, the woman behind the man, the man behind the woman, facing each other, but never together, never close... Or they would face each other and begin to spin around, to twirl quickly, and coming back around they would open their arms once again, stretch them out, jump and push their chests forward.... Those who stood around watching the skilful dancers showered then with handkerchiefs and hats and when they ran out of handkerchiefs and hats someone, perhaps to win their favour, would throw them a necklace to see who would pick it up first, the man or the woman, without losing the rhythm.

Suárez's keen observation of African music and dance prefigures the nationalistic interest which such cultural forms were to inspire in later Cuban writers, especially those of the 1920s *negrista* movement. At first glance the scene might appear to originate from a voyeuristic position. Suárez's description is remarkable in its dramatic content. But he describes the performance using a neutral and transparent vocabulary, without the hyperbole, sensationalism and grotesque animal imagery for which the *negrista* writers would become famous. This account also captures the active participation of the spectators with the performers. Given the anti-African tenor of the dominant proslavery worldview at this time in Cuba's history, the absence of any trace of white ethnocentrism in the comparison of the African folk forms to Euro-Creole cultural practice is remarkable. His enlightened vision is a far cry from the jaundiced perspective of the Havana sugar planters who, in 1790, reported to the Spanish king that 'the favourite entertainment of the Negroes is the dance in the barbaric style of their native countries' (La diversión a que se inclinan los negros es el baile al estilo bárbaro de sus patrias) (García 71). One discerns, instead, an approving tone in the language of Suárez's account, suggesting openness to the African roots of the slaves' cultural difference and a will to understand it in their terms.

Suárez displays more than a momentary interest in the African origins of such activities of the slave community. In a detailed exposition of the varied uses of song, he notes the persistence of some African forms:

> Pero hay tonadas que no varían, porque fueron compuestas allá en África y vinieron con los negros de nación; los criollos las aprenden y cantan, así como aquéllos aprenden y cantan las de éstos … Lo singular es que jamás se les olvidan; vienen pequeñuelos, corren años y años, se ponen viejos, y luego, cuando sólo sirven de guardieros, las entonan solitarios en un bohío, … se acuerdan de su patria aún próximos a descender al sepulcro (Suárez y Romero 65).
>
> But there are songs that never change, because they were composed over there in Africa and come with the African-born Negroes. The Creoles learn and sing them, in the same way that the former learn and sing the songs of the latter…. What is remarkable is that they never forget them. They come when they are very young, many years go by, they grow old, and then when they can only serve as watchmen, they sing them alone in some hut .... They remember their home country even when they are one step from the grave.

This description bears witness to two of the processes that slavery entailed for the African: resistance and accommodation. Whereas the emphatic tone used to underline the resilience of this cultural expression translates metaphorically into the slaves' defiance of their bondage, the parenthetical allusion to cultural interchange between African and Creole slaves attests to a concurrent adaptation to the alien environment. Such recognition of the validity and vibrancy of a distinct Africa-derived counter-culture may be interpreted as attribution of a self-constructed cultural identity to the slaves. Its durability is a contrast for Francisco's ephemeral acculturation as a domestic slave. The author's fascination with African song and dance makes unavoidable a comparison with the cultural void in the Euro-Creole world described in the novel.

Africa provides a structural frame for Francisco's life story. It is first evoked through the autobiographical memory of an idyllic homeland from which the young slave protagonist had been plucked. The theme of an idealized Africa makes a strategic reappearance at the end of the novel in Francisco's final thoughts before his death, where his self-identification as a slave and a black son of Africa involves both separation from his imposed New World identity and reconnection with his African roots. Here Suárez promotes the minority Romantic view of Africa found in Western, and especially European, literary discourse. Of greater significance than the obvious mythologizing of the African home, however, is the author's imaginative interpretation of the meaning of slavery to the slave. Understood in a longer view, these details signal an early recognition in colonial Cuban literature of the slave's connection to a vital African past, associated with freedom and personal dignity. This perspective was to become a major theme of postcolonial discourses on slavery. That Suárez lacked the knowledge and language to write about the real Africa does not diminish the importance of his thinking.

Commentaries on Antonio Zambrana's *El negro Francisco* (1875) have concluded that the qualification 'negro' in its title reflects the importance given to the protagonist's ethnicity and allegiance to Africa, and that this is a means of distinguishing his story from Suárez's *Francisco* to which it owes much of its inspiration. Subversion inheres in the Africa-centred construction of the second slave protagonist's identity. Zambrana's Francisco is not characterized as a *bozal* (the derogatory label assigned to slaves from Africa), but is referred to more fittingly as 'negro de nación,' or a native negro, embodying the spirit of African nationalism.

In his bid to rehabilitate the image of the African slave Zambrana portrays Francisco with many of the attributes of the noble savage stereotype. Upon his first entrance Francisco responds without any sign of subservience to the power of the accusatory gaze of his superiors. Angle of vision is carefully chosen to unravel the stereotype of African savagery. From their elevated balcony, slave owners look down on Francisco in the patio below. Yet their gaze is not sufficient to diminish him. Rather, all eyes are drawn, involuntarily, to admire this embodiment of regal pride and defiant dignity. But his portrait goes beyond patronizing Romantic cliché. Zambrana makes strength one of Francisco's defining attributes, even while he avoids the reductive labour value with which it is invested by the economic self-interest of the slave owners. The idea of the slave's endurance transcends the physical mystique. Francisco combines his strength as a warrior with strength of character, muscles of steel with a heart made of granite ('músculos de acero y corazón de granito') (23). Taken in conjunction with the expectation that slavery would have destroyed the soul of the enslaved Africans, this view is consonant with the postcolonial emphasis on the myriad (surreptitious) ways in which slaves subverted the designs of their owners. With the establishment of the protagonist's mental and emotional fortitude the personal overlaps with the political, for Francisco's survival of physical brutality is attributed to the strength of his will. And though it is a despairing act immediately motivated by the frustration of his love for Camila, his suicide also figures as an act of willing his own death: 'Pensó en dejarse morir.' (156).

Zambrana pays greater attention to the Cuban slave's African origins than his predecessor. Transatlantic slavery, in literary accounts and as a matter of historical fact, is primarily the story of Europeans' forced transfer of Africans to the Americas. In his novel Suárez had implied such a scenario for his Francisco, a victim of the foreign predators, many of whom, we now know, waited for parents to leave for work in their fields to kidnap their children. Zambrana's Francisco, on the other hand, is the fictional representative of another group of Africans who were captured in warfare and sold into slavery by their compatriots. This practice has become one of the awkward issues in contemporary debates about slavery. It has been argued that the traffic in slaves brought economic gain to both sides, and some even suggest that it became a reason for war. Some contemporary African historians have attempted to explain away this discomfiting reality by pointing out that in Africa local slavery was 'less ugly' because such slaves would have been assimilated into the master group. In a spirit reminiscent of Fanon's postcolonial thinking, Zambrana, on the other hand, does not shy away from the uncomfortable truth about the slave trade and the slave's African past, even while he is engaged in combatting the racism in Eurocentric discourse on Africa. He construes Francisco's stoicism as a soldier's courageous acceptance of his bondage as part of the rules of the game of war. Making Francisco accept his status as a prisoner-of-war slave amounts to neither justification of his enslavement or disapproval of the African practice. As we are reminded by Orlando Patterson, writing about this category of slaves 'as soldiers, one would hardly expect them to be shocked at being taken prisoners of war' (147).

Zambrana has mastered that fundamental novelistic strategy of allowing the reader to see the world through the eyes and the emotions of a character without sharing that character's vision of the world. So it is that Doña Josefa, the xenophobic slave mistress, articulates the classic defense of slavery as a civilizing project through which Africans were rescued from Africa's 'barbarism.' Moreover, this character uses country of birth to establish a slave hierarchy in which the local-born (Creole) slave takes precedence over the 'negro de nación.' Zambrana, on the other hand, is careful to portray the slaves as a community in which such differences are dissolved. Though only glimpsed, an underlying solidarity among the slaves inheres, for example, in the Creole slaves' acceptance of the African-born Francisco, and in the respect they accord him as the incarnation of their African nationality, the only one to which they could lay claim. This proposal of solidarity between Africa and the New World culminates in the *rapprochement* between Francisco and the mulatto slave Camila.

The love union of the two slaves gives a different slant to the idea of African continuity in the New World. Francisco's initial resentment of Camila's identification with her white heritage and denial of her African connection reverses the anti-black racism displayed by her owners. It also weaves another antislavery thread into the novel's theme. Camila is drawn to Francisco and through him to her African heritage and an antislavery consciousness. Francisco is the raconteur and repository of memories of the African past, which he applies as a potent antidote for his mulatto lover's cultural malaise. This act of reverse acculturation acquires tacit but potent political meaning in a context where European cultural mores were in the ascendancy and suppression of African traditions was an important mechanism for control of the enslaved. Viewed, moreover, against the background of the mulattoes' legendary wish to be white, Camila's choosing to identify with the 'savage' African way is an unheralded snubbing of the dominant Euro-centred ideal. At the same time the fact that Francisco capitulates to Camila hints at endorsement of the *rapprochement* between native Africans and Afro-Creoles, a *sine qua non* of which is the latters' affirmation of their African roots.

Zambrana's issues his stoutest challenge to slavery by eroding the Eurocentric ideology embedded in the language that sustains the institution. His repeated application of the epithet 'savage' to Africans and African culture is central to his portrayal of Francisco. In colonial discourse the word describes not just the person who inhabits a space outside the pale of European civilization, but more specifically the inferior 'other,' deficient in the ways of a superior Western culture. An adequate decoding of the intention behind the author's association of the word with his slave protagonist needs to consider the ways in which it is inflected and to what end. In a manner that is now routine in postmodern writing, Zambrana appropriates the discourse of African savagery but only to simultaneously dissociate himself from its Eurocentric ideology. When after describing the ineffable power of his love for Camila the author concludes 'ese hombre era un negro, era un salvaje, era un esclavo. No importaba' (56) (That man was a negro, he was a savage, he was a slave. It did not matter), the repetition of proslavery discourse is distinctly parodic (in the ridiculing sense of the term), and forces the reader to join in questioning the myth of African savagery. Such examples are far too numerous for the reader to miss this cornerstone of the novel's theme. Francisco is human first, a normal man ('un hombre cualquiera') and only incidentally black ('un negro oscuro'). His story can be any man's story.

Using savage with its Eurocentric meaning would collide with Zambrana's liberal self-image. From the author's perspective, the African slave's difference is not defect or inferiority. This process of inscribing new meaning in the word begins in the novel's first chapter, where, as in the case of Suárez's novel, the protagonist is introduced *in absentia.* Here Dona Josefa's description of Francisco as ignorant and coarse is simultaneously discounted by her own son who defends the slave's intelligence. Used subsequently by the narrator, the word takes on more defiant overtones. In an implicit or overt manner, the 'savagery' of the African stands opposed to a notionally 'civilized' European-derived way of being. The civilized / savage binary is used, at least ostensibly, to invoke this antithesis between the two slave lovers - Camila, the fine product of civilization and Francisco, the creature of African barbarism. But by appropriating the vocabulary of savagery in order to validate it as the African's conscious resistance of Western culture the author makes it liable to an antislavery interpretation. Francisco chafes at the hegemony of European-derived civilization: '¡Cuanto mejor hubiera vivido en su tierra agreste, en su selva desgreñada, mandando guerreros valerosos y teniendo por compañera una hija de los bosques que le reverenciara y le adorase! (79-80).' (How much better would he have lived in his wild and untamed land, commanding warriors and having as his companion a daughter of the forest who would honour and adore him!) The irony in his description of his African homeland as wild and untamed extends to the intractable Francisco - not unable, but *unwilling* to be 'tamed.'

If the savagery of the African is questioned and given new meaning, so too is civilization, which was assumed to be a European preserve. Civilization, for Zambrana, equates to the improvement of character through education, echoing a theme that runs through much of the liberal political discourse in nineteenth-century Cuba. Savagery, for him, therefore describes destructive instincts to be tamed through education. As such it is not linked inextricably to ethnicity or nationality, for the character who is said to look savagely at Camila is the European-descended slave master Carlos. Moreover, in the narrator's loaded description of the erstwhile 'king of the [African] forest' turned ironically a prisoner of civilization, Francisco's cultural status as a prisoner of civilization supersedes his political fate as a prisoner of war. Such a characterization both valorizes his pre-slavery condition and puts paid to the idea of slavery as an enlightening experience for those who had been brought out of African 'darkness.' The author goes to great length to demonstrate the relativity of the savage / civilized binary. Referring to the runaway slaves who live easily for extended periods in the forest, he notes that their inability to adapt to New World culture is hardly a sign of their deficiency. It is not so much that the slaves have a hostile attitude to civilization, as Lorna Williams (145) has argued, but that they find the ways of civilization alien to their spirit. Civilized and savage, Zambrana seems to say, are not spatially determined conditions. Both descriptors must therefore be (invisibly) bracketed for ironic treatment because they have been given the fluidity of constructs rather than the fixity of absolute essences

El negro Francisco bears testimony to the author's understanding of slavery in terms that have become commonplace in postcolonial cultural history: that the slaves found various surreptitious and passive ways to defy the authority of their enslavers and to preserve and transmit their ancestral culture. Through Francisco Zambrana also expands the picture of African cultural continuity in the New World. He adds to the African dance and musical traditions expressed in live performance in Suárez's novel, the stories transmitted orally to Creole slaves by their African-born peer. Looking beyond the slave's chattel status, Zambrana imagines Francisco's continuing allegiance to Africa, something which his enslavers were not eager or pleased to contemplate. After twenty years of enslavement, he retains his identity as a 'negro de nacion,' a pedigree that earns him the recognition and respect of his fellow slaves. The narrator lauds Francisco's recall of African ancestral religious rites, interpreting it as an index of a patriotism which exposure to European culture cannot extinguish. The conspiracy of silence surrounding the African past is construed as the slaves' dual response to slavery. It is, on the one hand, a pragmatic move for self-preservation based on their insight into slave-owner psychology, and, on the other, an exclusionary strategy to safeguard their cultural integrity from contamination by exposure to their enslavers.

That the slaves' connection to Africa hardly features in Gertrudis Gomez de Avellaneda's *Sab* (1841) is hardly surprising. This lone female in the ranks of antislavery writers builds her story around the love of Sab, the almost-white mulatto slave, for his young mistress Carlota. His identity is marked by a high level of absorption of Euro-Creole cultural values, leading to his inability to connect with his African heritage. One of the novel's sporadic allusions to the African past, however, is the liaison between the protagonist's slave mother and his slave-master father. Sab's evocation of his mother's life story accentuates briefly the suffering caused by her violent uprooting from Africa, and contests the stereotype of African savagery. Africa, the land of the slave woman's royal birth is associated with freedom, a place where race does not mediate social relations, a country governed by civilized values, the antithesis, it is implied, of Cuba, a land ruled by barbaric 'traffickers in human flesh.' However, her love for her white owner magically renews the slave woman's 'African soul;' suggesting retention of an original African essence as a prerequisite of accommodation. In his lack of this essence, one may infer, lies the root of Sab's psychological turmoil.

Africa as a centre and source of national and personal identity surfaces only in Sab's political rhetoric as an expression of his disgruntlement with his society's prohibition of cross-racial love. He constitutes slavery as transportation from a paradise of racial homogeneity into a state of dispossession, alienation and exile. African 'savagery' is once again bracketed for ironic effect: 'No tengo tampoco una patria que defender, porque los esclavos no tienen patria. Si al menos los hombres blancos ... le dejasen tranquilo en sus bosques, allá tendría patria y amores porque amaría a una mujer de su color, salvaje como él' (257). (Nor do I have a country to defend, for slaves have no country. If only the white man ... had left him in peace in his forests, there he would have and a country and love because he would love a woman of his own colour, uncivilized like himself). Sab, however, entertains no thoughts of personal reconnection with Africa. It is Martina the old and demented Amerindian woman who points the way. Her militant voice invokes his African heritage to inspire him to resist his bondage, in contrast to the emasculating effects of his implied identification with his white European heritage: 'Levanta tu frente hijo de la esclava, las cadenas que aprisionan las manos no deben oprimir el alma' (308) (Lift up your head, son of a slave; the chains that bind your hands must not shackle your heart.)

In a manner suggestive of the postmodern notion of unity in difference, Avellaneda links Cuba's African heritage to its pre-Columbian past when Martina predicts that African slaves will avenge their Amerindian predecessors. Noting that in the early period of colonization escaped these slaves made common cause with the Amerindians in attacking the Spanish colonists, Caribbean cultural historian Nigel Bolland has recently argued for greater acknowledgement of 'African-Amerindian side of the colonial triangle.'[il] A similar reckoning of the African contribution to Cuban history would be incorporated into political discourse in post-Revolution Cuba more than a century later with the view of the struggle against slavery as the continuation of a line of resistance originating in Amerindian struggle against the Spanish conquistadores.

Resistance marked every stage of the enslavement of Africans in the New World. In his little-studied novella *Romualdo: uno de tantos,* written in 1869 but published only in 1891, Francisco Calcagno provides a robust testimony to this defiance. The actions of the African-born maroons in this story are a powerful assertion of their free will. However, the author's conscious intention of presenting an enlightened image of *marronage* is sabotaged by his unconscious Eurocentric bias. Adopting a posture akin to ethnographic surveillance, he observes keenly the nuances in the human and social elements of maroon existence. Surveillance, as theorized in postcolonial studies, is one strategy of imperial dominance, for it implies a viewer with an elevated vantage point from which to project a particular understanding of what is seen and to fix the identity of the viewed (colonized subject) in relation to the surveyor (colonizer). In one sense Calcagno's observation of the maroons assumes such a position of superiority.

An obstinate Negrophobia struggles with the author's antislavery intent and clouds his perception of the maroons' Africanness. He cannot contain the revulsion evoked in him by these 'hellish monsters' who are indistinguishable from an equally monstrous nature. The alliterative force of the language that describes the maroon leader distils the author's disgust: 'era tan friamente feroz su alma como feas y repugnantes todas sus facciones' (350). (His heart was as callously cold as all his features were ghastly and repugnant.) Josefa Lucumi, the female maroon, fares no better; she is a 'horrible specimen of the African woman' (horrible ejemplar de la hembra africana). These descriptions show no trace of the authorial distance with which proslavery ideology is exposed elsewhere in the story. Rather, they rival and surpass the most grotesque images of African people commonly found in the early Hispanic literary tradition. Calcagno resorts to deliberate negative stereotyping in the physical description of their leader whose given name, Juan Bemba, recalls the blubber-lipped image of the African created by the Spanish burlesque tradition. Close-up shots of individual maroons create the most hideous effects. Their leader is picked out by the author's eye for sharp focus. The adjectives used to describe him are deceptively neutral at first: 'nariz aplastada, labios gruesos, frente pequeño, cuello corto, dientes blanqísimos.' (flat nose, thick lips, small forehead, short neck, very white teeth). But thereafter, the author reveals his aesthetic prejudice with parodic malice: 'Juan Bemba era un bello modelo de su raza; por lo tanto feo, si comparado con la circasiana.' (Juan Bemba was a beautiful model of his race, that is, ugly, when compared with the Caucasian.) The portrayal of these Africans as fearsome bespeaks the morbid dread of a mythical 'African barbarity' felt and propagated by white society. Calcagno's perception of the Africa-derived religion practised by the maroons is a mixture of awe and contempt. He is hard-pressed to hide his disdain for the difference in the maroons' African cultural retentions.

But there is more than racist prejudice in Calcagno's portrait. The depiction of the maroons in their world seems designed, simultaneously, to affirm the bond created by their common adversity despite ethnic differences. He challenges and reverses their official depiction as predators and as threats to the social order by counterposing an image of harmless, beleaguered 'savages' escaping ironically from the 'civilized,' doing what they need to survive and defending their right to freedom.

Calcagno's account poses an interesting paradox, for it is both an anathema in its Negrophobia and a monument to the heroism of the African slaves who fought against their oppressors. Yet the Eurocentric prejudice that colours his perception is not sufficient to render null and void his expression of admiration for the maroons' courage. His celebration of their recalcitrant spirit is no less potent a protest against slavery than his more direct denunciation of the slave trader and the overseer elsewhere in the story. Calcagno has captured in his group of fugitives the characteristic spirit of the maroons: defiant, freedom-loving, self-reliant, and preferring death over a life of bondage. Where the slave in other narratives must resort to submission and accommodation, or seek freedom as a gift, Juan Bemba and his band fight to maintain their autonomy. Ultimately, therefore, their indwelling spirit of defiance assumes more positive significance as an antislavery statement than the pessimism that might be conveyed by their eventual defeat. Utter disgust describes the author's vision of both maroon leader and slave trader, but while the moral repulsion aroused by the latter is implacable, the frank admiration for the maroons' bravery takes some of the burlesque edge off his aversion to their physical appearance and cultural expressions.

His awareness of the signifying power of the language of representation also manifests itself in the author's references to the maroons. He refrains from alluding to them as mere 'slaves,' preferring instead more politically appropriate names such as 'africano,' 'apalencado,' (palenque dweller) and 'negro,' and 'esclavo prófugo' (fugitive slave). In this context even the more controversial designation of 'salvajes,' with its connotation of wild or untamed and uncivilized, seems to be an affirmation of their intransigent struggle for autonomy. The story takes on a dramatically charged tempo in the final episode, rising to a near-epic climax in the showdown between the maroons and their adversaries. In his heroic last stand Juan Bemba comes to represent fearlessness rather than a fearsome savagery.

The close-up shots used for individual portraits combine with longer shots of the maroons in the environment that they created for themselves. Carefully avoiding the temptation to collapse them into a single (stereo)type the author describes the mixed motivations of the members of the maroon village. For the author these maroons, hunted so mercilessly as criminals, constitute a *society* of families with their distinct customs and cultural expressions. Calcagno's maroons are not rebels without a political cause. A community of diverse national constituencies, they are united in their uncompromising demand for autonomy and their rejection of the plantation regime: 'no querían más funche, ni más mayoral, ni más cuero, ni más esclavitud: que querían morir allí antes que volver al ingenio; que los dejaran quietos en las sierras ; y que se les diera la erial llanura inmediata, donde vivirían sembrando viandas y sin meterse con nadie' (373). (They wanted no more *funche*,[ii] no more estate administrator, no more beatings, no more slavery. They would rather die than return to the estate. They wanted to be left alone in the mountains and to be given the uncultivated land on the plain nearby where they would live, growing their food and interfering with no one.) Maroon society, removed from the divisiveness of the plantation slavery dynamic, fosters a counter-culture of collaboration and harmony. As a community and in their consciousness these African rebels are the answer to their lone-wolf counterpart Esteban Montejo, memorialized in Miguel Barnet's *Biografía de un cimarrón.*

Focussing on the maroons also affords the author an alternative mode of expression of his antislavery views. Where denunciation characterizes his treatment of the slave trader, in the maroon episode affirmation becomes the dominant idiom. When, for example, the narrator characterizes their attempt to defend themselves as an act of 'madness,' he intends it not as a negative judgment, but as a remark on the incredible courage of these rebels even in defiance of the dictates of prudence. Further destabilizing the ideological foundations of slavery, Calcagno links the maroons to a pre-slavery past. He pictures their commune or *palenque* as both an emblem of resistance and as a site for the preservation of an African identity – a little Africa of sorts ('una especie de pequeña Africa'). His depiction also provides a first glimpse of the process of cultural interchange which Fernando Ortiz would latter refer to as transculturation. In the maroon settlement Calcagno perceives the signs of the process of Africanization of Cuban culture. By casting the maroons in the role of agents of cultural transformation, the author has provided an alternative to the image of Africans as inert objects of Eurocentric acculturation.

An allegorical reading of the story's denouement is tempting. There is no pathos in the death of the maroons. Like the heroic warriors of epic literature, they sacrifice their lives in a fight for freedom. Gone are the tragic feeling and despair that mark the end of earlier narratives with an antislavery theme, for the maroons are not honourably outdone but cravenly betrayed. Their demise itself might be a concession to the awesome power of their oppressors, but their heroism removes the pessimistic traces from their deaths. Slave resistance in Calcagno's eyes is both warranted and worthy of admiration, even where it is futile.

Calcagno's resolve to display a consistent attitude is repeatedly threatened and sometimes thwarted by contradictory urges. His ambivalence towards the maroons may be usefully understood, however, in the light of the tension between centripetal and centrifugal impulses which Mikhail Bakhtin (271-3), Russian literary theorist cited by many postmodern scholars perceives at the heart of virtually all aspects of experience, including language and ideology. Bakhtin theorizes that a centripetal tendency towards coherence and unity must always contend with a centrifugal movement in the opposite direction of disunity and dispersion. The confluence of aversion and admiration in Calcagno's attitude, his wavering between empathetic involvement and detached voyeurism is evidence of this syndrome. If this work is outstanding for its antiblack fear-mongering, it is, paradoxically, just as outstanding for the antislavery resonance of its defence of *marronage*. The one cannot be acknowledged without the other. Caribbean historian Gordon Lewis (159) reminds us that in their struggle for independence the emergent Cuban bourgeoisie embraced the liberal philosophies of their European counterparts, adding racist prejudice to their class-based bias. The racism that compromises Calcagno's antislavery efforts might appear to be no different from the racism of the advocates of slavery. *Romualdo, uno de tantos* has shown, however, the inflections in his representation that stand in the way of a complete equation of the two. It is possible to decry his Eurocentric leaning while recognizing the value to be found in his antislavery perspective. Writing more than a century after him, Lewis places Cuba's antislavery novel and its 'morally inspired social analysis critical of the slavery institution' in the same politically subversive category as *marronage* which posed a challenge to the sovereignty of the emerging European nation-state (236). His post-colonial view may be seen to coincide with Calcagno's view from the centre of the colonial scene.

The antislavery authors reviewed in the preceding pages, their ambivalence notwithstanding, repudiate any notion of New World slavery as beneficial to the transplanted Africans. In no case do the slave characters, African-born or Creole, experience it as such. The studious marking of a difference between the image of Africa that emerges from the slaves' consciousness and the one constructed by their enslavers, is a strategy that counters the specious justification of slavery as a civilizing project. Feebly or forcefully, each narrative offers a diachronic perspective of slavery, acknowledging what the authors imagine to be the slaves' link to their pre-slavery past, as well as the relation of that past to their present circumstances. Taking the slaves out of Africa, the writers seem to say, was the manageable part of the story of slavery. Taking Africa out of the slaves was a far more difficult proposition.

References

Ashcroft, Bill, Gareth Griffiths, and Helen Tiffin (2000). *Post-Colonial Studies: The Key Concepts*. London: Routledge.

Bakhtin, M. M. (1981) *The Dialogic Imagination.* Trans. Caryl Emerson and M. Holquist University of Texas Press.

Barnet, Miguel (1966). *Biografía de un cimarrón.* rpt. Madrid. Ediciones Alfaguara S.A., 1984

Bolland, Nigel (2006) 'Caribbean Cultures and Identities: Interpreting Garifuna Stories,' The 22nd Elsa Goveia Memorial Lecture, University of the West Indies, Kingston Jamaica, March 29.

Calcagno, Francisco (1891). *Romualdo: uno de tantos* in *Noveletas Cubanas*, rpt. Havana: Editorial de Arte y Literatura, 1977.

Fanon, Frantz (1967). *Black Skin, White Mask.* Trans. Charles Markmann. New York: Grove Press.

García, Gloria (1996). *La esclavitud desde la esclavitud.* Havana: Instituto Cubano del Libro.

Gómez de Avellaneda, Gertrudis (1841). *Sab.* Havana: Instituto Cubano del Libro, rpt.1973.

Lewis, Gordon K (1983). Main Currents in Caribbean Thought. The Johns Hopkins University Press.

Zambrana, Antonio (1875). *El negro Francisco.* rpt. Havana: Editorial Letras Cubanas, 1979

Patterson, Orlando (1973). *The Sociology of Slavery.* London: Granada Publishing Ltd.

Suárez y Romero, Anselmo (1838). *Francisco.* rpt. Havana: Instituto Cubano del Libro, 1974.

Williams, Lorna (1994). *The Representation of Slavery in Cuban Fiction.* University of Missouri Press.

---

[i] Nigel Bolland, 'Caribbean Cultures and Identities: Interpreting Garifuna Stories,' The 22nd Elsa Goveia Memorial Lecture, University of the West Indies, Kingston Jamaica, March 29, 2006.

[ii] A dish prepared from ground corn, water, salt and lard.

Chapter 2

The Representation of a Black Cuban Slave and Literary Transculturation in *The Autobiography of a Runaway Slave* by Miguel Barnet

Miguel Arnedo-Gómez

The existence of large populations of African-descent in Cuba has its origins in the 1500s when the Spanish and the Portuguese began to bring African slaves to the New World to work as slaves in sugar, coffee, tobacco, cacao and cotton plantations of the Caribbean, Atlantic and Pacific coasts (Andrews 2004: 13). In the nineteenth century in particular, slave shipments increased substantially in order to meet the increase in the international demand for Cuban sugar after the collapse of Saint Domingue and by 1841 blacks comprised more than 50 percent of the total population of the island (Paquette 1988: 298). As in other parts of Latin America, Africans and their descendants in Cuba created a unique culture out of elements brought over from their native societies and the Spanish culture that their white oppressors imposed upon them.[i] Afro-Cuban culture is a rich and varied compendium of cultural forms that includes dance and music forms, ritual forms, theatre and oral literatures, and these have been extensively documented in numerous studies[ii].

Throughout the Cuban Colonial period Afro-Cuban culture was generally excluded from Cuban literature, which tended to be written and controlled by the white dominant sectors of Cuban society. Thus, the world views of Cuba's Africans and their descendants that were expressed through Afro-Cuban cultural forms were not reflected in the dominant literature.[iii] Rectifying this exclusion became one of the objectives of the Castro-led socialist regime in the early years of the 1959 Cuban Revolution. In a 1961 speech entitled 'Palabras a los intelectuales' (Words to the Intellectuals) Fidel Castro hinted at one of the interests that should be pursued in the intellectual field:

In recent days we had the experience of meeting an old woman who was 106 years old and had just learnt to read and write. We suggested to her that she should write a book. She had been a slave and we wanted to know how a slave would have seen the world, what her first impressions of life were, of her masters, of her fellow slaves. I think that this old woman could write something about her time that would be as interesting as anything any of us could write. It is possible that she will become fully literate within a year and that she will write a book at the age of 106. (Castro 1987: 41)

In 1966 a Cuban writer named Miguel Barnet seemed to be following Castro's lead when he decided to write a *testimonio* novel entitled *The Autobiography of a Runaway Slave* (*Biografía de un cimarrón*) in order to reproduce the view of Cuban history of 105-year-old Esteban Montejo, who had been a runaway slave during the Cuban colonial period. As the critic Elzbieta Sklodowska points out, Barnet's project was one of the first Latin American *testimonio* novels, a genre that did not acquire worldwide recognition until the publication in 1982 of Elizabeth Burgos's *Me llamo Rigoberta Menchú y así me nació la conciencia*. Burgos's book narrates the life experiences of Rigoberta Menchú, a Quiché Indian Woman from Guatemala who was an activist in the struggle of the Quiché Indians and who went on to win the Nobel prize for peace in 1992. As an early precursor of this type of literature Barnet is partly responsible for establishing the method for producing a *testimonio* work that Burgos and others would later follow (Sklodowska 1992: 9). In order to write *The Autobiography of a Runaway Slave*, Barnet had a number of meetings with Montejo and interviewed him about his life experiences. He recorded the interviews and on the basis of the recordings he wrote a stylised narrative in the first person singular from Esteban's perspective. *The Autobiography of a Runaway Slave* recounts Esteban's time as a slave, and then as a runaway slave living in the forest. The book also includes Esteban's recollections of the post-emancipation period, during which he returned to mainstream society as a free worker. The last historical period featured in Barnet's book is the Cuban War of Independence against Spain and the triumph of the independentist forces, aided by the last-minute intervention of the United States. The Cuban War of Independence lasted from 1895 to 1898 and Esteban fought on the independentists' side along with many other black Cubans who hoped that Independence from Spain would bring about a more equitable Cuban society.

Barnet and other *testimonio* authors believed that through this genre they were able to produce an authentic representation of the subjects' discourse. In a 1998 essay entitled 'Para llegar a Esteban Montejo: Los caminos del cimarrón' (How to Arrive at Esteban Montejo: The Paths of the Runaway Slave), Barnet revisits his *testimonio* project and explains that 'Esteban's soul is in this book'. He then argues that he was able to totally identify with Esteban to the extent that the book almost wrote itself. These perceptions are all present in the following extract:

> I know that Esteban's soul is in that book. You only need to look at the hand-written pages that the Cuban National Library asked me for, and which are now there in a safe place. You only need to look at those pages; there are hardly any crossings-out. They are very clean drafts because the recording came out like this, flowing so easily. Before I started to write I had identified so deeply with Esteban and his language that the book was coming out by itself. [...] What I mean to say is that the book transcends the book, so that it becomes more than just an object that one reads for entertainment or in order to acquire knowledge, or for any other reason. The book becomes a talisman of communication between human beings and that is where it acquires its purposefulness and its message is complete. (Barnet 1998a: 146-47)

According to Francesca Denegri, *Testimonio* literature was initially conceived by United States and European critics as the possible answer to the question posed by Gayatri Spivak 'Can the subaltern speak?' (Denegri 2003: 230). This, combined with the urge to find a 'new Latin American discourse', led many critics to defend the idea that *testimonio* was a genre through which the subject was able to express his / her testimony directly through the writing of the intellectual (Sklodowska 1992: 11). This notion recurs throughout John Beverly's and Marc Zimmerman's 1990 essay 'Testimonial Narrative". These authors refer to 'the erasure of authorial presence in *testimonio*' and argue that 'since this is the discourse of a witness who is not a fictional construct, in some way the testimony speaks to us directly, like a real person could speak to us' (Beverly & Zimmerman 1990: 176, 177).[iv]

This conception of the genre diverts attention from the fact that in the process of writing a *testimonio* work, the editors do not merely 'reproduce' the discourse of the subject in all its purity; they influence it and modify it in a number of ways. Some of the transformations involved are a natural consequence of transposing an oral discourse to the written word. This transposition implies, first of all, the elimination of a number of non-verbal codes that are part of oral discourse. Martín Lienhard's 1994 paper on methods for studying literary representations of orality in Latin American literature lists some of the non-verbal codes of an oral performance that cannot be reproduced on the written page, such as musical and choreographic codes, gestures and tonal and rhythmic variations. Orality, according to Lienhard, includes codes that require the audient to engage all the five senses. Thus, the 'transcription' of an oral performance, even when complemented by audio-visual documents, must not be confused with its concrete and corporeal reality, which includes the text 'written' by the actors, time, space, and the auditorium. An oral performance, he concludes, can only be experienced in full by witnessing it (Lienhard 1994: 372).

As an oral narrator Montejo would have resorted to many of the non-verbal codes mentioned by Lienhard and since all these could not be faithfully reproduced in *The Autobiography of a Runaway Slave*, it becomes difficult to support the view that Barnet's *novela-testimonio* was an exact representation of Montejo's testimony.

Secondly, the formal characteristics of the verbal elements of the subject's discourse are also modified by the editor of a *testimonio* work in order to adapt them to the requirements of a written narrative. Oral discourse and oral narratives have formal characteristics that stem from the dynamics of orality. For example, as Walter Ong explains, when composing an oral text or producing oral discourse the producer must bear in mind that the audient will not be able to glance back over a written text in order to go over something that was missed the first time around. In oral discourse 'there is nothing to back loop into outside the mind, for the oral utterance has vanished as soon as it was uttered'. 'Hence', Ong continues, 'the mind must move ahead more slowly, keeping close to the focus of attention much of what it has already dealt with. Redundancy, repetition of the just-said, keeps both speaker and hearer surely on the track' (Ong 1982: 39-40). Although, as Sklodowska points out, Barnet's written narrative does employ some repetition, it is clear that this and other oral formal characteristics of Esteban's verbal testimony had to be modified by Barnet in order to make the testimony 'readable' (Sklodowska 1992: 126). Barnet himself wrote the following in his introduction to the 1968 edition of *The Autobiography of a Runaway Slave*:

Throughout the entire narrative the reader will be able to appreciate that we have had to paraphrase a great deal of what Esteban told us. If we had faithfully reproduced his language the book would have been difficult to understand and extremely repetitive. (Barnet 1968: 8)

Another way in which Barnet modified Montejo's original testimony was by presenting it as a narrative monologue in the first person when, in reality, Barnet was Montejo's interlocutor in the interviews. Barnet's aim in doing this, as Lienhard points out, was to give the reader the illusion that he or she is in the presence of an oral narrator and listening to a spontaneous account (Lienhard 1996b: 21). But this illusion contradicts the self-questioning that is now part of modern ethnography, where there has been an effort to incorporate the dialogue between ethnographer and subject to the final text (Sklodowska 1992: 118). It is useful at this point to compare Barnet's strategy in representing the Other with the strategies employed by his fellow Cuban ethnographer Lydia Cabrera. Cabrera has been praised for creating an ethnographic method for representing Afro-Cuban discourse that anticipated by 30 years or so the self-questioning which is now an integral part of modern ethnography. Martín Lienhard's lucid analysis of Cabrera's treatise on Afro-Cuban religions *El monte* ('The Forest' in Cuban Spanish) shows that one of the reasons for her reputation as an innovative ethnographer is her use of a wide array of different techniques for representing the discourses of her informants. This allows the reader to see how these discourses interact with Cabrera's own discourse in a variety of ways. As Lienhard explains, Lydia Cabrera sometimes transcribes the testimonies of her informants with all their phonetic peculiarities, but other times she simply summarises them in her own words. Other times she transcribes descriptions of Afro-Cuban rituals and stories about Afro-Cuban deities that she finds in Afro-Cuban *libretas*, notebooks used by Afro-Cuban practitioners to record and preserve essential information about their religious traditions. Lienhard also points out that whilst making the reader aware of the presence in the text of her own discourse and that of her informants, Lydia Cabrera often blurs the boundaries between them. In many cases she does not identify the provenance of the voices that she quotes or their religious and ethnic affiliation, and she mixes up voices from members of different Afro-Cuban ethnic groups. To make matters even more complicated, sometimes the voices that she introduces introduce or quote other anonymous discourses. Lienhard's analysis shows that Cabrera's 'anti-method', as he refers to it, highlights the presence of many different discourses within her text and allows the reader to see some of the different ways in which the discourses interact: sometimes they fuse, but other times they are distinct; sometimes her discourse is dominant, whereas other times her informants' voices take over. In addition, by exposing the modes of production of her texts, Cabrera allows the reader to question himself (or herself) about the nature of the relationships between the 'witnesses' and the editor, and the underlying power dynamics present in these relationships (Lienhard 1996b: 30-31).

Barnet's decision to write *The Autobiography of a Runaway Slave* as if it were Esteban's monologue has exactly the opposite effect, i.e., it obscures the author's influential presence in the interviews on which the book is based. In the introduction to the first edition of the book Barnet explains that after having initially met with Montejo around six times, he started to widen the thematic field of the interviews by guiding him with specific questions about slavery, his life in the slave barracks and his life in the forest as a runaway slave. Once he obtained 'a general overview of Montejo's life', Barnet decided which were the most noteworthy aspects. Then Barnet started to formulate more questions intended to guide Montejo to the parts of his life that were of interest to him, like the social environment in the slave barracks and his celibacy whilst being a runaway slave (Barnet 1968: 6-7).

The fact that Barnet's mediating role is not acknowledged in any way in the final text that is *The Autobiography of a Runaway Slave* is particularly problematic in the context in which the book was written, as it is evident that the dominant Cuban revolutionary discourse imposed certain ideological parameters that would have led Barnet to 'edit' the final text so as to avoid censorship.

What could have happened to Miguel Barnet if he had written a *novela-testimonio* that did not fit in with the expectations of the Cuban regime? The case of the North American anthropologist Oscar Lewis as related by Sklodowska provides some hints. Oscar Lewis was an anthropologist who went to Cuba in 1969 to study how a series of Cuban families were adapting to their new lives in a new neighbourhood built by the government as part of a programme of poverty eradication. After studying the situation of these families he concluded the following:

It is clear that in this neighbourhood many elements from the culture of poverty persist. I think I was excessively optimistic in some of my former conclusions about the disappearance of the culture of poverty under the socialist system. (As cited in Sklodowska 1992: 21)

According to Sklodowska, In July 1970 the Cuban government put an end to Oscar Lewis's project and he was accused of being a CIA agent. Many of his materials were confiscated and one of the informants was imprisoned. The Cuban government's accusations have not been proven to this day (Sklodowska 1992: 21). This incident took place only three years after Barnet published *The Autobiography of a Runaway Slave*, so it can serve as an indication of the constraints that he was working under. William Luis argues that when writing *The Autobiography of a Runaway Slave* Barnet may have been seeking to ingratiate himself with the Cuban government after a group of poets known as El Puente, to which he belonged, fell out of grace with the regime for 'stressing the aesthetic over the political' (Luis 1989: 485). The publication of *The Autobiography of a Runaway Slave* was a national and an international success and Barnet rejoined the Cuban literary establishment and became an important writer in Cuba thanks to it. Barnet's reinsertion into the Cuban cultural establishment may have been facilitated by the fact that *The Autobiography of a Runaway Slave* would have been viewed as a worthy contribution to the revolution at a time when acknowledging the importance of Afro-Cubans in Cuban history and in the formation of Cuban culture was one of the Revolution's concerns. However, Luis also claims that becoming an important international figure may have been a more significant factor (Luis 1989: 485).

Barnet certainly spelt out how *The Autobiography of a Runaway Slave* fitted in with Revolutionary expectations. In his 1969 essay on the *novela testimonio* ('La novela testimonio: socioliteratura'), Barnet points out that the purpose of this literary genre is 'to provide the reader with an awareness of his / her own tradition, to provide him / her with a useful and advantageous myth that can be a model from which to categorise' (1998a: 23). Such a statement presents the *novela testimonio* as an ideal artistic instrument in the context of a socialist society that, as Moore points out, was trying to radically transform the consciousness of its citizens in order to create an 'hombre nuevo' or 'new man'. In the dominant state ideology this was an individual with 'a profound consciousness of his role in society and his duties and social responsibilities' and as 'a person capable of constructing Communism and living with it' (Moore 2006: 142). In the introduction to the book, Barnet also felt that it was necessary to stress that Montejo was a model revolutionary and a member of the Cuban Socialist Party, despite the noticeable individualism that he displayed throughout his life:

His revolutionary spirit is not only evident throughout the narration, but also in his present attitude. Esteban Montejo at the age of 105, constitutes a good example of revolutionary behaviour and qualities. His tradition as a revolutionary, first as a runaway slave, then as a freedom fighter in the Cuban War of Independence, and later as a member of the Cuban Socialist Party, is manifest today in Montejo's identification with the Cuban Revolution. (Barnet 1968: 10)

The issue of how Barnet may have modified or edited the content of Esteban Montejo's accounts in order to stay within Revolutionary parameters is explored in detail in William Luis's 1989 article 'The Politics of Memory and Miguel Barnet's *The Autobiography of a Runaway Slave*'. William Luis's analysis centres on the conspicuous absence in the book of Montejo's views of two key events in Cuban history that were of great importance to Cuban blacks. The first of these events is the violent repression in 1912 of the black armed revolt staged in response to the ban of the Independent Party of Coloured People (Partido Independiente de Color or PIC). The ban of the party and resulting black protests occurred at a time when Cuban blacks were resentful about the fact that despite having played a decisive role in the struggle for independence, their conditions had not improved sufficiently under the early Cuban Republican governments. Fearing that the United States government would retake control of Cuba, as it had threatened to do every time that the threat of a black revolt had emerged since Independence, President José Miguel Gómez decided to send armed forces to quash the black uprisings. Violence escalated and various massacres of black protestors took place. Particularly ruthless was the assassination with machine guns of 150 peaceful black peasants on 31 May 1912 in the small town of La Maya in the region of Oriente (Helg 1995: 194, 210-11).

As Luis points out, Montejo definitely shared his impressions of the 1912 Race War with Barnet in the interviews on which *The Autobiography of a Runaway Slave* was based, as he would later reproduce them in another *testimonio* book entitled *La canción de Rachel* (Rachel's Song). Montejo's views display a defiant and militant fervour for the cause of the PIC and for the black protestors who, like him, took part in the revolt:

> And what the hell did they think? That we were going to hand ourselves in, all tame, and that we were going to hand over our weapons and take our trousers down for them? That was not going to happen, and we proved it to them. They called us savages, and used other racist insults against us, but when else in the history of this nation has there been a political party that has offered to the Cuban people a political programme that is as democratic as that of the Independent Party of Coloured People? (as cited in Luis 1989: 487)

Montejo's attitudes with respect to this historical event may indeed be the reason why they were not reproduced in *The Autobiography of a Runaway Slave*. Luis substantiates this idea in the following extract from his above-mentioned article:

The period surrounding the Partido Independiente de Color may have proven to be problematical for an overall understanding of blacks in Cuba and Barnet's reintegration into literary production in the Revolution. It may have been politically expedient not to rekindle the racial debate and conclude the novel at the end of the Spanish-Cuban-American War, thus alluding to the triumph of the Cuban Revolution. Under Slavery, during the Ten Years' War and during the Spanish-Cuban-American War, the enemy was a foreign power. But the Race War of 1912 was a national problem. Though Rachel claims that the war came to an end because of the threat of U.S. invasion only Cuban nationals were directly involved in the massacre of 1912. It was a campaign of Cubans against other Cubans sufficient to discourage any black movement for many decades. By ending the narration after the Spanish-Cuban-American War, Barnet leaves us with the impression that, at least from Montejo's point of view, Cuban problems were foreign related. (Luis 1989: 488)

The second event that is strangely absent from the book is the 1959 triumph of the Cuban Socialist Revolution. As Luis points out, documenting Montejo's views of the improved conditions for blacks under the Revolution would have fitted nicely with Barnet's description in the prologue of Montejo's life trajectory from runaway slave to model revolutionary (Luis 1989: 486). This silence immediately brings up questions about Montejo's real opinion of the Cuban Socialist Regime. William Luis ventures the following hypotheses:

In spite of the extensive conversations between Montejo and Barnet, the informant has not revealed the whole story. Montejo says: 'If I could, I would come right out and tell the whole story now'. Did Montejo tell the whole story? Was he aware that no matter what he said, Barnet would write his recollection, that is, his own version of the story? By ending the autobiography has Barnet controlled and therefore silenced parts of the ex-slave's life and voice? Yet the end recalls the early years of Montejo's life, years before the time of the narration, in which he felt he needed to be silent. Is Montejo a silent witness of the Cuban Revolution? (Luis 1989: 490)

But, it is interesting to note that there are many traits of Montejo's personality and behaviour that seem to clash with the dominant ideology that *The Autobiography of a Runaway Slave* was written under. Throughout the book, Montejo comes across as a close observer of the customs of Cuban people, of their popular and folkloric cultural practices; but he rarely participates in them and he always describes them as the activities of 'los negros' (the blacks), using the third person as if he was not one of them.[v] The reader gets a very strong sense of his individualism, which seems at odds with the values of cooperation, collectivism and camaraderie that are normally promoted in socialist societies. In addition, Montejo repeatedly expresses his desire to govern himself.[vi] In one part of the book he also explains that when he was a runaway slave, many other blacks wanted to befriend him. They always asked him what he did being a runaway slave but he always replied 'nothing' because he always valued his independence (Barnet 1998b: 63). In another part of the book, Montejo remembers playing card games that would almost invariably turn into heated arguments from which he used to walk away because he had 'always been a separatist' (Barnet 1998b: 93). Luis tries to explain how Barnet reconciled in his mind Esteban's rebellious and independent nature with the values of the Revolution by arguing that 'Montejo's independent nature, his rejection of slavery, and his opposition – first to Spanish occupation and later to U.S. intervention – recall the position of the Cuban revolutionary government'. But, as various critics have pointed out, at the same time Montejo did not even choose to join other maroon slaves when he was a runaway (Geisdorfer-Feal 1990: 107-8, González Hechevarría 1980: 261). This was not only because of the greater risk of being caught if he became part of a group; it was also because he enjoyed the tranquillity and the freedom of being by himself (Barnet 1998b: 54). Sklodowska also brings attention to the contradictions in Barnet's project that stem from his description of Montejo as a representative of a class of people who have experienced moments in history that mark the Cuban psychology and his claim that the book 'narrates experiences that many Cuban men experienced' (Sklodowska 1992: 15). Indeed, if Barnet really wanted to convey a view of history that would be representative of the perspective of Cuban blacks, or even of the Cuban people in general, Montejo was an odd choice. He was not even a good representative of the slave sectors as runaway slaves were a very small minority.

As Sklodowska points out, the ideological contradictions of *The Autobiography of a Runaway Slave* are difficult to decipher (Sklodowska 1992: 15). One possible explanation is that Barnet was interested in telling the story of Montejo because he was an outstanding and unique character but he felt that he had to make certain modifications and remarks in order to make sure that the project fitted in with the Revolution. If this was the case, *The Autobiography of a Runaway Slave* cannot be conceived of as the perfect expression of the Cuban Regime's ideology, but rather, as Barnet's attempt to resolve the tensions between his specific artistic and ethnographic interests and those of the reigning ideological discourse.

Transculturation in *The Autobiography of a Runaway Slave*

The problematic elements of Barnet's representation of Esteban Montejo's discourse described in the previous section severely undermine the *novela testimonio.* This type of literature was envisaged as the means by which the Latin American intellectual could finally help those without a voice, the disempowered, to introduce their perspectives into the dominant literature. By contrast, the above criticisms could lead one to assume that *testimonio* is an instrument of exploitation by which the middle-class intellectual appropriates the discourse of the disempowered and manipulates it in a number of ways to promote his or her own agenda. However, I would now like to bring attention to a parallel process at work in *The Autobiography of a Runaway Slave* in which Esteban Montejo and his Afro-Cuban oral culture played a much more active role in the production of the novel than the above image suggests. I am referring to a phenomenon known as narrative transculturation, as defined by Uruguayan critic Ángel Rama. In his 1982 study *Transculturación narrativa en América Latina* Rama defined the concept with reference to a number of Latin American authors, such as José María Arguedas, Gabriel García Márquez, Juan Rulfo and Augusto Roa Bastos. What Rama revealed about these writers is that they were producing literary works that opened the way for a distinctive Latin American modern literature by utilising elements of rural and popular cultures of their regions as guiding formal principles whilst, at the same time, also employing the literary techniques of the European and US literary avant-gardes (Rama 1982: 32-56). In this way, what Rama highlighted throughout his study, and particularly in his analyses of José María Arguedas's *Los ríos profundos*, was that transcultural novels are characterised by a polyphony of voices, discourses and perspectives. In some sections of these works, indigenous, African or popular cultural elements predominate over European elements, but in others European elements are the dominant ones. In certain parts the elements are in conflict with one another and in other parts Rama brings attention to the presence of mixed, hybrid, or *mestizo* perspectives, which could be understood as instances of fusion between disparate cultural elements.[vii]

A similarly wide array of relationships between elements of Barnet's culture (the Europeanised literary culture of the Cuban white intellectual) and elements of Montejo's (Afro-Cuban oral culture and Afro-Cuban belief systems) is actually present in *The Autobiography of a Runaway Slave*. In the previous section of this essay I highlighted aspects of this work that betray Barnet's editorial interference and manipulation of Esteban's discourse, but there is also evidence of the ex-slave's influence on the final text. Noteworthy examples are the sections in which the narrative voice describes 'magical' or spiritual phenomena that are part of the Afro-Cuban belief system. In the following extract, the narrator (Montejo-Barnet) describes how he learnt to 'manufacture' a 'little devil' (*diablito*) that helps those who carry it in their pockets in a small glass jar:

> I learnt to make the little devil and I also learnt how to raise it and everything. In order to do that, one has to have heart, above all; a heart as hard as a fish. It is not difficult. You take a chicken egg with a blood spot; it has to have a blood spot, otherwise it is no good. You leave the egg in the sun for two or three days. When it is hot you put it under your armpit three Fridays in a row. On the third Friday a little devil comes out of the chicken instead of a chick. [...] Then you put the little devil in a small and transparent glass jar so it can be seen, and you pour dry wine in it. Then you put it in your trouser pockets but you make sure it is firmly secured because these little devils tend to be fighters. (Barnet 1998b: 131)

Throughout the narration 'superstitious' or 'magical' Afro-Cuban beliefs are described from this same perspective; that is, the perspective of someone who wholeheartedly shares these beliefs. The fact that this is the only perspective from which the book is written is an example of transculturation that resembles one of the transcultural features of Gabriel García Márquez's masterpiece *Cien años de soledad (100 Years of Solitude)*. As is well known, the Colombian writer's novel is also written from the point of view of a narrator who shares the magical, religious or superstitious beliefs of the characters, instead of one who adopts an 'objective' western, scientific standpoint. This implies a transculturation because it means that one of the formal lineaments of the novel (the narrative point of view) comes from the popular culture of the Colombian rural popular sectors represented in the novel (Rama 1982: 45, Higgins 1990). Curiously, whereas in Gabriel Garcia Marquez's novel, this technique has been praised as a highly original transcultural strategy, Barnet's adoption of Montejo's world view in *The Autobiography of a Runaway Slave* (one year before *100 Years of* solitude was published) has not been acknowledged as an example of transculturation. The only critic who touches upon the correlation between these two texts is Sklodowska, who remarks upon the fact that Esteban's humorous tone when relating 'magical' events resembles Gabriel Garcia Marquez's tendency to juxtapose recognisable mundane details like a white sheet, or a cup of hot chocolate, with extraordinary events, such as the levitation of Remedios La Buena in *100 Years of Solitude* (Sklodowska 1992: 133).

In the previous section of this essay I explained that the production of *The Autobiography of a Runaway Slave* involved Barnet's processing of a number of oral codes in Esteban's discourse in order to respect the formal conventions of a written narrative text. Whilst there is no doubt that Esteban's discourse was stripped of many of its oral formal qualities, the final text at times also betrays oral influences. Despite Barnet's concern with avoiding the repetitiveness of Montejo's testimony, the narrator of *The Autobiography of a Runaway Slave* does make use of redundancy and repetition, and as Sklodowsaka points out this is probably a mnemonic device characteristic of oral culture and also a way of substantiating the authenticity of facts and claims invoking the authority of the oral community.[viii] Luis also remarks upon the oral nature of the repetitions in the text. He argues that 'the repetitions in *The Autobiography of a Runaway Slave* are a part of the resurgence of history, but also of African oral tradition and of Montejo's own recollections' (Luis 1989: 477). Another formal influence from Esteban's oral discourse is the chronological order of the narration. Barnet pointed out in the prologue that his intention was to write a book in which the things that happened to the protagonist were recounted in the chronological order in which they happened to him throughout his life. But when conducting the interviews Barnet was confronted with digression, which is another characteristic of oral discourse that clashes against the chronological conventions of the traditional written narrative:

Frequently, a word, an idea, awakened in Esteban's mind memories that often made him get off the subject. These digressions ended up being very useful because they brought to the conversation elements that perhaps we would not have found. (Barnet 1968: 6).

These digressions undermine the historical chronological order that Barnet attempted to impose on the narrative by dividing into three distinct historical periods: Slavery, Abolition and the War of Independence. Throughout the narration Esteban's memories move outside of the historical periods assigned to each section. An example mentioned by Luis is found in the first section of the book, which deals with the slavery period. The narrator is recounting the period during which he lived in a cave when he was a runaway slave, but suddenly he breaks with the chronology of the narration and starts describing something that happened to him after Abolition, an occasion on which he told a Congolese black that he had lived with bats (Barnet 1998b: 52). Luis concludes his analysis of this particular episode by stating that 'the narration cannot be conceived as interviews with a historical development, but as a discourse which breaks with history and is subject to the strategies of memory' (Luis 1989: 478).

All these examples of transculturation could be a conscious attempt on the part of Barnet to introduce into *The Autobiography of a Runaway Slave* aspects of Esteban's narration, which would not challenge the notion that Barnet had total control over the characteristics of the final text. But there is also the possibility that some of these elements became part of the final text without Barnet necessarily meaning them to. Indeed, it would not be necessarily easy to exert total control over Esteban's narration, and in the whole production process of the book there would have been many occasions when Esteban could have imposed aspects of his ideology and his culture upon Barnet. It is significant in this respect what Barnet wrote about Esteban's conduct during the interview:

After just a few weeks of meetings, Esteban became very affable [...]. He spoke with fluidity and he himself on many occasions chose the theme that he thought was the most important. Many times we agreed on which were the important themes. On one occasion, he was puzzled that we had forgotten to ask him about the Chinese in Sagua la Grande. He kept looking at our notebook and he almost forced us to write down everything he said. (Barnet 1968: 7)

To assume that Esteban Montejo did not play a significant role in the overall production of *The Autobiography of a Runaway Slave* would underestimate the resourcefulness and perspicacity that the old man displayed throughout his life (his life as portrayed in *The Autobiography of a Runaway Slave*, that is). The above extract from Barnet's introduction provides an idea of the ways in which the interviewed subject can exert some control over the content of the interviews. It also points to the fact that, like the author-editor, the subject of a *testimonio* project has his / her own agenda. Montejo may have regarded Barnet as an instrument through which to perpetuate his life story and achieve fame, money or recognition. It is not surprising that the overall portrait of Esteban is of course very favourable to him as a person. We will never know Esteban's intentions in participating in this project but the controversy about the accuracy of Rigoberta Menchú's account of her life that emerged 17 years after the publication of *Me llamo Rigoberta Menchú y así me nació la conciencia* certainly suggests that the *testimonio* subject is capable of manipulating the intellectual-editor in order to further his / her own objectives.[ix] Something that would make it particularly easy for them to do so is the fact that often the authors of *testimonio* works seem to idealise the subjects as 'pure' and 'innocent' beings incapable of being dishonest. This is apparent in the prologue to *The Autobiography of a Runaway Slave.* Whilst making sure to point out that Esteban's account is only the ex-slave's personal vision of things, Barnet also remarks upon Esteban's honesty, which he claims is apparent in many episodes in his life (1968: 10). This amounts to stating that 'Esteban Montejo is honest because he told me so'.

To conclude, the above arguments suggest a picture of *The Autobiography of a Runaway Slave* as a space in which Montejo's voice and Barnet's discourse interact in a number of ways. Sometimes the two voices are in conflict and one of them needs to silence the other, as suggested by Luis's treatment of the absence of references to key historical events. Other times there is a harmonious or successful fusion of the two perspectives, as in those cases in which Barnet has consciously used Afro-Cuban culture as a guiding formal principle in the narration. Barnet failed to produce a book that expressed Esteban's testimony in a totally authentic manner, but *The Autobiography of a Runaway Slave* stands as a perfect example of a transcultural work of literature as defined by Rama and this certainly adds considerable value to the book within the field of Latin American literature.

References

Andrews, George Reid, 2004. *Afro-Latin America 1800-2000* (New Cork: Oxford University Press).

Arias, Arturo, ed. 2001. *The Rigoberta Menchú Controversy* (Minneapolis: The University of Minnesota Press).

Barnet, Miguel, 1968. *The Autobiography of a Runaway Slave* (Barcelona: Editorial Ariel).

____, 1998a. *La fuente viva* (Havana: Editorial Letras Cubanas).

____, 1998b. *Cimarrón. Historia de un esclavo* (Madrid: Ediciones Siruela).

Beverly, John & Zimmerman, Marc, 1990. 'Testimonial Narrative', in *Literature and Politics in the Central American Revolutions* (Austin: University of Texas), pp. 173-211.

Brown, David H., 2003. *Santería Enthroned. Art, Ritual, and Innovation in an Afro-Cuban Religion* (Chicago and London: The University of Chicago Press).

Castro, Fidel, 1987, 'Palabras a los intelectuales' in *Pensamiento y política cultural cubanos (II)*, edited by Nuria Nuiry Sánchez and Graciela Fernández Mayo.

Davis, Darién, 1995. *Slavery and Beyond. The African Impact on Latin America and the Caribbean* (Wilmington, DE: Scholarly Resources Inc).

Denegri, Francesca, 2003. 'Testimonio and its discontents', in *Contemporary Latin American Cultural Studies*, Stephen Hart and Richard Young, eds. (New York: Oxford University Press), pp. 228-38.

Geisdorfer Feal, Rosemary, 1990. 'Spanish American Ethnobiography and the Slave Narrative Tradition: "*The Autobiography of a Runaway Slave*" and "Me llamo Rigoberta Menchú"', *Modern Language Studies*, 20.1: 100-111

González Echevarría, Roberto, 1980. '*The Autobiography of a Runaway Slave* and the Novel of the Cuban Revolution', *NOVEL: A Forum on Fiction*, 13. 3 (Spring): 249-63.

Gugelberger, Georg and Kearney, Michael, 1991. 'Introduction: Voices for the Voiceless: Testimonial Literature in Latin America', *Latin American Perspectives*, 18. 3 (Part I, Summer): 3-14.

Helg, Aline, 1995. *Our Rightful Share. The Afro-Cuban Struggle for Equality, 1886-1912* (Chapel Hill NC & London: The University of North Carolina Press).

Higgins, James, 1990. 'Gabriel García Márquez: *100 Años de soledad*', in *Landmarks in Modern Latin American Fiction*, Philip Swanson, ed. (London: Routledge), pp. 141-60.

Lienhard, Martin, 1991. *La voz y su huella. Escritura y conflicto étnico-cultural en América Latina* (Hanover: Editorial del Norte).

——, 1994. 'Oralidad', *Revista de Crítica Literaria Latinoamericana*, 40: 363-74.

——, 1996a. 'El fantasma de la oralidad y algunos de sus avatares literarios y etnológicos', *Les Langues Neó-Latines*, 11.297: 19-33.

____ 1996b. 'La représentation de l'oralité populaire ou marginale dans des textes modernes d'Amerique latine et d'Afrique lusophone', *Versants*, 30: 9-30

Luis, William, 1989. 'The Politics of Memory and Miguel Barnet's *The Autobiography of a Runaway Slave*', *MLN* 104. 2: 475-491.

Moore, Robin, D., 1997. *Nationalising Blackness: Afrocubanismo and Artistic Revolution in Havana, 1920-1940* (Pittsburgh: University of Pittsburgh Press).

——, 2006. *Music and Revolution. Cultural Change in Socialist Cuba* (Berkeley, Los Angeles, London: University of California Press).

Ong, Walter, 1982. *Orality and Literacy. The Technologizing of the Word* (London and New York: Methuen).

Palmié, Stephan, 2002. *Wizards and Scientists. Explorations in Afro-Cuban Modernity and Tradition* (Durham and London: Duke University Press).

Rama, Ángel, 1982. *Transculturación narrativa en América Latina* (Mexico DF: Siglo XXI Editores).

Rodríguez-Mangual, Edna M., 2004. *Lydia Cabrera and the Construction of an Afro-Cuban Cultural Identity* (Chapel Hill and London: The University of North Carolina Press).

Sklodowska, Elzbieta, 1992. *Testimonio Hispanoamericano* (New York: Peter Lang).

Stoll, David, 1999. *Rigoberta Menchú and the Story of all Poor Guatemalans* (Boulder: Westview Press).

---

[i] Various examples of African-derived cultural forms throughout Latin American can be found in Davis 1995.

[ii] Examples of recent studies on Afro-Cuban culture include Brown 2003, Moore 1997, 2005, and Palmie 2002.

[iii] This is in fact a phenomenon that affects most populations of indigenous and African descent throughout Latin America. Thus, a chief concern of Latin American writers with a social conscience has been to try and incorporate the perspectives of these subaltern sectors into the dominant literature of their nations. Martín Lienhard describes this phenomenon in the Andean regions of Latin America, where written literature has tended to reflect mostly the perspectives of the educated, white social sectors because subordinate groups have tended to privilege non-written forms of verbal expression, or at least forms of verbal expression that do not conform to the traditional European concept of 'literature'. As Lienhard points out, the construction of the official literary histories or canons of these nations reflected the role of the written word as an instrument of exclusion and domination because they only included the written literary production of the learned, mostly white dominant classes (1991: 30-31). Since the very concept of literature is the product of societies that were graphocentric or that fetishised the written word and considered it superior to other forms of verbal expression in non-western societies, the construction of the official literary canons was based on a denial of the validity of orality and its varied manifestations (Lienhard 1994: 371). This leads Lienhard to suggest that the rescuing of the oral texts of the marginalised sectors must be a part of any serious program of cultural decolonisation (Lienhard 1994: 372).

[iv] See also Gugelberger and Kearney 1991: 9.

[v] See, for instance, Barnet 1998b: 29-30.

[vi] See, for example, Barnet 1968: 58.

[vii] A section of *Transculturación narrativa en América Latina* where this conception of the transcultural novel is clear is section 3 of chapter seven, which deals with José María Arguedas's novel *Los ríos profundos*. In this section Rama emphasises the simultaneous presence of a number of perspectives or world views in Arguedas's novel which often correspond to different socio-cultural formations within the Peruvian nation. At the beginning of chapter 3 Rama outlines the three conceptual or 'perspective levels' that can be identified in the novel (Rama 1982: 289). His analyses of each level bring to light the simultaneous presence of ideological elements of European origins and of indigenous origins, and of perspectives that are based on a mixture of both. Whereas Rama's analyses of the first and third perspective levels reveal interactions in which the European perspective is dominant, in the second level Rama highlights the presence of perspectives that are

a mixture of indigenous and European elements, such as the mythical concepts of the characters of the novel, that is, Ernestos's and those of the younger children of the Abancay school (1982: 292, 296). Thus, at this level, for Rama, *Los ríos profundos* does represent a *mestizo* worldview based on elements from the dominant culture and the subordinate indigenous sectors. But even when analyzing this particular level, Rama also brings our attention to the conflicts between incompatible elements. This is the case of his analysis of the students' performance of an act of indigenous 'magic' in chapter VIII of *Los ríos profundos* (Rama 1982: 293).

[viii] Sklodowska is referring to the narrator's repetition of statements such as: 'This I know to be definitely true because it was told to me many times' (Sklodowska 1992: 126).

[ix] The controversy was unleashed by the publication of David Stoll's study *Rigoberta Menchú and the Story of all Poor Guatemalans*. Stoll interviewed survivors of the political violence in Guatemala in the late 1980s and began to come across testimonies and evidence that contradicted parts of the life story narrated in Burgos's book. According to Stoll, Rigoberta wanted to show that the Guatemalan Guerrilla Army of the Poor (EGP) was a defender of the rights of Guatemala's indigenous peasants and had with their full support. By contrast, many of the witnesses Stoll interviewed talked about constant repression from both the government and the Guerrilla Army of the Poor (EGP). Many of the atrocities committed against the peasants were in fact attributed to the EGP and, in addition, many indigenous people actually accused this guerrilla movement of starting the violence (Stoll 1999: 8-11). On the Rigoberta Menchú controversy, see also Arias 2001.

Chapter 3

Tenacity and Taboo: Africa-Inspired Narrative in *Biografía de un cimarrón*

Mario André Chandler

Few narratives have emerged out of the Latin American slave experience to provide a firsthand account of the conditions under which blacks toiled, labored and struggled in territories south of the Rio Grande. Though the number of Africans brought to Hispanic colonies and Brazil pales the quantity of those trafficked to the United States, it is curious that the latter has yielded a more prolific corpus of slave narratives penned by men as well as by women of African descent. Of equal importance is the role that such narratives served as testimonies of the resistance exhibited by Africans and their American descendants. Moreover, the widely distributed antebellum narratives of Frederick Douglass, Harriett Jacobs and William Wells Brown, to name a few, were instrumental in the abolitionist effort in the United States. While in Latin America, inclusive of Brazil, it has been argued that the conditions of slavery in its colonies were harsher than in the United States[i], the slave narrative was not the most commonly employed literary instrument of resistance used in the fight against the peculiar institution in its Latin-American incarnations.

Considering the difference between the utility and prevalence of the slave narrative genre between Latin America and the United States, two important questions can be asked: Why were there far fewer slave narratives to emerge from the Latin colonies? Why were other instruments of resistance, including alternative literary genres, preferred and cultivated by blacks in the freedom struggle in Latin America? While a comparison between Latin America and the United States is not the focus of this project, these questions merit further serious exploration.

With respect to the limited cultivation of the slave narrative genre in Latin America, Cuba stands out as an exception from its Latin American neighbors. Juan Francisco Manzano's *Autobiografía de un esclavo* and Esteban Montejo's *Biografía de un cimarrón* are two Cuban texts that provide richly harrowing portraits of slave life on the island. Manzano's narrative is unique in Spanish colonial letters as it has the distinction of having been penned by the hands of a slave protagonist himself, while the latter is unique for different reasons altogether. Montejo's *Biografía de un cimarrón*[ii], compiled by Cuban ethnographer Miguel Barnet, details the 105-year-old narrator's observations and recollections of his experiences as slave, as *cimarrón* (maroon), as emancipated citizen, and later as fighter for the independence of a country that had only recently implemented his rights as a citizen. The narrative is a compilation of the ex-slave's memories as reconstructed and preserved in written form by the biographer-ethnographer, Barnet.

Biografía de un cimarrón shares with its genre equivalents in the north, the emphasis on the slave's escape from bondage told by means of a captivating narration that satisfies "the public desire to read about the experiences of slaves, and an increasing interest in the first-person accounts of the effects of slavery on individuals" (Sterling Lecater Bland xiii-xiv). More accurately, *Biografía de un cimarrón* falls under the label of testimonial novel[iii]. The opening third of Montejo's testimonial, covering the period of slavery in Cuba, reveals the protagonist as an interrogator of African identity preserved and cultivated in the American homeland of the narrator, a Cuban-born slave, a *criollito* (18), only a generation removed from Africa. Montejo's narrative is replete with references that witness the preservation of cultural and spiritual practices deriving from Africa that are familiar, salient and contemporary in the narrator's Cuba. African cultural continuity revealed in the rites, practices and worldview sentiments, as lucidly recalled by Montejo, illustrates a form of resistance that was essential to the narrator's survival as well as his re-edification of an identity that had been fragmented by the institution that had enslaved him.

In the process of re-edifying a fragmented racial identity, blacks from throughout the diaspora often seek bedrock in some notion of lineage or connection to Africa. The details provided to us by Montejo regarding his paternal origins in particular, serve the purpose of anchoring his identity in an African ancestral pedigree. Between the two parents, information about his mother is the most ambiguous. Montejo remembers that her name is Emilia, yet regarding where she's from, he only knows that his mother "was a slave of French origin" (17), implying that she was probably from the French-speaking Antilles, perhaps from Haiti, but this is unclear.

In contrast to his mother's ambiguous background, Montejo's paternal origins are vividly and proudly recalled by the narrator in great specificity. Montejo informs: "My father was called Nazario and he was Lucumí from Oyó" (17). The designation, "Lucumí", references Yoruba spiritual systems that originate from Nigeria, and whose roots give rise to the development of Cuban *santería*. Moreover, Oyó pinpoints a specific state located in southeastern Nigeria. Ibadan is the capital of this powerful state, which has tremendous historical importance sharing with the Benin and Dahomey states, the distinction of being three foundational kingdoms of the Yoruba empire (De La Torre 160). Indeed, the most direct and personal link between Esteban Montejo and Africa is established by means of the African-based rites and rituals that he sees in practice in Cuba as witnessed through the lens of his father's African background. The narrator draws a great deal of personal pride in his identification with Africa. More importantly, his identification with things African is an important pillar which sustains the spirit behind Montejo's *cimarronía*[iv], the driving force of the text.

While Montejo's spiritual worldview is syncretic, as it clearly recognizes the existence of Christian as well as African deities, he believes the African deities to be stronger and more influential in worldly matters. The narrator's syncretism is clear when explaining humankind's limitations in the face of nature:

> You see, I know it all depends on Nature, everything comes from Nature, even what can't be seen. We men cannot do such things because we are the subjects of a God; of Jesus Christ, who is the one most talked about. Jesus Christ wasn't born in Africa, he came from Nature herself, as the Virgin Mary was a señorita.
>
> The strongest gods are African. I tell you it's certain they could fly and they did what they liked with their witchcraft. I don't know why they permitted slavery. (15-16)

Rather than mankind, white or black, being responsible for the institution of slavery in Africa, the African gods, according to Montejo, permitted its existence. The black deities' reasons for allowing slavery are beyond the narrator's knowledge. Ironically, instead of placing blame for the introduction of slavery on his white

Cuban masters or the Portuguese slave trading agents, whose presence he situates in his father's Nigerian homeland (16), the narrator cites the capricious nature of the black gods for allowing slavery to happen in the first place.

Nonetheless, Montejo in no way exonerates whites for the horrors and abuses that they committed against the black slaves on the plantations in Cuba. In describing the barracoons, or dwelling spaces provided to the slaves by their masters, the narrator expresses disgust with the unsanitary conditions that whites found acceptable for their human chattel:

> The masters, of course, said they were as clean as new pins. The slaves disliked living under those conditions: being locked up stifled them...And there was no modern ventilation there! Just a hole in the wall or a small barred window. The result was that the place swarmed with fleas and ticks, which made the inmates ill with infections and evil spells, for these ticks were witches. (21-22)

Montejo does not hold back in his criticism against the living conditions in the barracoons. The undesirability of being contained not only describes the sentiment of his fellow slaves, but more importantly it foreshadows Montejo's eventual flight and pursuit of the life of a maroon. Moreover, it is notable that while the white masters created and endorsed the inhumane conditions in the living quarters, evil forces beyond the human realm are able, according to Montejo, to thrive in that squalid environment, and wreck further havoc on the physical health and spiritual well being of the slaves. Like in many African contexts, in Montejo's reality, the spiritual and the worldly are inseparable, and incapable of functioning independent of one another.

Montejo's inspiration by Africa is not only evidenced in the frequent mention of the power of spirituality from the continent, but also it is evident when the narration highlights the African-based affinities that are preferred by Montejo as well as by his Afro-Cuban contemporaries. Montejo's descriptions of certain natural scenes that are lacking in Cuba frequently take the form of yearned reverie of a nostalgic African landscape. The nostalgia is amplified by the barrenness of the slave quarters as described by the narrator: "There were no trees either outside or inside the barracoons, just empty solitary spaces. The Negroes could never get used to this. The Negro like trees, forests" (22).

A spiritual personification of trees is described by Montejo later when he is full-fledged maroon. Trees, and to a lesser degree other figures of nature such as birds, bats and insects, become surrogates for the human contact that is absent from the caves where runaway slaves are forced to live in hiding, sustaining the narrator in his frequent moments of darkness and solitude in the forest according to his own words: "I got used to living with trees in the forest. They have their noises too, because the leaves hiss in the air. There is one tree with a big white leaf which looks like a bird at night. I could swear that tree spoke" (57).

Montejo seems to be aware of the symbolism that trees have in the African worldview[v]. Though he never visited the continent, Montejo indeed plugs into an arbor iconography with profoundly African roots: "Africa was full of trees, god-trees, banyans, cedars" (22). It is interesting that Montejo immediately follows his Africa-affirming statement with the interjection of contrastive opposition against Chinese-Cubans, who were brought to the island to serve in a state of indentured servitude. He compares: "But not China—there they have weeds, purslaine, morning-glory, the sort of thing that creeps along" (22). At various points throughout the text, Montejo virulently attacks Chinese-Cubans[vi], who he deems inferior to blacks in many respects. Where African agricultural fertility produces lush plants and tress, China produces only weeds. Where most black Cubans found strength and fellowship through rhythmic drumming rituals like *mayombe* (26) and *yuka* (29), their Chinese counterparts, according to Montejo, were collectively insular, having, "no ear for drums," preferring to stay, "in their corners" (29). Finally, in contrast to the black Cubans, whose urge and effort to return to Africa was a force rivaling an "obsession," says Montejo, the Chinese-Cuban, on the other hand, had no desire to return to his native country. Escape for Chinese indentured servants, if they so desired it, only came in the form of suicide, which Montejo abhors as a weakness never chosen as an option by blacks. Montejo views the mere suggestion that blacks found escape in suicide as a "fabrication." He claims to have never witnessed black suicide in Cuba. Montejo defends:

> "The Negroes did not do that, they escaped by flying[...]they disappeared by means of witchcraft[...]There are those who say the Negroes threw themselves into rivers. This is untrue" (43-44).

The notion of suicide as a weakness or defect in personal fortitude is common in many cultures, but appears to be particularly pervasive throughout the black diaspora in communities where a superhuman alter-identity has been constructed to counter the dehumanizing stripping and attacks on black personhood that accompanied slavery and colonialism. That this sentiment is echoed in Montejo's testimonial and projected upon a group, the Chinese, who the narrator deems to be far weaker than blacks, is illustrative of what I call, a *diasporan taboo*, which reveals itself in the text. A *diasporan taboo*, more so than simply describing practices that are frowned down upon by members of a community from within the diaspora, in reality, serve the function of constructing a collectively sanitized identity that is projected to achieve, interiorly, solace, and exteriorly, social armor for blacks who have experienced the psychological trauma of the slave or the colonial experience[vii].

A second *diasporan taboo* that emerges in *Biografía de un cimarrón* involves homosexuality, a subject that receives curious treatment in the text. The subject is first introduced among Montejo's descriptions of Afro-Cuban games and entertainment diversions. One game in particular described by Montejo is a competition with a homoerotic bent. The narrator details the competition with an uncharacteristically impersonal tone:

> Another competition was the jug game. You took a large earthernware jug with a hole in the top and stuck your prick into it. The bottom of the jug was covered with a fine ash, so you could see whether a man had reached the bottom or not when he took it out again. (28)

Unlike other ritual descriptions where Montejo presents himself as an active subject in the activity, here, Montejo prefers the role of informed and detached observer. Moreover, different from other diversions described, which have clearly African origins, the homoerotic "jug game" is generic with no African etymology whatsoever. Does this imply that homoerotic male bonding or homosexual acts themselves among black Cubans were, in reality, purely American-born practices that had no African origin or equivalent? Montejo seems to think so. The narrator opines, but with noticeably less certainty than his stance on suicide: "I don't think it [homosexuality] can have come from Africa, because the old men [the black elders] hated it. They would have nothing to do with queers" (41). If we think for a moment that Montejo's statement reeks of homophopic rhetoric from an elderly black Cuban traditionalist, his comical follow up says otherwise: "To tell the truth, it neer bothered me. I am of the opinion that a man can stick his arse where he wants" (41).

Though Montejo exhibits a great deal of personal liberalism toward the subject, the taboo is exposed in the narrator's explanations for the practice. He suggests that some men turned to homosexuality in Cuba in reaction to the unstable sexual requirements that either slavery or custom originating from Africa imposed on the male slaves. Montejo states "They [the black elders] said a man should wait until he was twenty-five to have experiences. Some men did not suffer much, being used to this life. Others had sex between themselves and did not want to know anything of women. This was their life—sodomy" (41).

In spite of Montejo's liberal attitude regarding homosexuality, he is very careful not to indict himself in the practice, maintaining a narration that is impartial and distant from the act. He equates homosexuality with "effeminate" weakness. Femininity, then, would represent the antithesis of the crafted image of a rugged, independent *cimarrón* whose presentation within the text is an exclusively masculine and wholly virile construct. Montejo personally doesn't reject the homosexual taboo, yet his narrative must somehow, distance the practice from Africa in order to maintain a representation of masculinity that would inhibit, if perceived too soft, an ethos of resistance grounded in a patriarchal notion of African fortitude. The *diasporan taboo* remains in tact.

It has been previously discussed that the ethos of resistance permeating *Biografía de un cimarrón* is also closely related to the labels of inferiority and weakness that Montejo attaches to certain groups. It is important to note that a number of African groups described in the text are also painted as inferior. Like with his critique of whites and Chinese Cubans, Montejo's criticism of certain groups of Africans in Cuba who lack a value system consistent with the values that he preferences, are called out and contrasted against the superior system with which he identifies. Montejo accomplishes in his African critique what he realizes with his non-black critiques: a carefully constructed and at times, group-specific African ideal that forms the vital force of his narrative of black resistance on the island.

The narrator frequently contrasts Africans originating from the Congo with those sharing his father's Yoruba background. For Montejo, Lucumis, like his father, exhibited values and attitudes more consistent with the spirit of the *cimarrón*. The narrator differentiates the Lucumis from his Congolese rivals: "The Lucumis didn't like cutting cane, and many of them ran away. They were the most rebellious and courageous slaves. Not so the Congolese; they were cowardly as a rule[…]There is a common rat called Congolese, and very cowardly it is too" (37).

While Montejo attacks the Congolese for a lack of courage and rebellious nature compared to the Lucumis, he takes nothing away from them with respect to their spiritualism, which he finds powerful in many ways (33). Still, as a runaway, Montejo prefers a spiritualism that contributes to the freedom struggle rather than one that exists for its own sake. This is the basis of the narrator's distrust, and outright rejection of the Roman Catholic religion (59). The ideal of African fortitude present in *Biografía de un cimarrón* draws from Montejo's internalization of values, semiotics and taboos derived from Africa. The resistance and recollection which motivate the narrator's actions for survival in Cuba evidence cultural persistence and preservation originating from the African homeland of his father. In some ways, the narrator exhibits bias in favor of his Yoruba background. In other ways, his grounding in a generic Africanity contributes a countervoice to the dominant white Cuban discourse. In other ways yet, it is clear that Esteban Montejo is indeed the product of a slave reality that molds and shapes a new Afro-Cuban character. The double consciousness grounded in African and American experiences is evident in this Cuban manifestation of the slave narrative genre.

References

Bland, Jr., Sterling Lecater, ed. *African American Slave Narratives: An Anthology.*
Westport: Greenwood Press, 2001.

Conrad, Robert Edgar. *Children of God's Fire: A Documentary History of Black*
Slavery in Brazil. University Park: Pennsylvania State University Press, 1994.

De La Torre, Miguel A. *Santería: The Beliefs and Rituals of a Growing Religion in America.* Grand Rapids: William B. Eerdmans Publishing Company, 2004.

Gugelberger, Georg and Michael Kearney. "Voices for the Voiceless: Testimonial
Literature in Latin America." *Latin American Perspectives.* 18 (1991): 3-14.

Manzano, Juan Francisco. *Autobiografía de un esclavo.* Bilingual edition. Trans.
Evelyn Picon Garfield. Detroit: Wayne State University Press, 1996.

Montejo, Esteban. *Biografía de un cimarrón.* 1966. Ed. Miguel Barnet. Madrid: Ediciones Alfaguara, 1984.

-----. The Autobiography of a Runaway Slave. Trans. Jocasta Innes. New York: Vintage Books, 1973.

Mungazi, Dickson A. *Gathering under the Mango Tree: Values in Traditional Culture in*
Africa. American University Studies Series. New York: Peter Lang, 1996.

Ogunyemi, Olatunji. "The Implications of Taboos Among African Diasporas for the
African Press in the United Kingdom." Journal of Black Studies. 37.5 (2007):
630-654.

---

[i] In his book *Children of God's Fire: A Documentary History of Black Slavery in Brazil*, Robert Edgar Conrad argues the extreme conditions of slavery in Brazil and other Latin American countries.

[ii] All citations from *Biografía de un cimarrón* that appear in this paper come from Jocasta Innes' English translation, *The Autobiography of a Runaway Slave*.

[iii] The testimonial represents a literary form commonly used in modern Latin American writings that gives voice to marginalized communities by legitimizing their recollections, perspectives and experiences in light of the "official" national accounts that frequently subvert them. See the Gugelberger and Kearney article: "Voices for the Voiceless: Testimonial Literature in Latin America".

[iv] Here the term *cimarronía* is used, not as "maroonage", the literal translation in English, but rather to describe the essence or spirit of Montejo's rebellion and resistance.

[v] Professor Dickson A. Mungazi prefaces his book, *Gathering under the Mango Tree: Values in Traditional Culture in Africa*, with an African-inspired proverb: "The sight of the Africans gathering under a mango tree symbolizes the values of the African culture."

[vi] Chinese immigration to Cuba began as early as the 1840s when Spanish colonialist contracted indentured servants from China to work in the sugar plantations alongside African slaves. The interaction (at times conflictive) between Chinese and black servants is reflected in Montejo's statements.

[vii] Olatunji Ogunyemi's article, "The Implications of Taboos among African Diasporans for the African Press in the United Kingdom" discusses extensively the social impact of collective taboos maintained by Africans in diaspora.

Chapter 4

Nicolás Guillén's Women (And Men): Another Look at Some Early Poems

Conrad James

Guillén criticism is often centred on questions of race, nationalism, and black aesthetics. This is hardly surprising since his is the most influential voice of an African-centred consciousness in Cuban writing since the end of the colonial period. Early work by Afro-Hispanists tended to examine the poetry of Guillén against the tradition of 'negrista' poetry in order to establish its continuity with or divergence from the main tenets of this movement. Over the last three decades, in addition to countless articles on the subject, major books have presented cogent analyses of his poetry through comparison variously with African American creative discourse (Kutzinski, 1987), negritude aesthetics (Kubayanda, 1990) and the contestatory cultural traditions of the wider Caribbean (Smart, 1990). Of course the foundational critical texts produced in the early 1980s, Lorna V. Williams's *Self and Society in the Poetry of Nicolás Guillén* (1982) and Keith Ellis's *Cuba's Nicolás Guillén: Poetry and Ideology* (1983) already had established firmly the poet's socio-historic significance.

That the dynamics of gender in Guillén were hardly prioritized in most of these earlier assessments of his work has been noted sufficiently elsewhere and as such does not need to be repeated here. In *Sugar's Secrets* (1993) Vera Kutzinski energized significantly the discussion on the gender politics inherent in Cuban national tropes. The book provides a convincing explanation of the national discourse of 'mestizaje' as an unstable construction of 'interracial masculinity which hides behind racially mixed femininity' (p.16). Guillén's pivotal participation in this discourse serves Kutzinski well in her explication of the complicating factors within the 'ideological volatility in Cuban society' (p.172); things that have to be kept hidden in order to facilitate the presentation of a harmonious national narrative. Thus the poet's leitmotif of 'Cuban colour' is confirmed as paradigmatic of tropes of racial mixing which elide female participation.

But even after *Sugar's Secrets* and later critical work on Guillén, the gendered power relations implicit in *Motivos de son* and *Sóngoro cosongo* can still accommodate further interrogation. By placing the black Cuban woman within a clear socio-political milieu the 'motivos' distinguish themselves from the one-dimensional exotic portrayal of the black woman that defined 'negrista' poetry written by many of Guillén's contemporaries[i]. However, as my discussion of these poems show, they inscribe several other gender-related problems.

The most salient feature of the texts in these two early collections, according to Antonio Benítez-Rojo, is that the black voice sets out to invest 'the plantation' with 'its desire and its resistance' (1992, p.123). Guillén intends to 'impregnate society with the negro's libido – his libido - transgressing the mechanisms of sexual censorship that the plantation imposed on his race' (p.123). Clearly, the poetic deployment of the desired black female body becomes indispensable in this process. In these collections, as indeed in later ones such as *La paloma de vuelo popular* (1958) and *La rueda dentada* (1972), the black woman as muse serves key corrective ideological and artistic functions. Through this medium Guillén redraws significantly the aesthetic/poetic mappings within early twentieth-century Cuban literature. Nineteenth and early twentieth-century Cuban literature (as well as lived history) is replete with sexual liaisons between white men and black women. And the propensity of nineteenth-century black Cuban poets to write the desired white or Mediterranean woman is well known. The black Cuban woman, 'a composite of transcontinental and Antillean mysteries', (Benítez-Rojo, p.124) as the centre of the poetic/historical text thus constitutes a radical political shift. But in his interpretation of black life in 1920s Cuba, Guillén's attitude to black and mulatto women emerges as highly contradictory; if they are central to the articulation of a transgressive discourse they are also, at least partially, constrained by it. And it is also illuminating to examine the images and attitudes of men in the *motivos* not only as members of the black urban poor but as men vis-à-vis the women with whom they are necessarily in constant negotiations, battles or, as Gordana Yovanovich (2001) would put it, play. I shall return to Yovanovich later.

The snapshots of the lives of the black Cuban underclass which are provided in the 'motivos' capture the way politics of gender in male/female domestic relationships further complicate lives in the margins of society. Ellis's early observation of the way the love relationships between man and woman in the 'motivos' are frustrated by 'unrelentingly hostile social forces' (Ellis, p.66) might therefore be productively extended to include an examination of the relative pressures suffered by man as opposed to woman and more importantly to consider the way the economic pressures faced by each are exacerbated by gendered socio-cultural codes.

In both 'Negro bembón' (1974, 1: p.103)[ii] and 'Mulata' (1: p.104) the poet might be regarded as being complicit with the objectification of the women presented; this is implied since they are only used to articulate the psychological state of the male subject without any reference to their own. In the first poem the reassuring presence of Caridá is evoked as a means of allaying the man's psychological insecurities about his racial identity:

> 'Bembón así como ere
> tiene de to;
> Caridá te mantiene,
> te lo da to'
> (Big-lipped as you are / you have everything; /Caridá takes care of you, / she gives you everything you need)[iii].

Inserted as a refrain in the segments of the poem which call attention to the black man's poverty and sense of shame about being black, it is the utility rather than the complete personhood of Caridá that is evoked to pacify this crisis in black masculinity. Similarly, though the second poem is named 'Mulata' after the apostrophized object of male desire, it is the man or, more correctly, the masculine psyche which is the subject of the poem. The rejection is articulated definitively in the poem as a racial issue and the gender aspect of the dilemma is silenced rather than problematized. In his coming to terms with rejection by the mulatto woman the utility of the black woman is again articulated to counter the sense of inadequacy experienced by the black man. Therefore, both the *mulata* who spurns him and the *negra*, whom he possesses and on whose presence he relies as a psychological prop, are really conduits which facilitate the staging of male emotional insecurities and identity crises.

The two central preoccupations in *Motivos de son,* socio-economic marginalization and black male psychosis, coincide in 'Si tú supiera' (p.105) through the motif of jealousy. Harsh material circumstances cause the woman to desert the speaker for someone who is more economically secure, at least temporarily. The damage to the male ego is evidenced through the expression of the concern that the woman will be giving the sexual favours once reserved for him to the new lover:

> 'A é tu le hará como a mí,
> que cuando no tube plata
> te corrite de bachata,
> sin acoddadte de mí'
> (You going to do to him what you used to do to me, / cause when I ran out o' money / you went out on a spree / without thinking about me).

Female autonomy is obviously not an option. More crucially female agency is vilified since her refusal to be confined to a love life of economic hardship is what precipitates his suffering.

The amplification of economic oppression by gender socialization is a significant feature of 'Si tú supiera'. The notion of the male as provider coupled with the increased profile of money as the symbol of masculinity in Cuba of the 1920s (Williams 1982) compounds the crippling effect which the male ego suffers because of the loss of the woman to a male rival. An added dimension of this is seen in 'Búcate plata' (p.108) where the woman's tolerance of economic difficulties has reached breaking point:

> Búcate plata, búcate plata,
> poqque no doy un paso má:
> etoy a arró con galleta, na má'
> (Go get money, go get money / because I cannot go one step further: / Am down to rice and crackers, that's all.).

In addition to pointing up the societal ethos which prescribes the male partner as provider, this poem is more sensitive to the predicament of the female character than poems like 'negro bembón' and 'mulata'. Her speech act points to double jeopardy; in addition to economic destitution she is expected to bear the burden of respectability:

> Depué dirán que soy mala,
> y yo me quedrán tratá,
> pero amó con hambre, biejo,
> ¡qué bá!'
> (Dey will all say am bad / won't want to have anyting to do wit me, / but love on a hungry belly man, / to hell wit dat!).

Her implicit refusal to have her future determined by a set of social prescriptions (both racialized and gendered) is one instance in the motivos which anticipates the more progressive attitudes towards women's self-determination which would come to define some black Cuban women's writing much later in the twentieth century.

The question of reputation as a controlling device for the woman had already been evoked in 'Sigue,' (p.106) the fourth 'motivo'. In this poem the woman who rejects the male speaker, and thus challenges the proprietorial expectations inherent in the brand of masculinity which he represents, is accorded pariah status. The speaker warns the implied male interlocutor:

> Sigue y no te para,
> sigue;
> no la mire si te llama,
> sigue;
> acuéddate que ella e mala,
> sigue'
> (Keep on walking and don't stop, / carry on, / don't look if she calls out to you, / carry on, / don't foget she is a bad woman.).

Ostracism and defamation are the penalties paid by the 'mala mujer. As a contaminating force she must be avoided at all cost. But Guillén in these early poems also bears witness to a wider social panorama in which male anger, violence and the endangered female body are dominant features. Poems such as 'Secuestro de la mujer de Antonio' and 'Chévere' from *Sóngoro cosongo* reveal much about the insecurities at the heart of the performances of masculinity which often obtained in the marginal communities of the republic. Hemmed in by a variety of gender-based expectations the 'chévere' is able to deal with almost every form of defeat except the infidelity of his woman. Female infidelity not only makes of a woman a person of ill repute but it also puts the reputation of the 'macho' at stake.

Largely through the work of African-American and Caribbean feminist criticism we have become highly attuned to the use of the idea of the inordinately strong and interminably resilient black woman as an insidious means of control. The paternalism of the male speech in 'Hay que tené voluntad' gestures towards this tendency as it simultaneously controls with advice and absolves itself from responsibility. But where this image is complete and most problematic is in one of the most controversial poems in *Motivos de son* is 'Mi chiquita'.

La chiquita que yo tengo
tan negra como e
no la cambio po ninguna,
po ninguna otra mujé.

Ella laba, plancha, cose,
y sobre to, caballero.
¡cómo cosina!

Si la bienen a bucá,
pa bailá,
pa comé
ella me tiene que llebá,
o traé.

Ella me dise: mi santo,
tú no me puede dejá;
bucamé,
bucamé,
bucamé
pa gozá.

Black as she is,
I wouldn't trade
The woman I got
For no other woman.

She wash, iron, sew,
And, man,
Can that woman cook!

If you want her
to go dancing
or go eat,
she got to take me,
got to bring me back.

She say: 'Daddy,
You can't leave me 't all,
Come get me,

Come get me,
Come get me,[iv]
Let's have a ball.'

Obviously, the declaration of commitment contingent upon exemplary domesticity constitutes a manipulative *machista* discourse. What the ostensible praise for and celebration of his *negra* reveals is the male ego-centricity which is at the core of the spoken text. In addition to being a domestic phenomenon the faithful woman is not only available for his sexual pleasures but also makes sure to give the speaker the extra satisfaction of expressing to him his desirability. Not surprisingly, this prevailing image of possession has been the subject of much strident criticism by feminist scholars for decades. The domestic slave (la esclava doméstica) (Fuentes, 1994, p.88), to mention just one example of this trend, is for some the only image that successfully emerges despite any attempt to mythify the *negra* in this text. In rejecting the indignity of poverty and hunger through threatening to opt for the infamy of the street rather than the respectability of self-sacrificial domesticity, the woman speaker in 'Búcate plata' suggests the possibility of an agentic position not prioritized by the black woman in 'Mi chiquita'.

It might be argued that if the psychological power of male over female is shifted at all in *Motivos de son* it is in the final poem 'Tú no sabe inglé'. In this poem the lack of linguistic competence on the part of the black Cuban male prevents him from succeeding in his seduction of the American (presumably white) woman. The lack of ability to speak English for which the man is ridiculed effectively becomes an attack on his masculinity. But if the power balance is shifted here, far from serving a female-centred agenda of empowerment it only reminds us of the cultural imperialist dominance of the United States over the Cuban republic. Thus the woman here becomes a symbol of the castrating effects of North American imperialism on the Cuban nation.

More importantly, 'Tú no sabe inglé' foregrounds the politics of Cuban homo-sociality and its constituent capacities for both solidarity and ridicule which are at the heart of several of the poems in *Motivos de son*. Together these poems imply either conversations or contests between men in which women serve as the opportunity for consolidating one's machismo or challenging that of others. The men console each other through the evocation of the functionality of their black women ('Negro bembón'), they warn each other of the danger embodied in the tainted mulata ('Sigue'), they deride each other when they are proved lacking in the dynamics of seduction ('Tú no sabe inglé') and they proclaim their status as 'supermachos' through staging the industry and sexual dependency of their women ('Mi chiquita').

Gordana Yovanovich has read these poems rather differently. For her, they are best read as instances of imaginative play which are borne out of the necessity to mitigate difficult circumstances and endure (p.16). It is through play, she suggests, that the black women in Guillén's poetry escape the fate of being just slaves. And play is the mechanism through which 'in ontological terms she finds her dignity and realizes her humanity' (p.16). Yovanovich quite correctly warns of the of the dangers of imposing Anglo-American feminist reading criteria on texts such as Guillén's and insists that the cultural context of women's subordination be taken into account. Thus in the reading which she activates, the Afro-Cuban woman in poems such as 'Mi chiquita' is best seen as being in a relationship of co-dependency. She is not a victim but an agent. Quite apart from being simply evidence of her subservience, 'the pleasures furnished by the Afro-Cuban woman… are also forms of seduction'. Her duties are also in fact a form of foreplay and she is thereby empowered (p.17).

According to this account the woman, who 'displays a healthy self esteem', (p.18), has power, and above all sexual power. And this is indicated through the female sexual leadership which is implied in the text. What is omitted from the analysis, however, is the fact that the audience/reader is never privy to the voice of the woman. We never hear her side of the story and as such the reader is forced to gather all of the information concerning the dynamics of work/play/sex from the male speaker. Despite its astuteness and originality, then, this approach to the text runs the risk of over-determining the discursive and undermining important aspects of the materiality in which it is inscribed. Concretely, allowing the focus on conjugal play in 'Mi chiquita' to necessarily supersede the silence and acquiescence (voluntary or coerced) of the Afro-Cuban woman indicates a perspective which takes as given black female resilience; one which assumes that power always miraculously emerges from suffering. While certainly not patronizing in this instance, this attitude comes dangerously close to the essentialist glorification of black female strength which often appears in a range of more problematic critical contexts.

Like 'Negro bembón,' 'Mi chiquita' reveals the racial crisis and insecurity of the Cuban macho assuaged to some extent by the comfort drawn from his assumption of the safety and security of the gender order. Early twentieth-century Cuban society conceives of very limited roles for women. In the case of non-white women these roles, all somatically determined, are even fewer. At best, in 'Mi chiquita' the speaker's initial introduction of his woman, (tan negra como e / black as she is) is an instance which reveals his indeterminacy towards the value (aesthetic at least) of blackness. At worst it might be read as an occasion of blatant racial shame. Clearly, at the centre of his discourse is the plantation episteme which designates the black woman's body as a tool of labour. Ultimately the woman in 'Mi chiquita' becomes an amalgam of the race/gender stereotypes available to the male speaker within his cultural milieu. Hence the celebrated woman combines the fortitude of the black female workhorse with the supposed sensuality and eroticism of the *mulata*.[v]

While Yovanovich acknowledges that the women in Guillén's early poems are more abused than men in the social panorama that they present, the premise that the woman's being 'at the centre of everything' (p.27) implies some reconstructive empowering outcome remains unconvincing. In these early poems the black woman as muse becomes one of Guillén's sources of reconstituting the black male image and an opportunity thereby to construct a new androcentric black nation. The creative energy drawn from the woman is not redeployed in ways that reward its female source.

These are not texts of female empowerment. Women's bodies are certainly at the centre of the poems but women's voices are not. Women's images adorn the texts but any ideology which promotes female directivity remains at their margins or beyond their borders.

Interestingly, the black woman does not necessarily fare better in much of the Afro-Hispanist criticism of this poetry. What characterizes most of this strand of criticism is an overwhelming zeal to celebrate Guillén's putative authenticity as a voice for black pride and a source for the recuperation of a lost African identity in new world poetics. Emblematic of this approach are the critical reflections offered on the women in the much discussed poems from *Sóngoro cosongo*, 'Mujer nueva' and two poems, both entitled 'Madrigal'. Deified figures, these women are symbols of strength and a tireless repository of pristine African culture. Within the Afro-Hispanic interpretative tradition especially, though not exclusively, 'Mujer nueva' is seen as an un-problematically redemptive representation of black womanhood. For Jackson it is an early poetic representation of respect for the black woman (1976, p.125); Ellis sees it simply as a celebration of 'the elemental beauty of the black woman' (1983, p.73) and Smart discusses the poem as a highpoint in a process of humanizing nature (1990, p.130). Despite his acknowledgement that some of the reductive characteristics of 'negrista' poetry feature in the poem therefore, Smart contends that Guillén's images are 'evocative not provocative' (p.131) and the 'mujer nueva' thus becomes a positive figure of 'telluric mysticism' (p.132).

The fact is that the women in 'Mi chiquita' and the supposed new women in *Sóngoro Cosongo* have far more in common with the exoticized and often deformed female figures imagined and propagated by most white practitioners of negrista poetry than many early Afro-Hispanists cared to admit. These commentaries by leading Afro-Hispanists all reveal, to a greater or lesser extent, a critical practice that is caught up in the very crisis in which the texts themselves are embroiled. As though forced to choose between competing loyalties, what appear as or are intended to be reconciliatory critical strategies ultimately result in any possibility of a feminist reading being necessarily superseded by Afro-centric nationalist readings. I am not convinced, for example, by Lorna Williams's argument that the 'machista' portrayal of the black woman in 'Mujer nueva' is somehow tempered by the ascription of her sensuality to African atavism (Williams, p.21).

Simply put, this is a critical practice in which race trumps gender in any attempt at prioritizing a political analysis of the texts. In an understandably overwhelming zeal to pay homage to the celebration of Africa and the African in these texts some critics felt the need to deliberately supplant a feminist agenda with a black nationalist agenda. Others were hardly aware of the crisis that the texts presented and still others failed to problematize the issue sufficiently. The result is that the very premise of an African centred practice of critical analysis is undermined within these readings. In particular, the three aforementioned poems from *Sóngoro cosongo* together constitute a discourse on reason and the body in which the black woman's physicality precludes any capacity for thought or knowledge. The extent to which these poems, and much of the early criticism of them, are able to serve a redemptive racial agenda is therefore seriously attenuated by their extremely reactionary gender perspective. As Vera Kutzinski has aptly stated in response to Gustavo Pérez Firmat's analysis of the 'madrigals', 'when you think with your thighs you don't speak (1993, p.177).[vi] Thus this celebration of the black woman forecloses her possibilities for agency.

Conclusion: *La rueda dentada*, Guillén's Real New Women?

La rueda dentada (1972) falls within what Benítez-Rojo refers to as the subversive phase in Guillén's poetry. Published four decades after the poems discussed above, the collection addresses concerns of social justice in both national and international contexts from the perspective of a mature poet towards the end of his career. Firmly anti-imperialist in stance the collection is an integral part of Guillén's poetry of revolutionary consolidation. Thirteen years after the inception of the revolutionary process there is still no appetite to forgive or sympathise with the fallen bourgeoisie 'los burgeses vencidos' ('Burgueses'). In paradigm shifting texts European cultural elitism is ridiculed ('Problemas del subdesarollo') and a range of atrocities endorsed by the United States is condemned through poems occasioned by the murder of heroes such as Che Guevara and Martin Luther King. Several poems in this collection are celebrations of women and I wish to use this closing segment of my discussion to suggest that perhaps it is in later collections such as these that we might perceive the emergence of a progressive new image of the black woman in Guillén's poetry. If in the early poems the black woman appears simply as muse or trope in order to consolidate a male-centred vision of racial or cultural resistance, it is possible to read women in some of the later texts as part of a more nuanced political landscape in which gender is also a recognized site of struggle. Several poems in *La rueda dentada* are dedicated to women (real or imagined) but perhaps 'Nancy' and 'Angela Davis' might be the most useful in demonstrating the points with which I intend to conclude.

The personal portraits in *La rueda dentada* all serve as conduits through which Guillén filters convictions of a progressive racial and revolutionary politics. This is equally true in the case of elegies to dead men (Martin Luther King, Che Guevara, Martín Dihigo)[vii] as to the celebratory texts written in praise of living black women (Nancy Morejón and Angela Davis). In '¿Qué color?', for example, satirizing the multitply problematic, if 'well intentioned' white patronage and outrage at the assassination of Martin Luther King, Guillén questions what for some is the inevitable nexus between whiteness and purity and praises the murdered leader for his soul that was as black as coal, 'negra como el carbón'. In death Che Guevara becomes a ubiquitous symbol of inspiration for all just liberation struggles ('Che comandante') and the simultaneous mourning of Martín Dihigo's death and celebration of his past vitality are executed through symbols which are distinctly indigenous or African, 'ácana', 'guayacán', and 'ébano'[viii]. Thus the poems constitute a radical epistemological shift which simultaneously denounced oppressive power dynamics and sought to reconfigure the anti-black bias, what Stuart Hall refers to as, 'the ethnic scale' which continues to determine social relations in the Caribbean, the United States and beyond.

In the poems dedicated to them, Nancy Morejón and Angela Davis, figure as significant symbols used to articulate the epistemological/political process in which Guillén is engaged. However, unlike the earlier poems discussed in this essay in which the black woman becomes little more than a trope deployed for representational expedience, in 'Nancy' and 'Angela Davis' the women are invested with a greater degree of personal subjectivity. Nancy Morejón appears as the quintessence of the Cuban national spirit in 'Nancy'. She also stands for an African-centred perspective, faithful to her roots as she becomes the epitome of a progressive class politics. It is principally through somatic images that these ideas are articulated. For example, the poet/speaker praises her un-straightened, 'natural', hair. This is a tangible symbol that separates her from the women of an ideologically maimed black Cuban bourgeoisie, mocked in the poem for remaining enslaved to deceptive hairdressers ('esclavos del peluquero engañador'). In addition to hair, skin, eyes, breasts and flesh all feature in 'Nancy', a poem which encompasses personal love and politics equally. The beloved in the text is imaged as an anteleope, a gazelle with innocent eyes and culpable breasts ('senos breves y culpables'). Throughout the poem love is expressed both for the body and the soul of the younger female poet and its ending establishes the poet/speaker's deep admiration of the woman subject in terms which are both personal and political. Her identity is grounded physically and becomes indistinguishable from that of the nation.

Nancy is seen and the sight of her is a source of pleasure. More importantly she is heard and the poem celebrates her powerful whisper. Voice, woman's voice, becomes a crucial pivot around which revolves Guillén's poetic gesture of solidarity with the African American philosopher and freedom fighter, Angela Davis. Written in response to Davis's highly controversial imprisonment in 1970 for conspiracy, kidnapping and homicide, the poem dismisses the oppressive state apparatus as clumsy and condemns its attempts to silence Davis to bitter failure. Imaged deliberately as male, the enemy fails to extinguish Davis's voice which is described variously as lightning, fire and thunder ('rayo, incendio, relámpago'). Ultimately, the attempt to silence Davis will be ineffectual. In 'Angela Davis' the (white male) US justice system is rendered weak and clumsy against the strength and intensity of Davis's (black female) voice and its global reach[ix].

The poem becomes an occasion to highlight the regressive politics of the United States, the proliferation of racism, the haunting presence of the Klu Klux Klan and what Davis herself has referred to as the 'Jail, Courtroom, Prison Apparatus' which today, more than ever, remains central to the quotidian social dynamics of that country.[x] This is contrasted in the poem with the speaker's celebration of the progressive politics of Revolutionary Cuba. It is from the vantage point of the new progressive nation, a utopia of the present in which constraining prison walls are replaced by the openness of the Caribbean Sea, that the poet/speaker forms an alliance with Davis and pledges his allegiance to her.

As in 'Nancy', the delineation of the body (face, smile, skull) is highly significant in the construction of the liberatory message of the text. Nancy Morejón's un-processed hair symbolises for the poet a body/style politics which enunciates the then ideologically correct message 'Black is beautiful'.[xi] And Angela Davis's smile, in the poem, encapsulates hope for black liberation struggles in a trans-national context. Of course, in both poems there is a clear tension between sensuality and politics, between libidinal desire and social desire. This is present from the very first line of 'Angela Davis' with the simultaneous evocation and erasure of the significance of the body as a site of sensuality; of the poet as desiring subject and the woman as the textualized subject of desire.

> Yo no venido aquí a decirte que eres bella
> Creo que sí, que eres bella,
> Mas no se trata de eso.
>
> I have not come here to tell you that you are beautiful
> I believe so, that you are beautiful,
> But that is not the issue now.

The speaker himself is acutely aware of the tension and it might be argued that the politics of desire threaten to de-stabilize the wider project of Black Atlantic solidarity which the text sets out to inscribe. I prefer to read 'Angela Davis' and 'Nancy' as examples of textual economies which have the capacity to accommodate both libidinal and political desires productively. In these later poems (un)thinking thighs are replaced by body, mind and voice; the woman not only serves as muse but she is also agent and protagonist.

Nicolás Guillén wrote numerous poems in which women feature centrally. Perhaps most interesting are those written not for public consumption but as private expressions of love and admiration.[xii] Here we have perhaps the most nuanced portrayal of the gamut of sensibilities which informs his poetic inscription of the connections between women and men. The exploration of these poems is beyond the scope of this essay. However the poems in *La rueda dentada*, despite the political militancy of the collection, already begin to suggest the complexity with which Guillén would later present the female dynamic in such poems. Both desired subjects and potent creators and leaders, it is here and not in the poetry of the 1930s that we might begin to find Guillén's real new women.

References

Benítez-Rojo, Antonio *The Repeating Island* (Durham: Duke University Press, 1992).

Ellis, Keith, Cuba's *Nicolás Guillén: Poetry and Ideology* (Toronto: University of Toronto Press, 1983).

Fuentes, Ileana, *Cuba sin caudillos: Un enfoque feminista para el siglo XXI* (New York: Linden Lane Press, 1994)

Guillén, Nicolás, *Obra poética* 2 vols. (La Habana: Letras Cubanas, 1974).

Jackson, Richard, *The Black Image in Latin American Literature* (Albuquerque: University of New Mexico Press, 1976).

Kubayanda, Josaphat, *The Poet's Africa: Africanness in the Poetry of Nicolás Guillén and Aimé Césaire* (London: Greenwood, 1990).

Kutzinski, Vera, *Sugars Secrets: Race and the Erotics of Cuban Nationalism* (Charlottesville: University of Virginia Press, 1993).

-------------------*Against the American Grain: Myth and History in William Carlos Williams, Jay Wright, and Nicolás Guillén* (Baltimore: Johns Hopkins University Press, 1987).

Smart, Ian, *Nicolás Guillén: Popular Poet of the Caribbean* (Columbia: University of Missouri Press, 1990).

Williams, Lorna, *Self and Society in The Poetry of Nicolás Guillén* (Baltimore: Johns Hopkins University Press, 1982).

Yovanovich, Gordana, 'Play as a Mode of Empowerment for Women and as a Model for Poetics in the Early Poetry of Nicolás Guillén' in *Hispanic Review*, Vol. 69, No.1, 2001, pp. 15- 31

[i] I do not subscribe to the thesis of authenticity which has defined the approach of many Afro-Hispanists to the poetry of Nicolás Guillén. Thankfully this discourse has been dismantled successfully by Miguel Arnedo-Gómez in his recent book *Writing Rumba: The Afrocubanista Movement in Poetry* (2006).

[ii]Nicolás Guillén *Obra Poética* 2 vols. (1974). All subsequent references to Guillén's poems will be taken from this collection and referred to by page number only.

[iii] All translations, unless otherwise stated, are my own.

[iv] Translated by Roberto Márquez in *Nicolás Guillén: My last Name and Other Poems* (London: Mango, 2002), p. 47.

[v] For an extensive analysis of these images as they appear in Spanish Caribbean literature see Claudette Rosegreen Williams *Charcoal and Cinnamon: The Politics of Colour in Spanish Caribbean Literature* (Gainsville: University of Florida, 2000).

[vi]In a curious attempt to separate language and poetics from gender Pérez Firmat suggests that in the 'madrigals' Guillén is talking about his poetry and therefore to be offended by the portrayal of black women is to take the poems too literally. See Pérez Firmat (1989, p.90).

[vii] Known as 'El Inmortal', Martín Dihigo (1906-1971) was one of the most outstanding Cuban baseball players of the twentieth century and a very close friend of Nicolás Guillén's.

[viii] Ácana, guayacán (lignum vitae) and ébano (ebony) are all hardwood trees found in the Caribbean.

[ix] The movement to free Angela Davis in 1970 gathered momentum rapidly and soon became global. Much of the information concerning the scope, composition and activities of the movement has been chronicled in *Angela Davis: An Autobiography* (London: The Women's Press, 1974).

[x] Davis has for decades been one of the leading thinkers exploring the philosophy underpinning prison in the US justice system. See for example, her book *Are Prisons Obsolete?* (Open Media, 2003).

[xi] Of Course this position of keeping one's hair 'natural' as an indication of authentic African identity seems retrospectively ironic given much of the work done on hair, style and black identity politics by cultural theorists since the 1990s. One of the earliest and best examples of this scholarship is Kobena Mercer *Welcome to the Jungle* (London: Routledge, 1994).

[xii] Here I am thinking specifically of the poems written over many years to his lover Sara Casal. These poems were collected, translated and published in a bilingual edition by Keith Ellis. *New Love Poetry?Nueva Poesía de amor* (Toronto: University of Toronto Press, 1994).

Chapter 5

The Eusebia Cosme Show: Translating an Afro-Antillean Identity

Emily McGuire

In 1939, V. B. Spratlin, Professor of Romance Languages at Howard University, wrote a brief but enthusiastic review of a recent performance he had attended:

> Students and the general public were so delighted with the incomparable art of Señorita Cosme that I am impelled to pass along the good news of her presence in the United States. The remarkable thing about the recital was the enthusiastic response of the audience, despite the fact that the great majority of those present did not understand Spanish. All are agreed that the artist's personality is so engaging, her mastery of pantomime so complete, and her sense of rhythm so refined that the linguistic element is secondary – or at least not essential to the enjoyment of her art.[i]

"Señorita Cosme" was Eusebia Cosme, an Afro-Cuban ("mulatta") declaimer and one of the most well-known public interpreters of the so-called *negrista* and "Afro-Antillean" poetry.[ii] Spratlin's editorial is significant for a number of reasons. First, it testifies to the popularity of Cosme as a performer outside her native Cuba and even beyond the Caribbean. The division of the audience into "students" and "the general public" suggests that her performance held a popular appeal as much as a potentially academic one. Perhaps Spratlin's most interesting comment, however, is his observation that the "linguistic element" of Cosme's performance was *secondary* to the physical one. That is, Cosme's performance communicated something beyond (or in addition to) the poetry she recited, and furthermore, that something was perceived to be equally – if not more – important than the poetry itself. A reader of Spratlin's comments is forced to ask herself just what the physicality of Cosme's performance – her "pantomime" and "refined" sense of rhythm – communicated, with what aspects of the recitation this North American audience found themselves identifying. Could it have to do with representations of gender? Of race?

When we think about how ideas travel, what we are frequently thinking of is how texts travel, the ways in which communities of readers are formed, and engage in dialogue both within and across national, regional, and above all linguistic borders. In his investigation into the artistic and intellectual communication between African American writers of the Harlem Renaissance and the African and Caribbean writers who found themselves in Paris, Brent Edwards argues that "the cultures of black internationalism can be seen only *in translation.*" (7). As much as these encounters took place thanks to certain similarities, Edwards emphasizes that "one can approach such a project only by attending to the ways that discourses of internationalism *travel,* the ways they are translated, disseminated, reformulated and debated in transnational contexts marked by difference" (7). In his analysis of the work of writers such as René Maran and Alain Locke, Paulette Nardal and Claude McKay, Edwards highlights the mis-readings and cultural differences that framed and guided both the cultural encounters between these figures and their understanding of what a universal black culture might mean. Edwards's analysis focuses on discourses of racial identity as differentiated and defined by texts, but many times the transnational journeys that tie such movements together are enacted not just by texts or 'ideas' but by physical bodies, sometimes bodies who actively mediate these ideas.

Eusebia Cosme was one of these bodies. For nearly 30 years, between 1930 and 1957, she performed a solo show, the central attraction of which was the recitation of poetry whose unifying characteristic was the presentation of a black racialized identity. Cosme's show was notable for the fact that it brought together the work of poets whose ideologies and aesthetic approaches to blackness did not always coincide but who were united through her performance. As Spratlin's observations indicate, Cosme's own performance – the public persona that she created and the ways in which she chose to embody a particular racialized identity – is also significant, both for the choices Cosme herself made in that representation and for the ways in which those choices were read. As it examines the multiple ways that Cosme was "translated" in different cultural contexts, this paper looks at how we might read Cosme's performance, both in relation to the poetry she recited and as separate from it, as a communicative gesture in its own right.

Biographical Interlude

Eusebia Adriana Cosme y Almanza was born in Santiago, Cuba's second largest city, in 1911. After her parents died, she was taken in by a well-to-do family who brought her to Havana, where she was given the opportunity to study music, elocution, and declamation. It was in Havana that she came to the attention of the Spanish actor José González Marín, who eventually sponsored her debut performance at the Teatro Payret. The performance was well-received and Cosme continued to perform throughout Cuba and the Spanish-speaking Caribbean, developing a poetic repertoire that focused almost exclusively on poetry with Afro-Cuban or Afro-Caribbean content. She eventually became something of an international star, performing in Europe, South America, and the United States. In 1940, she left Cuba for New York City, where she had her own radio program, "The Eusebia Cosme Show", on CBS's "Las Cadenas de las Américas". Her career entered its third incarnation when she was offered the role of Angustias in a Mexican theatre company's production of "El derecho de nacer", by the Cuban writer Félix Caignet. The play spawned a movie version, in which Cosme also starred, and she went on to appear in several other Mexican films, as well as in Sidney Lumet's "The Pawnbroker".[iii] Cosme remained in Mexico until shortly before her death, when she returned to the United States. She died in Miami in 1976.

While much could be said about the Mexican movies such as "Mamá Dolores" (1971) and "El derecho de nacer", in which Cosme was frequently slotted into stereotyped roles – the long-suffering servant, the wise maternal figure – my interest here is in Cosme's first career as a declaimer. Rather than providing a dry recitation of erudite verse, Cosme's show was a carefully crafted, well-rounded performance ("Espectáculo", literally "spectacle", the Spanish word for show, might be an appropriate description) in which Cosme herself had a surprising amount of directorial agency. Her recitations were accompanied by colorful sets and music, both of which she had a hand in designing. All of these elements served to augment Cosme's stage persona, described by Cuban intellectual Fernando Ortiz as a "mulata sandunguera" – a witty, gregarious mulatta ("¿Quién es Eusebia Cosme?" 1). While this figure had strong cultural connections to Cuba, the mulatta figure was in itself a translative gesture, allowing Cosme to perform/interpret Afro-Caribbean identity for a wide range of audiences (both national and international) and to unite the sometimes conflicting constructions of black Caribbean subjectivity displayed in the poetry she chose to recite.

While it would be easy to dismiss Cosme's stage persona as a stereotype, to accuse her of exoticizing the figure of the mulatta (and thus creating a kind of vaudeville spectacle of Afro-Caribbean culture), her performances form an interpretive framework linking the archive of poetry and what Diana Taylor has termed "the repertoire", the body of culturally encoded performances that in themselves communicate meaning (27). We cannot go back in time to witness one of Cosme's performances, yet an examination of the "scene" of those performances, the ways in which they were read and their relationship to the archive, reveals overlapping and contradictory shades of meaning.[iv] For Cuban writers and critics such as Nicolás Guillén and Fernando Ortiz, Cosme was the embodiment of a vision of a racially harmonious society that many of these writers were struggling to imagine or narrate.[v] But Cosme also created a speaking black female subject whose vocal presence visibly contested the objectification this same female figure receives in much *negrista* and Afro-Antillean poetry. For foreign audiences, Cosme's performances acted on the one hand as messengers of a certain kind of international black identity, exposing audiences to a specific corpus of poetry, and to the gendered black body speaking these texts. On the other hand, as we have seen through Spratlin's comments, her recitations also carried a message in themselves, that was not necessarily dependent on (and that may have been quite different from) that of the poetry. The contradictory evidence we have for reading her performances suggests that Cosme's staged readings can be identified as what Daphne Brooks names acts of "Afro-alienation", performances that work to "render racial and gender categories 'strange' and to thus 'disturb' cultural perceptions of identity formation" (5). Rather than speaking to one image of racial identity, whether stereotyped or harmonizing, they speak instead to the many acts of translation – to the *articulations* or disjunctures – inherent in representations of racial identities.

Poesía mulata: Race in Cuba

To understand how Cosme's performances might be read, and in particular how she came to claim the particular poetic corpus that she did, it is necessary to take a brief detour through the history of early racial politics in Cuba. Although arguments for Cuban unity clearly trumped race in defining national identity from Independence onward, Alejandro de la Fuente argues that the common element in early definitions of Cubanness was "a shared belief that 'race' was at the core of the nation" (23). Cubans of all races had fought in the War for Independence, yet post-Independence political discussion revealed a variety of opinions over the definition of an egalitarian society, and how that society should be created. Early racial discourse – in part influenced by the U.S. occupation and North American ideas about race – frequently emphasized the need to "whiten" Cuba, diminishing both the presence and visibility of Afro-Cuban elements. The formation of the Partido Independiente de Color (the Independent Party of Colour) in 1908, the strongest attempt to increase Afro-Cuban agency through the creation of a racialized political group, ended in tragedy four years later when attacks on the party degenerated into the "Guerrita del '12" (the "Little War of '12"), widespread violence and attacks on black Cubans that both observers of the time and recent historians such as De la Fuente, Ada Ferrer, and Aline Helg have identified as a race war.[vi] While Afro-Cuban social clubs, such as the elite *Club Atenas*, continued to exist well into the middle of the 20th century, the "Guerrita del '12" ended the Afro-Cuban bid for consolidated political influence. Segregation never became official Cuban policy, but until the Revolution of 1959, many elite establishments (the Havana Yacht Club, luxury hotels, etc.) refused to accept black patrons.

Outside of the political sphere, much of the interest in Afro-Cubans or Afro-Cuban culture in the early part of the twentieth-century came from a eugenicist or criminological perspective that tried to show Afro-Cuban culture and religious practice in particular, as marginal to the rest of Cuban society.[vii] Strongly influenced by Italian criminologist Cesare Lombroso, Fernando Ortiz acknowledges in the prologue to his first ethnographic monograph, *Hampa afrocubana. Los negros brujos* (*The Afro-*

Cuban Underworld. Black Witches, 1906) that Afro-Cuban religious practice (*brujería*) needs to be studied as a preventive measure, so that its practitioners may be more easily incorporated into the general population.

> Observemos con escrupulosidad microscópica y reiterada – *cum studio et sine odio* – nuestros males presentes, que la consideración de su magnitud nos producirá la pesadilla que ha de despertarnos más prontamente de nuestra modorra y nos ha de dar valor y fuerzas para alcanzar la bienandanza futura.
>
> Let's observe our present evils with microscopic and reiterated scrupulousness – *cum studio et sine odio* – so that the consideration of their magnitude produces in us the nightmare that must soon awaken us from our stupor and give us the strength and courage to reach our future prosperity.[viii]

Although published ten years after Ortiz's first study, Israel Castellanos's *Brujería y ñañiguismo desde su punto de vista médico-legal (Brujería and Ñañiguismo from a Medico-Legal Perspective*, 1916), argued that the *ñáñigo* (Afro-Cuban religious practitioner) was a criminal type (as opposed to the *brujo*, or witch), and attempted to produce a generalized physical and psychological profile (Bronfman 63). It should be noted that the criminological perspective expressed by these social scientists was in complete accordance with the way in which distinctly Afro-Cuban religious practices were treated under the legal system; a gathering of people engaged in an Afro-Cuban ceremony could be arrested for "illicit association", and could have their religious objects confiscated. As Alejandra Bronfman notes, this often led to a disavowal of these practices by middle and upper-class black Cubans: "Many black and mulatto politicians, mindful of a modernist nationalist vision, tended to downplay, if not excoriate, African-derived religions, which many of them deemed primitive and uncivilized" (19).

Against the backdrop of actual social prejudice and repression of black Cubans, however, certain elements of Afro-Cuban culture gradually found their way into mainstream Cuban culture – particularly into music and literature – in the first decades of the twentieth century. This can be seen in part as the result of an anxiety toward establishing the parameters of a distinctly national identity against increasing social and political pressure from the United States. In an attempt to define what was inherently Cuban, writers and musicians included Afro-Cuban elements in their poetry and the use of these cultural elements both set Cuban music and literature apart from their North American counterparts while simultaneously gesturing toward a narrative of racial harmony that Cubans could claim as uniquely theirs.[ix] Although the United States had strongly influenced Cuba's racial policies, it remained for many Cubans the symbol of a failed racial narrative, its segregation practices the symbol of all that Cuba had managed to avoid. The poet Nicolás Guillén, in his essay "El camino de Harlem" ("The Road to Harlem"), holds up the racially-divided neighborhoods of New York City as an example of a failed racial democracy, and warns of the danger of creating similar segregated social spaces within Cuba. He ends his essay imploring his readers to apply themselves to "la hermosa tarea de actuar en cubano" ("the beautiful work of acting in Cuban") defining work towards a mutual respect and a shared understanding as a *national* behavior (*Prosa de prisa* 5-6).

In their desire to depict Cuba as a space of racial harmony, writers and intellectuals frequently chose to view Afro-Cuban culture within the broader context of a culture of *mestizaje*, or racial mixing. These ideas reached their apogee in Fernando Ortiz's concept of transculturation (*transculturación*), a theory that views culture – and Cuban culture in particular – as formed by a dynamic process of give and take, in which dominant cultures are still affected by (and take on some aspects of) the cultures that they dominate. This idea, developed by Ortiz in his *Contrapunteo cubano del tabaco y el azúcar* (*Cuban Counterpoint Between Tobacco and Sugar*, 1940), allowed him to acknowledge the presence of Afro-Cuban culture, while showing it to be safely incorporated into the broader (read: whiter) Cuban society.[x]

Influencing the rise in the presence of Afro-Cuban elements and subject matter in poetry and music from a different direction was what Petrine Archer Straw has identified as "Negrophilia", the vogue of things African that swept Europe (and particularly France) in the 1920s.[xi] This was the decade in which Josephine Baker became the toast of Paris, and in which visual artists such as Pablo Picasso, Man Ray and Jacques Lipschitz incorporated African iconographic elements into their work. Unlike the recognition of African-derived elements in the Caribbean, however, the European avant-garde was attracted to Africa primarily because of what they saw as its foreignness – the "primitive" nature so different from European bourgeois society.

The first *negrista* writers may have employed Afro-Caribbean themes in the interests of national culture, but their writing has indeed frequently been accused of exoticizing and objectifying their black subjects in a manner similar to that of their European counterparts. Speaking of Emilio Ballagas' *Cuaderno de poesía negra* (*Notebook of Black Poetry* 1934), which was, along with Ramón Guirao's *Órbita de poesía afrocubana* (*Orbit of Afro-Cuban Poetry* 1938) one of the first anthologies of *negrista* poetry to appear in Spanish, Luis Duno Gottberg observes, "Se trata de una mirada epidérmica, centrada en lo exterior, en el gesto, en el sonido exótico, en el pigmento" ("We're dealing with an epidermic gaze, focused on the exterior, on gesture, on exotic sound, on skin color"89). The Puerto Rican writer J. L. Diego Padró, writing of the Afro-Puerto Rican elements in his compatriot Luis Palés Matos's *negrista* poetry, observes, "Es más bien un sencillo y primitivo espectáculo, una escenificación vital más o menos pintoresca, a base de color, gestos, y timbalismo" ("It is, rather, a simple and primitive spectacle, a more or less picturesque, lively staging centered around colour, gestures, drum rhythms" 94). A brief look at "Elegía de María Belén Chacón" ("Elegy for María Belén Chacón), one of Ballagas's most famous *negrista* poems, illustrates the legitimacy of this critique:

MARÍA Belén, María Belén, María Belén,
María Belén Chacón, María Belén Chacón, María Belén Chacón,
con tus nalgas en vaivén,
De Camagüey a Santiago, de Santiago a Camagüey.

En el cielo de la rumba,
nunca habrá de alumbrar
tu constelación de curvas.

MARÍA Belén, María Belén, María Belén,
María Belén Chacón, María Belén Chacón, María Belén Chacón,
with your hips swaying back and forth
from Camagüey to Santiago, from Santiago to Camagüey.

In the heaven of the rumba,
they never need illuminate
your constellation of curves. (78-9, translation mine)

In these first two stanzas of the poem, Ballagas explicitly plays with rhythm of the rumba dancer's name until the name itself seems to lose all connection to the woman herself, degenerating into pure rhythmic sound. The only thing left her is her physical shape – first shown as a pair of disembodied buttocks – "nalgas en vaivén" – notable for their movement, yet separate from the woman herself, and then as a silhouette of curves. As Vera Kutzinski has pointed out in readings of similar *negrista* poetry, the woman here is not a whole woman, but a collection of parts, linked to a musical rhythm (164-5).

While rhythm would be a defining characteristic of *negrista* poetry, not all poets focused exclusively on surface or visual aspects that could be labeled as Afro-Cuban or Afro-Caribbean. In his "Motivos de son" ("*Son* Motifs"), a collection of twelve poems first published in 1930, Nicolás Guillén created a brief series of dialogues, all set to the rhythmic structure of the *son* musical form, in which a series of speakers address their interlocutors in the first person in direct, colloquial Cuban speech. In "Búcate plata", for example, a woman speaks in the first person to someone who appears to be her husband:

Búcate plata,
búcate plata,
poqque no doy un paso má:
etoy a arró con galleta,
ná ma.

Look for dough,
Look for dough,
Because I'm not takin' one step more:
I'm down to rice an' crackers,
That's all.[xii]

Next to Ballagas distant vision of the rumba dancer's curves, Guillén's woman is a speaking subject who clearly articulates her problems and perspectives in a popular vernacular. We learn more about her circumstances – and her reaction to her circumstances –

than we do about her physical identity. Critics have consistently identified Guillén's poetry from *Motivos de Son* through *West Indies, Ltd.* (1945) as Afro-Antillean, but Guillén himself frequently emphasizes the hybrid nature of both his poetry and the racial identities of the people he portrayed. As much as he is interested in Afro-Cuban subjectivity, he seldom recognizes a racialized Afro-Cuban identity apart from the context of Cuba as a mixed or "mulatto" nation. He says of the poems in *Motivos de son*, for example, "[C]ada uno trata de ser un cuadro breve, enérgico y veraz del alma negra, *enraizada profundamente en el alma de Cuba*" ("[E]ach one tries to be a brief, energetic, and true portrait of the black soul, *profoundly rooted in the soul of Cuba*" *Prosa de prisa,* 37, emphasis mine). Earlier in the same essay, he states, "Aquí todos somos algo mulatos en lo íntimo, y no está distante el día en que también lo seamos a flor de la piel," ("Here we are all somewhat mulatto inside, and the day isn't far off when we will also be on the surface of the skin" *Prosa de prisa,* 36). This statement can almost be seen as an argument against articulating an Afro-Cuban subjectivity, since it implies that racial difference can no longer be recognized any way but visually.

The Performance

This poetic corpus – both the "picturesque" and *"costumbrista"* poetry that treated the exoticized surface elements as well as poetry that dealt with the struggles of black speaking subjects – was the archive from which Cosme drew the bulk of material for her performances. Cosme's first public appearances were not solos. She frequently performed in the variety shows that were popular in Cuba in the late 20s and early '30s, and playbills from the era frequently list her as simply performing *coplas*, or "verses". By the time she began touring regularly as a solo performer, however, she had developed a fairly standard show format. The show was divided into three parts, each featuring five or six poems. Cosme favored longer narrative poems, particularly those with a sad theme such as Guillén's "Velorio de Papá Montero" ("Papa Montero's Wake"), or Luis Cané's "Romance de la niña negra" ("Poem for the Black Girl"), in which an impecably dressed black child is snubbed and ignored by the neighborhood children, only to die and go to Heaven, where God commands the angels to play with her. The poems almost never seem to be grouped according to any particular logic other than perhaps the performative; the program consistently mixes poems from different countries (Cuban authors such as Guillén and Ballagas appear alongside Puerto Rican writer Luis Palés Matos and the Spanish writer Alfonso Camín), and poems of differing quality. No one today would confuse Guillén's elegiac lyricism for Papá Montero – "Quemaste la madrugada / con fuego de tu guitarra" ("You burned the dawn / with the fire of your guitar") – with Cané's narrative of the "little black girl". The poems are connected by their racialized subject matter, regardless of whether blackness appears in the form of an individual subject (such as Papá Montero) or as a stylized African presence, as in Palés Matos's "Danza negra" ("Black Dance") :

Calabó y bambú.
Bambú y calabó.
El Gran Cocoroco dice: tu-cu-tú
La Gran Cocoroca dice to-co-tó.

Calabo and bamboo.
Bamboo and calabó.
The great Cocoroco says: tu-cu-tú.
The great Cocoroca says: to-co-tó. (7)

While some poems carry within them a social message (a portrayal of the sad effects of poverty or racism), others, like those of Palés, take pleasure in conjuring up the visual and rhythmic effects of a carnival-like dance or celebration.

Besides the theme of race, the other principal element uniting this somewhat disparate poetic corpus is a sense of rhythm. All of the poetry that appears in Cosme's programs is governed by a strong rhyme scheme or sense of an internal beat. If Cosme's programs are the expression of a particular racial identity, this is an identity generated through performance, poetic narratives incarnated in a particular way by Cosme. A quote from the Cuban writer Jorge Mañach, used on several of her playbills, highlights precisely the shared use of rhythm in both the poetry and the performance:

Para recobrar a Eusebia en su propia ley, hay que escucharla luego en esas poesías de tono rumbero, como "La mujer de

Antonio", en que el candor negro se calienta, como el piel del bongó, a la llama del instinto. El verso se rompe con los ritmos de la cadera, se aprieta nervioso en el "camina así"... Y Eusebia Cosme se hace entonces la encarnación de toda la picaresca negra: la voz de una lírica que ya el trópico podrá reclamar orgullosamente como inalienablemente suya.

To recover Eusebia in her own law, you then need to listen to her in these "rumba-tinged" poems, like "Antonio's Woman", in which the black candor heats up, like the drumskin, at the call of instinct. The verse breaks with the rhythms of the hips, pulls itself tight nervously at "walking like this"...And Eusebia Cosme then becomes the incarnation of the black picaresque: the voice of a lyric that the tropics will now be able to proudly reclaim as inalienably theirs.[xiii]

In Mañach's description, rhythm seems to be responsible for racializing Cosme's performance, travelling as it does from the verses to her body. She undergoes a transformation into the "black picaresque" through what sounds like an act of (racial) possession.

If one can draw any conclusions about Cosme's performances from her programs, then, it is that the central performance of racialized identity is that of Cosme herself. While Mañach's portrait emphasizes her performance of blackness, other elements of her presentation send more ambivalent messages. The frontspiece of several of her programs shows an ink drawing of a woman's figure that Cosme used as a kind of trademark icon throughout her career. The drawing is resolutely feminine, and at the same time racially indeterminate. The woman's slim silhouette suggests the figure of a dancer, and while the layered skirt seems to hover somewhere between a traditional rhumba costume (possibly suggestive of Afro-Cuban culture) and a flamenco dancer's dress, the spareness of the drawing as well as the line delineating her legs almost go so far as to suggest that she is not clothed at all. The "E" from "Eusebia" winds sensuously up her body, perhaps as a snake or a bird might, forcing the curve of the body into a pose that could be either triumphant or awkward. Other than the skirt and the dancer's figure, there is nothing in this image to suggest what the performance will consist of, other than femininity.

The willowy abstractness of this illustration contrasts with the photographs of Cosme that appeared in some of her other programs. In these, Cosme can be racially identified through both her physical features and her costume. In a playbill from 1936, she appears in a kerchief, large hoop earrings, and a brightly patterned cotton dress. Her arm is suggestively raised, less in triumph than if she had been caught mid-conversation. Her eyes look away from the camera, and the clearest feature of her face is her smile. While the stylized pose of the woman's body in the drawing suggests mystery and distance, this photograph reveals a studied kind of intimate informality.

Despite their differences, both the drawing and the photographs highlight one element of Cosme's performance in direct contrast with her written program – her gender. Without exception, Cosme's repertoire was made up of texts by male writers. While some of the poems, such as Ballagas's "Elegía de María Belén Chacón" ("Elegy for María Belén Chacón"), are addressed to women, or use them as narrative protagonists, as in Jorge de Lima's "A negra Fuló" ("The Black Woman Fuló"), none of them featured a woman as a speaking subject or a narrative voice explicitly identified as female. (Those poems that do, such as Guillén's "Búcate plata", curiously do not seem to have been part of her repertoire.) By choosing to emphasize her gender in a visible way, Cosme not only performed a black Caribbean identity through the recitation of this poetry, but performed it as a speaking black female subject. If, as Vera Kutzinski has argued, *negrista* poetry consistently presents the mestizo nation "as a male homosocial construct" in which the black woman is largely absent and the mulata, while symbolically present, is a cypher through which a masculinist ideology is represented (165), Cosme's stage persona genders the speaking voice of these poetic narratives as female, breaking through the homosocial environment erected by the written corpus.

Visions of Eusebia

In the previous section, I have attempted my own reading of Cosme's performances from the traces of them that remain in the archives. But if we are to understand the ways in which Cosme embodied a Black Diaspora – and the ways in which her performances were translated, transposed, and (mis)read, we must return how she was read by her contemporaries, and to the ways in which her repertoire has re-entered the archive. In 1954, rather late in Cosme's career, the ethnographer and public intellectual Fernando Ortiz was asked to introduce a performance of Cosme's at the Lyceum, a women's literary and cultural organization located in the wealthy Vedado neighborhood of Havana. Cosme had given numerous previous performances in distinguished venues of the Cuban capital, but the Lyceum was a particularly important site, in that it in many ways represented the epicenter of white feminine privilige in the city. Nearly a quarter-century after she began her career as a declaimer, Cosme had finally "arrived" for this group of women.

Despite an already two-decade-long career, Ortiz, in his brief essay of introduction, treats Cosme as if she were indeed a new phenomenon: "¿Quién es Eusebia Cosme?" ("Who is Eusebia Cosme?") being how he chooses to open his discussion, promising to clarify this for the Lyceum members (1). Yet he goes on to add, "Acaso tenga que decírselo a ella misma, cuya propia sinceridad ella siente, sabe y vive sin poderla explicar" ("Perhaps I will have to tell Eusebia herself who she is, since she feels, knows, and lives her own sincerity without being able to explain it" 1). Cosme, Ortiz intimates, does not know her own greatness, an implication both complementary – see how modest she is! – and infantilizing. Ortiz thus appoints himself the interpreter of the great meaning attached to Cosme's identity.

Cosme's importance for Ortiz is only partially due to her artistic talent, something he indicates from the beginning when he identifies her as "una artista recitante, una mulata nacida en un instante de síntesis pacífica en esa dialéctica de las razas" ("a declaimer, a mulatta born in an instant of pacific synthesis in that race dialectic", 1). It is crucial that Ortiz identify Cosme as a mulatta, because only in this way can her very existence lend credence to a narrative of racial harmony. His use of the word "sincerity" is significant here, since it implies that Cosme possesses an essential identity that despite the performative nature of her enterprise, is *not* put-on or feigned. For Ortiz, the harmony of Cosme's racial background is tied to her function as the herald of a new moment in Cuba's artistic development, the arrival of a "poesía mulata", a "mulatto poetry", an artistic production that can be said to be truly Cuban. "En ese proceso de comprensión, de adentramiento en nosotros mismos, de nacionalismo integrativo, esta artista significa una positiva aportación" ("In this process of understanding, of looking within ourselves, of integrative nationalism, this artist represents a positive achievement" 5). Cosme's performances are the sign that a truly popular Cuban art has arrived, that in drawing from both European poetic traditions and Afro-Cuban musicality Cuba has finally produced a national poetic form.

Ortiz characterizes Cosme as a cypher whose significance he can read, but it appears that he does not, in fact, see her at all. Despite - or perhaps because of – the apparent disconnect between the black performer and her wealthy white audience, Ortiz merely uses her as a signpost leading the way towards racial harmony. The substance of his talk deals not with her performance but with the "mulatto" poetry itself, and on a broader level, with the narrative of Cuban culture as profoundly transcultural, as absorbing influences to produce a new and genuine product. It is significant that Ortiz insists on identifying Cosme as "mulata", never as black or "afro-cubana"; for his narrative of racial harmony to work, she has to be a product of such a synthesis. Thus while it could be argued that Cosme's actual performance brings the black speaking (female) subject to the fore, Ortiz's introduction relegates her again to a position of invisbility.

Ortiz was not the only writer to use Cosme as the gateway to a broader meditation on the nature of Cuban culture. In an article that he wrote about her during the same period – "El regreso de Eusebia Cosme" ("The Return of Eusebia Cosme"), Nicolás Guillén, whose poetry Cosme frequently declaimed, identifies her clearly as "una negra venida del norte de la Isla" ("a black woman from the north of the Island", 1). However, like Ortiz, Guillén uses her to open a discussion on Afro-cuban poetry which emphasizes its transculturative elements: "Poesía 'afro-cubana' - ¿qué quiere decir esto? Considerar que existe lo "afrocubano" como expresión independiente y parcial del alma de Cuba es falso, pues estamos hechos de una conmixtión profunda de dos sangres" ("Afro-Cuban poetry – what does it mean to say this? It is false to consider that the "Afro-Cuban" exists as an independent and partial expression of Cuba's soul, since we are formed from the profound co-mingling of two bloods", 3). He goes on to add that, "No creo – nunca lo he creído – que exista entre nosotros una manera de ser "afrocubana", diferenciada de lo cubano" ("I don't believe – I have never believed – that there exists among us a way of being "Afro-Cuban" different from being Cuban", 4). The use of the feminine adjective here implies that Ortiz is responding to Cosme herself – and to her particular performance, attempting to reject the racial particularity of her stage persona and return it to a more culturally neutral space. While the comment is frustratingly vague, it is suggestive of the fact that Cosme was performing a particular *way* of being (Afro-) Cuban, and that Guillén, rather than responding favorably, sees it as a false attempt to isolate certain cultural elements. His essay thus performs a gesture of re-incorporation. No longer a racialized exile, Guillén's article "returns" Cosme to Cuba in both a physical and a cultural sense.

Ortiz and Guillén's need to connect and characterize Cosme and/or her performance as mulatta speaks to their shared preoccupation with a narrative of Cuban racial harmony, but their insistence on this portrayal is indicative of a certain anxiety that Cosme's performance may have created. An anxiety of a similar kind is visible in other Cuban accounts of her performances. Rafael de Zéndegui, in a brief article entitled "Las manos de Eusebia Cosme" ("Eusebia Cosme's Hands"), alternates between empasizing the declaimer's black attributes and portraying her as sophisticated and elegant.[xiv] His mention of the "exotic" contrast between her dark skin and ruby-red fingernails is coupled with an observation that she moves with "spontaneous distiction". While the recitation of certain poems causes her to move her hands "con el gesto primitivo y típico" ("with a primitive and typical gesture"), her hands also "brindan…en su silueta de belleza clásica, toda la fina aristocracia de aquellas manos femeninas de la frivola corte de los Luises" ("offer…in their classically beautiful silhouette all the fine aristocracy of those feminine hands in the Louis's frivolous court"). For De Zéndegui, Cosme's Afro-Cuban identity seems to be both seductive and dangerous. His praise of her sophistication seems placed to remind readers that while she may use "primitive" gestures, she is not truly primative.

De Zéndegui's descriptions reveal his own anxieties about race and class (and perhaps those of his readership), but his portrait also draws attention to the "Afro-alienating" nature of her performance. De Zéndegui openly comments on the ways in which Cosme's mulatta character interacts with masculine poetic voice of the texts observing of her hands, "En ellas he visto la irónica burla que hacían a la palabra fuerte y viríl…" ("In them I have seen the ironic fun they poke at the strong and viril word…"). If the "mahogany" colour of Cosme's skin visibly identifies her as Afro-Cuban, her costume, gestures, rhythm and voice allow her to both assume a racialized identity and comment on, modify, parody, and dialogue with that identity.

De Zéndegui's description hints at the ways in which Cosme's performances may have managed to elude and move beyond both his exoticizing impulses and Ortiz and Guillén's attempt to replace a black female subject with the less-threatening mulatta. One wonders if this performative fluidity, the irony present in Cosme's gestures, is what Spratlin means when he observes in his review that "the linguistic element is secondary". Did the audience at Howard University identify with Cosme's performance merely because they recognized her as a black woman, albeit one speaking Spanish? Were they responding to (and identifying with) a particular racial identity, or was their positive reception an acknowledgment of the ways in which Cosme's "engaging" performance managed to communicate a contestation of stereotypes?

Spratlin's review is too brief to tell us exactly how Cosme was translated for that particular North American audience. But taken together with the work of Ortiz, Guillén, and de Zéndegui, it reveals the complex ways in which her show mediated the literary representation of a black Caribbean subjectivity. Jehan Ryko (Alphonse Henríquez), a Haitain artist and writer, in a letter to Cosme herself observes, "Como el pelícano que dá, para devorar, sus entrañas a sus hijos, asimismo tú dás al público insaciable tu alma multiple de poetisa negra" ("Like the pelican, who allows her young to devour her own guts, so you give your insatiable public your multiple black poetess soul"). Ryko's characterization of Cosme is strange – a portrait of painful self-sacrifice seemingly at odds with the playful nature of her performance. Yet in the word "multiple" it hints at meanings that go farther than the poetry itself, at a multifaceted self whose gendered performance went beyond the archive, at the "something" that V.B. Spratlin mentions, yet cannot define.

References

Archer Straw, Petrine. *Negrophilia. Avant-Garde Paris and Black Culture in the 1920s.* New York: Thames and Hudson, 2000.

Ballagas, Emilio. *Obra poética.* Havana: Letras Cubanas, 1984.

Bronfman, Alejandra. *Measures of Equality: Social Science, Citizenship, and Race in Cuba, 1902-1940.* Chapel Hill: U of North Carolina P, 2004.

Brooks, Daphne. *Bodies in Dissent: Spectacular Performances of Race and Freedom: 1850-1910.* Durham: Duke UP, 2006.

De la Fuente, Alejandro. *A Nation For All: Race, Inequality, and Politics in Twentieth-Century Cuba.* Chapel Hill: U of North Carolina P, 2001.

Diego Padró, J. I. Antillanismo, criollismo, negroidismo". 1932. Rpt. *Luis Palés Matos y su trasmundo poético.* Río Piedras: Ediciones Puerto Saldaña, 1973. 93-97.

Duno Gottberg, Luis. *Solventando las diferencias: La ideología del mestizaje en Cuba.* Madrid: Iberoamericana, 2003.

Edwards, Brent. *The Practice of Diaspora: Literature, Translation, and the Rise of Black Internationalism.* Cambridge: Harvard UP, 2003.

Guillén, Nicolás. *Obra poética.* Havana: Letras Cubanas, 1995.

---. *Prosa de prisa, 1929-1972. Tomo I.* Havana: Arte y Literatura, 1975.

---. "Regreso de Eusebia Cosme." *El Nacional.* Caracas, 1951. Copy from the Eusebia Cosme Papers.

Kutzinski, Vera. *Sugar's Secrets: Race and the Erotics of Cuban Nationalism.* Charlottesville: U of Virginia P, 1993.

Ortiz, Fernando. *Hampa afrocubana. Los negros brujos. Apuntes para un estudio de etnología criminal.* 1906. Rpt. Miami: Ediciones Universal, 1973.

---. "¿Quién es Eusebia Cosme?" Talk presented at the *Lyceum*, Havana, 1954. The Eusebia Cosme Papers, The Arthur Schomburg Collection, New York Public Library. 1-6.

Palés Matos, Luis. *Tuntún de pasa y grifería.* 1937. San Juan: Universidad de Puerto Rico, 2003.

Taylor, Diana. *The Archive and the Repertoire: Performing Cultural Memory in the Americas.* Durham: Duke UP, 2003.

---

[i] Handwritten article, no publication references. The Eusebia Cosme Papers, The Arthur Schomburg Center, New York Public Library.

[ii] The term *negrista*, which will be discussed later in this paper, first appeared in the 1920s, and was used to refer to poetry written in Spanish which employed African or Afro-Caribbean elements. Many of the writers first identified as *negrista* – Emilio Ballagas, Ramón Guirao, Luis Palés Matos – were criticized for being white writers who employed African elements in a superficially stylistic way. The term *poesía afroantillana* ("Afro-Antillean poetry") came into parlance later, and implies a use of African-derived elements in Caribbean poetry that many include both stylistic conventions and the presentation of black subjects. While related, neither term is fully equivalent to the radical black subjectivity communicated by the French term *Négritude*.

[iii] These films included "Rosas blancas para mi hermana negra" (1970) and "El derecho de los pobres" (1973).

[iv] While a vocal recording of a performance of Cosme's at Northwestern University in January, 1940 is available (in the Archives of Traditional Music at Indiana University), I have been unable to locate any extant cinematic documentation of her performances.

[v] José Martí, in his essay "Nuestra América" ("Our America") was perhaps the first proponent of a Cuba (and a Latin America) so racially harmonious that "race" as a category ceased to exist. It was in the first decades of the twentieth century, however, that the question of race, and the idea of racial harmony, became a central preoccupation.

[vi] De la Fuente observes that the opinion at the time "was that Afro-Cubans themselves had broken the fragile boundaries of Cuban racial democracy" (76). See also Aline Helg's *Our Rightful Share. The Afro-Cuban Struggle for Equality, 1886-1912*, and Ada Ferrer's *Insurgent Cuba. Race, Nation, and Revolution, 1868-1898.*

[vii] The island's most prominent eugenicist, Dr. Francisco Fernández, was also the secretary of sanitation and the chairman of the first Pan American Conference on Eugenics and Homoculture, held in Havana in 1927 (de la Fuente, 43).

[viii] *Los negros brujos*, 7. This and all following translations are mine, unless otherwise identified.

[ix] Vera Kutzinski adds that Afro-Cubanism "contained and defused potential ethnic threats to national unification by turning them into original (and originary) contributions to Cuban culture (143).

[x] For a deeper exploration of transculturation as it relates to national identity and nation-state formation, see Gareth Williams's *The Other Side of the Popular: Neoliberalism and Subalternity in Latin America.*

[xi] This is the opinion of Cuban writers Eugenio Florit and José Olivio Jiménez (cited in Duno Gottberg, 85).

[xii] *Obra poética*, 90-91. I have chosen to provide my own translation of this poem over the controversial earlier version by Langston Hughes and Ben Carruthers. For a full discussion of the difficulties of rendering Guillén's colloquial Cuban Spanish into English, see Vera Kutzinski's article "Fearful Asymmetries: Langston Hughes, Nicolás Guillén and *Cuba Libre" Diacritics*, 34.3-4: 112-42.
[xiii] Program, 1934, The Eusebia Cosme Papers.
[xiv] While De Zéndegui was a frequent contributor to the Havana newspaper *Diario de la Marina*, this article, from the Eusebia Cosme Papers, has no publication information. It is accompanied by an illustration of two dark-skinned, clearly feminine hands.

Chapter 6

The 1960s Revisited: Art, Race, and Revolution at the Cuban Crossroad[i]

Lourdes Martinez-Echazábal

The 1960s were pivotal years for the development of contemporary Caribbean, African, and US African-American Black consciousness and their attendant intellectual production. This period witnessed the proliferation of African and Caribbean literatures and of the Black Arts Movement in the US. The 1960s also harboured social and political events that were to have profound repercussions in world history, giving new meaning to words such as *revolution* and *capitalism.*[ii]

When I refer to the 1960s, I am thinking not just of the years bracketed between January 1, 1960 and December 31, 1969. Rather, my periodization of the [Cuban] 1960s, one I drew long before reading Jameson's seminal article on the period, but which, nevertheless, bares resemblance to his, begins circa 1952 and extends beyond the decade (see appendix at the end of this essay).[iii] During this period, particularly from the late-1950s through the late-1960s, political idealism and revolutionary zeal, coupled with organized armed struggles, produced some of the most significant revolutions and social movements of the second half of the 20th century, among them, the Algerian and the Cuban revolutions, and the Civil Rights and Black Power movements in the United States.

Over a century after the formal abolition of the slave trade another "passage" came into existence, only this time it was a deliberate one carrying not just bodies, but new political subjects and/or their ideas of emancipation and decolonization back and forth across the Atlantic. The writings, speeches, and political activism of Ben Bella,[iv] Amilcar Cabral, Franz Fanon, C.L.R. James, Patrice Lumumba, Kwame Nkrumah, and Malcolm X, among others, the calls for civil rights and liberties voiced by Dr. Martin Luther King Jr., the cry for retaliation of Robert Williams in the US-South, and his subsequent broadcasting of Radio Free Dixie from Havana, Cuba, in the early 1960s,[v] the Black Power slogan "Black is Beautiful," the empowering statements conveyed by the

Afro hairstyle together with the incendiary messages of the Black Panther Party, among others, provided the moral impetus for the formation of African, African American, and Afro-Caribbean political consciousness and aesthetic production during this period and for years to come.

The 1960s fostered a sense of international solidarity absent in the West perhaps since the spread of fascism in the 1930s and the Spanish Civil War (1936-39). For the Cubans, as for Malcolm X, and later for the Black Panther Party, the enemy was said to be "one and the same." Speaking to leaders of African liberation movements in Dar-es-Salaam, Tanzania, during his three months trip to Africa in 1965, Commander Ernesto "Ché" Guevarra (hereafter referred to as Ché) would declare that the "the real issue [for the continent] was not the liberation of any given state, but a common war against a common master, who was *one and the same* in Mozambique, and in Malawi, in Rhodesia and in South Africa, in Zaire and in Angola" (Emphasis mine. Cited in Gleijeses 87). Similarly, in the petition he addressed to the second summit of the Organization of African Unity held in 1964, Malcolm X "called on African Americans and Africans to join together against their common enemy –in Alabama and in Zaire alike" (Cited in Gleijeses 131). In synergy with the views subsumed above, transnational thinking and international solidarity also characterized the philosophy of the Black Panther Party.[vi] According to poet LeRoi Jones (later known as Amiri Baraka), the Black Panther Party wanted to show that "the murder of Patrice Lumumba in the Congo, and of Medgar Evers [in Mississippi,] were conducted by the same people" (Cited in Quarles 323). But was the enemy really "*one and the same*"?

The transnational reasoning of Malcolm X (notably after his trip to Mecca and Africa), and of the Black Panther Party seem to suggest that Black radicalism in the US came closer to the model of international solidarity and militant rhetoric of Castro's Cuba than to that of the Civil Rights Movement, the NAACP, and its leaders. Nevertheless, it is my contention that the gist of Cuba's militancy in Latin America, as in Africa and the rest of the Third World, had little or nothing to do with race or with a racialized logic, *per se*, and much to do with *realpolitik* and with the Revolution's relentless anti-imperialistic crusade to redeem, as Fanon would have it, *les damnes de la terre* (the wretched of the earth) from the evils of US imperialism and internal colonialism.

Nevertheless, Cuba played the race card both wisely and strategically by offering support to those struggling against (European and US) imperialism and white oppression. It did so, as early as 1960, when, on the occasion of attending the Fifteenth General Assembly of the United Nations in New York, Castro and the Cuban delegation stayed at the Hotel Theresa in Harlem, were he met Malcolm X and other prominent leaders of the African American community. Castro's (and the Cuban delegation's) stay in Harlem endowed the Revolution with great symbolic capital in the eyes of many African Americans. Moreover, it produced a stunning "media spectacle" (Quiroga 40) whose images have traveled the world as a tangible testimony of Cuba's anti-racist logic and of its solidarity with, and support of, the struggles of people of African descent in the US, and, by extension, around the globe.[vii] Cuba played the race card again in 1965, when, at the request of Laurent Kabila, the Simba leader from northern Katanga, it sent a battalion of Black Cubans to fight in Zaire.[viii] It continued to do so throughout the decade and for years to come.

Undoubtedly, the Cuban Revolution afforded the most relevant model of international solidarity with the people, national liberation movements, and emergent nations in Africa, Latin America, and the rest of the Third World, including Black America. In fact, it might be argued that throughout the period no one rivalled the Cuban Revolution's symbolic capital within the Third World, except, perhaps, China's Maoist Revolution. But even before Cuba's first gesture of a concerted effort to launch an international solidarity campaign in June of 1959, "Castro sent Ché Guevara in an unprecedented three-month globe-circling tour" where he met with world leaders, among them President Nasser of Egypt (Halperin 112-113). Similarly, it has been argued that "[t]he imperialist subjugation of the Cuban people by the US had developed among North Americans [sic] a sympathy and a sense of fraternity [they] could never have for other third world peoples in their struggles" (Jameson 182). Perhaps this historic fondness –which undoubtedly predates the official beginning of the imperialist subjugation of the Cuban people by the US in 1898– would partially explain why in the late 1950s the epic of the bearded rebels of the Sierra Maestra mountains of Cuba, chronicled by the mighty lenses and pens of a handful of young, idealistic, and well-placed US journalists and/or guerrilla *wannabe*s (Herbert Matthews, Robert Taber, Donald Soldini), sparked the condition of possibilities that would produce the first Third World solidarity movement in the US in 1960: the Fair Play for Cuba Committee. For according to Van Gosse, the images and achievements of Fidel Castro (to whom he refers to as "a kind of Latin American White Knight" and "a rebel with a cause") and of the Cuban Revolution, together with the "peculiar conjuncture of 1950s America, produced the Fair Play for Cuba Committee, which became a locus for the New Left emerging from the ashes [of McCarthyism, and] of Kennedy's New Frontier."[ix] In short, Van Gosse credits Castro and the Cuban Revolution as one of the leading forces in the emergence of the New Left in the US.

Whether we agree with Jameson's claim or with Van Gosse's provocative reading of the decisive, if mostly symbolic, role of the Cuban Revolution in the emergence of the New Left and the student movement in the US during the early- and mid-1960s, respectively, or not, the undisputable fact is that from its inception the Cuban revolutionary government strove to build an internationalist profile. And it did so by 1) fomenting solidarity networks amongst progressive circles in the US, including the African American community, 2) supporting revolutions in Latin America (Venezuela, Argentina 1961-1964; Bolivia, Argentina 1966-1967), 3) launching covert military and civilian missions to Africa (Algeria, 1961, Zaire, the Congo, and Guinea-Bissau, 1965-1967),[x] and 4) building nexuses of solidarity with the Afro-Asian block, in order, to create a Third World force in which Cuba would play an important role and increase her stature in the nonaligned world. For, as Gleijeses has suggested, becoming a key player in the nonaligned world would allow Cuba to "draw significant political and psychological advantages in relation to the major socialist powers," and to "develop political support (including Afro-Asian votes at the United nations) that [would] force an easing of US policy towards Cuba" (80).

It is estimated that between 1961 and 1964 alone, 1,500 to 2,000 Latin Americans received either guerrilla or political training in Cuba (Gleijeses 23), as did members of various African liberation movements, though in much smaller numbers. As far as direct military and humanitarian aid to Africa is concerned, as early as December 1961, Cuba sent weapons to the National Liberation Front of Algeria (FLN), and gave shelter to "seventy-six wounded Algerian fighters" and "twenty children from refugee camps, most of whom were war orphans" (Gleijeses 31). Also in 1961, the first foreign scholarship students arrived in Cuba. They were from Guinea. Two years later, on May 1963, a Cuban medical mission consisting of 55 men and women, landed in Algeria, spearheading the Cuban civilian missions to the continent (Cited in Gleijeses 36). In exchange for its support, and until the fall of Ben Bella on October 19, 1965, asserts Gleijeses, "Algeria was Cuba's headquarters in Africa, its window to the continent" (51). But, most importantly, observes Darío Urra, third secretary of the Cuban embassy in that country in 1963, Algeria "served as a bridge for Cuba with Latin America" (cited in Gleijeses 51).[xi]

Notwithstanding the political links outlined above (and despite the emerging anti-war and woman's movements, and the burgeoning youth counterculture in the West), while it is possible to speak of the period as an influential one in the development of contemporary world history, the 1960s is far from being a monolithic decade, or a global epoch, except perhaps in the most general sense. Generally speaking, while the 1960s were marked by political restlessness and epistemic violence in many regions of the globe, and are by and large seen as progressive from the vantage point of leftist struggles, it would be misleading to conflate, for instance, the Bay of Pigs invasion in 1961 with the invasion of Czechoslovakia in 1968, or the assassination of Patrice Lumumba in 1961, in "the heart of darkness", with that of Malcolm X four years later, in the heart of Harlem, despite the overriding similarities between these events. Therefore I would suggest that we revisit the 1960s, first and foremost, within their local specificities and instantiations, ones that are intrinsically linked to global and/or transatlantic events and processes, yet always grounded within a given (regional and/or local) cultural context. Seen this way, there are, indeed, many 1960s![xii]

In Cuba, the 1960s moved from an unprecedented moment of political euphoria and idealism (1959-1961), too-revolutionary-to-be-true, so to speak, to the sovietization of the Cuban state after 1968 (and most definitely by 1971), leading to what has been referred to as "*el quinquenio gris*" ("the grey five years"), an authoritarian and dogmatic period spanning from 1971 through 1975. Although, according to Desiderio Navarro, the "*quinquenio gris*" lasted not five but fifteen years (from 1968 to 1983) and "was in fact not grey but Black for many intellectual lives and work" (198).[xiii] In contrast to Navarro's assessment, others, and perhaps for different reasons (Díaz, Casanova), have considered the 1960s (as in the decade) to have been the real *años duros*[xiv] (hard years) and not the 1970s, as is commonly accepted, or the 1990s, as has been recently suggested by Pedro Juan Gutiérrez.[xv] Irrespective of whether the 1960s, the 1970s, or the 1990s, were the actual hard years, the fact is that by 1968, when Cuba sided with the USSR by sanctioning her invasion of Czechoslovakia and the events of the Prague Spring, as "necessary," freedom of expression in art and other forms of cultural expressions, including expressions of religious and sexual difference, were dramatically curtailed by the iron claw of an authoritarian regime and its attendant police state. In other words, by the end of the decade, the Revolution congealed, losing its revolutionary zeal.

Until recently, my own impulse has been to view the Cuban 1960s through the prism of my youth; after all, my first coming of age took place on that island during the latter part of the decade, and my memories –as most "remembrance of things past"– are impregnated not only by nostalgia –as it is usually the case when we look back at our own youth, and more poignantly so from the vantage point of exile– but, most significantly, by the specter of an abundant vitality, and free-flowing *jouissance*. As I change lenses, and move closer and deeper into the subject of race, national culture, and the limits of racial politics during the 1960s, a different vision of those years emerges. This renewed vision of *Cuba's* 1960s and mine begins in 1952 the year of the military *coup* that brought Fulgencio Batista back to power for a second time, a local instantiation that would lead to the attack on the Moncada Barracks on July 26, 1953, to the Granma landing in 1956, to the beginning of armed struggle in the Sierra Maestra, and to the subsequent victory of the Revolutionary government in January 1, 1959.

The Cuban sixties stood as a *crossroad* where the North and South Atlantic worlds met through the constant ebb and flow of political bodies and revolutionary ideas. As previously mentioned,

Cuba became aggressively involved in South Atlantic politics and liberation struggles much earlier than her well-publicized presence in Angola in the mid-1970s. Attention to the Caribbean came later in 1972 when the island established "diplomatic and other relations with the Black English-speaking Caribbean countries" (Dominguez xiii). But it was not until the 1980s, in Grenada, that Cuba became militarily involved in Caribbean political affairs. Nevertheless, the cultural policies and politics of the Cuban Revolution during the 1960s were crucial to strengthening the notion of a Caribbean culturehood.[xvi] To this end, *Casa de las Americas* (an institution that served, and continues to do so, as a kind of clearance cultural house for the Third World), through its *Centro de Estudios del Caribe* (Center for Caribbean Studies), played a decisive role in agglutinating the otherwise cultural and linguistically atomized Caribbean intelligentsia, and disseminating their work in print and visual forms prior to setting up the aforementioned diplomatic and political links. There is no question, then, that by virtue of her involvement in African and African American political affairs, and of her support of Caribbean culture, Cuba became not only an icon but, what is more, a crossroad for progressive ideologies of Black liberation, decolonization, and aesthetics, emanating from both sides of the Atlantic.

The 1960s were indeed about the coming-of-age of new subjectivities (women, Blacks, ethnic minorities, gays and lesbians) and nations. In this sense, this essay is an attempt to understand what happened when some of these new subjectivities (for instance, Black subjectivities) crossed paths with more established ones (such as socialist or communist ones), in an attempt to create art, to craft a new culture that would bring together multiple subject positions and speak to and about those new subjectivities. The topic is an intricate one. And not only because it stands at the intersection of the personal and the political in the aesthetic process, of the local and the global in the political process, of individual biographies and the exigencies of a socialist state, of "art" and "revolutionary art", but, foremost, because it summons two fields or variables which in the context of Latin America have always competed for interpretative authority: race and class, or, if one prefers, color and social status.

Three texts have been particularly pivotal in forcing a productive reckoning with my initial reading of the 1960s and the Cuban Revolution. First and foremost, Carlos Moore's *Castro, Africa, and the Blacks* (1984). Moore's text is to the study of race in post-1959 Cuba what Reynaldo Arenas autobiography *Before Night Falls* (1992) is to the study of gender and sexuality during the same period. Like Arena's text, Moore's is also an impassioned and controversial book, an undiluted reading of race and racial politics during the first two decades of the Cuban Revolution. It is a compelling text, and –like Arena's overly obsessive critique of *el máximo leader*- one that cannot, nevertheless, be easily and uncritically dismissed, despite some of the negative (and equally impassioned) criticism received since its publication.[xvii] The others are John Clytus' *Black Man in Red Cuba* (1970), and Maurice Halperin's *Return to Havana* (1994). No one working on race in Cuba after 1959, or trying to understand the course of the Cuban Revolution –regardless of their ideological positioning– should uncritically dismiss the above texts. They undertake a compulsory, if profoundly personal, analysis of the revolution's Negrophobia (Moore, Clytus), and of Castro's "irrepressible ego" (Halpering 166), together with an examination of their corollary in the Revolution's cultural and political policies. Despite their differences in subject matter and styles, each text forces the reader to reckon with some of the issues that the Revolution has silenced: the generalized sense of white superiority still prevailing in the island among revolutionary leaders, the condescending paternalism of the ruling class towards the masses, the implicit Negrophobia of the state and the high degree of government corruption. Hence, even if one disagrees with some or most of their claims and/or methodology, one is, nevertheless, compelled to question, to abandon the idealistic tenor, to look at the Revolution right in the eyes without fear of becoming a pillar of salt.[xviii]

In *One-Hundred Years of Solitude*, Gabriel Garcia Marquez writes of a banana workers strike in Colombia (likely alluding to the 1928 banana worker's strike against the United Fruit Company, in which 1,000 workers were killed), the massacre that followed it, and the ensuing response of the *bananera* to inquiries about these events. In the novel what the *bananera* (the Banana Company) does in order to produce a plausible explanation of the events is to erase the referent, that is, *the workers*. For if there were no workers how could there have been a strike? And, consequently, the massacre could never have occurred. As in the Macondian world depicted in *One-Hundred Years of Solitude*, in post-1959 Cuba, topics like domestic racism and racial discrimination were virtually effaced from official discourse (except to reiterate their absence) for nearly twenty-five years. Like the "workers" in Garcia Marquez's novel, these topics also disappeared from public discussions in the island – even though they were and are as real as the banana worker's strike and the attendant massacre.

The erasure of race as a valid category of analysis during the Revolution comes as no surprise, first and foremost, given Cuba's (and Latin America's) longstanding denial of prejudice, racism, and other forms of "race-" or color-related practices of social exclusion and discrimination. The denial of race is best epitomized by the writings and philosophy of one of the most acclaimed political and intellectual founding fathers of the Cuban nation, and so-called intellectual author of the 1959 Revolution: Jose Martí (1863-1895). Martí, together with Juan Gualberto Gómez (1854 - 1933), his collaborator and political ally on the island, and, arguably, the most important Cuban Black activist of the era,[xix] strove to unify all Cubans, and overcome racial and social inequality by emphasizing "the transcendent aspect of nationalist ideology" (Bronfman 10) and promoting a raceless nationality, or, if one prefers, a national ethnicity: Cuban (Martinez-Echazábal 1998). Cuban people as well as race scholars are all too familiar with phrases or sayings such as: "In Cuba there is no racial hatred, because there are no races " (José Marti), or "the 'Black problem' is a social problem, not a racial one" (Jorge Manach). The aforementioned illustrate recurring claims by many Cuban intellectuals and politicians, black and white, since the late 19th century. Today, after more than *one hundred years of indoctrination*, most Cubans seem to embrace the idea that racial prejudice and discrimination are either class or culturally motivated, resulting, primarily, from the social position or status of a given individual in society and not from the value assigned to one's color and phenotype. However, the elaborate grammar of racial classification still prevailing in the island disproves these claims and, instead, points to a highly color-conscious society. It is well know, for instance, that in Cuba as in other Afro-Latin American countries, an individual deemed Black by US standards could be considered mulatto, *indio*, *jabao*,[xx] or even white, depending on his colour and/or phenotype. In more recent history, the denial of race also emanates from the state's adherence to Marxism, an ideology that traditionally has proclaimed class and class struggle (rather than race and racial oppression), as the mighty signifiers of difference and differentiation.

Rhetorically clinging to Martí's principles, the Republic (1902 – 1958) claimed to have institutionalized a nation "con todos y para el bien de todos" (A nation for all and for the good of all"). Paradoxically, after 1959, the Revolutionary government claimed that racism, racial profiling, and police repression, existed during the *pseudo* Republic (also referred to as *la República mediatizada*), but no longer after 1959, in the Republic dreamed by Martí and materialized by Castro and its Revolution. Shortly after 1959, the story goes, the Cuban government abolished institutionalized forms of racism previously existing in the island[xxi] and contended that, since racial discrimination had been eradicated, there was no longer any reason to address the issue. Similarly, as there was no reason to summon race or race-related issues, there was no need, outside history and folklore, to study them either. This belief, however, was not unique to the post-1959 period. Let us recall that racial integration became Cuba's foundational story in the 20th century, one parroted by virtually every political leader and demagogue since the beginning of the Republican period in 1902.[xxii] In fact, from the early 1900s until the present *every* government has considered expressions of Black cultural nationalism or discussions of domestic racial issues (particularly on the part of Black Cubans) to be anti-nationalistic, a form of reverse racism, counter-revolutionary,[xxiii] even a pathological response to the national (read socialist) project.[xxiv] In fact, it would not be ludicrous to suggest that the Black peril persists to date in the island's imaginary.

Notwithstanding the limits of racial politics that existed in Cuba during the first half the 20th century, many of the policies and practices enacted by the revolutionary government after 1959 encroached even further on Afro-Cuban politics, social activities, and religious expressions. By abolishing, for instance, the Black and Mulatto Mutual Aid Societies, and other civil organization such as the National Association for Economic Rehabilitation (of Black people), also known as the O.N.R.E., the revolutionary government disavowed black civil society, and prevented their political development. Also, like previous regimes, the Revolution circumscribed scholarship and artistic production pertaining to Blacks in Cuba to the study of folklore, music, dance, and/or the study of slavery. Scholarship on contemporary Black populations in Cuba, from the vantage point of the social and political sciences, for instance, was either never initiated or was promptly disavowed until the mid-1990s.[xxv] And yet, since 1960, the government has endorsed a foreign policy that buttresses the struggles of African people and of people of African descent in the US. In other words, while the Cuban government "remained intolerant of the independent expression of cultural and political ideas and behavior by Cuban Blacks," (Domínguez xv) it became deeply involved in African political affairs, and offered support, including political asylum, to African American leaders fleeing from the FBI and other repressive and racist institutions in the US.[xxvi]

So while Cuba's foreign policies celebrated and encouraged *racially* motivated struggles in Africa and in the US, domestic policies extolled class and class struggles at the expense of race, resulting in the effacement and/or ostracism, at home, of newly created Black subjectivities elsewhere. Similarly, the privileging of class over race in the configuration of the new society, prevented Black organizations in Cuba from re-signifying blackness *as a place* (rather than as an ontological condition) from which to prompt political interventions as part of the newly constituted Socialist state, whose top ranking leadership, incidentally, with few exceptions, was virtually all white and mostly bourgeois. How did these political and social contradictions impinge upon the first generation of artists, writers and filmmakers of African descent that came of age in Cuba during that period, is a pivotal question raised by this essay.[xxvii]

Under the rubric of first generation, I include people still living and working on the island, others living abroad, and others now deceased. Amongst those I include are: filmmakers Sara Gómez (1940 - 1974), Nicolás Guillén Landrián (1938 - 2003), and Sergio Giral (b. 1937); poets Nancy Morejón (b. 1944), Georgina Herrera (b. 1936), and Excilia Saldaña (1946 - 1999); novelist Manuel

Granados (1930 - 1998); playwrights Gerardo Fulleda León (b. 1944) and Eugenio Hernández (b. 1936); performer, critic and folklorist Rogelio Martínez Furé (b. 1937); journalists and writers Pedro Pérez Sarduy (b. 1943) and Manuel Casanova (b.1940). Considering their experience as Black Cubans and the historic gap between political rhetoric and practice, as well as the experience of being newly enfranchised social actors, it would seem predictable that their politics (racial and otherwise) as well as their art would grow out of this exhilarating, yet complex and contradictory, situation. But to draw attention to their predicament is obviously not enough; the relevant work to be done involves showing how this generation grappled with the intersections of Marxist ideology, essentialist racial ideology (or, if one prefers, black nationalism), individualist democratic ideology, perhaps gender and sexual orientation issues, and their individual biographies. One only needs to delve into their lives and works to grasp the multiple and complicated ways in which Afro-Cuban identity has been lived, written, and performed in contemporary Cuba. Paired together (lives and work), they offer a privileged site to explore the intersection of art (broadly defined as writing and other forms of cultural expressions), 'race,' and revolution during the period in question, and beyond.

In addressing the topics of race, and of race-related cultural policies and politics in Cuba, particularly during the 1960s, one encounters stumbling blocks. Most noted among them have been the lack of research and published materials on these subjects, as if in observance of the official silence on the topic. These barriers to critical inquiry, however, are rapidly disappearing, particularly since the turn of the new millennium, as the Cuban government itself has adopted a rather proactive attitude towards expressions of (*marketable*) Black popular culture, one quite different from the one adopted in the 1960s towards a similar (though not very marketable) phenomenon. As a result of what appears to be a sanctioning on the part of the state towards Black popular cultural expressions, more and more artists are performing race, and more and more critics (Cuban and otherwise) are exploring its various expressions in History and in the Arts. Similarly, anthropologists and sociologists (species that nearly became extinct in Socialist Cuba) are beginning to dig into the thick [cultural] rubble resulting from years of neglect in areas such as the political economy of race, the persistence of inequality among Black inner-city dwellers in Havana, and the political culture of race, particularly during the so-called Special Period in Times of Peace, and thereafter. Though many writers have discussed the various domestic cultural policies and politics forged after 1959, very few works have included race as a variable in their analysis. With a few notable exceptions (Moore 1988; Fernández Robaina (1990); Sarduy & Stubbs 1993, 2000; Howe 1995, 1999, 2004; Brooks & Castaneda Fuertes 1998; De la Fuente 2002; Luis 2003) most studies addressing race or race-related issues are sprinkled amidst books and journals dealing with broadly related subjects. Seldom has the topic been studied at length and in-depth.

I would like to propose nine key questions as conduits through which a greater understanding of the topic of race and cultural production in 1960s Cuba might be achieved:

1. Prior to 1959, how much awareness was there amongst Black Cubans, particularly amongst the Black *intelligentsia* and the middle class, of the aesthetic expressions and political struggles of Africans and of people of African descent in the Americas?
2. Similarly, how cognizant were Afro-Cuban youth (those who would come of age during the 1960s), of African and African American histories and struggles prior to 1959, including the struggles of Black Cubans?
3. Does the situation differ after 1959, and if so, why?
4. Did Afro-Cuban artists and intellectuals of the time embrace or reject the principles that informed the social, political, and aesthetic movements in Africa and its American diaspora, particularly their accompanying racial ethos?
5. Did contact between some of these young Cubans artists, filmmakers, and intellectuals, and political activists and intellectuals, primarily from the US, but also from Africa and the Caribbean, who came to Cuba either as official guests or "tourists" of the Revolution, or fleeing from persecution and imprisonment in the US, have an

imprint on their writings and/or other forms of cultural expressions?

6. Did the artists, filmmakers, and intellectuals of this period recognize themselves, and accordingly identify, as Black, as Cuban, or as Afro Cubans? Did the burden of the discourse of *cubanidad* and/or*cubanía*, and of the particular brand of racial formation in the island, have an impact on their self-identification? Were forms of self-identification, as Cuban, Black or Afro-Cuban, situational, that is, were they partially dependent on particular contexts and situations? Did individuals articulate different ident-ifications at different moments or in different political contexts?

7. Did the Revolution's domestic policies (cultural and otherwise) and the limits of racial politics established by the government conflict with this generation's enthusiastic reception *and* re-signification of racially motivated writings and struggles from abroad?[xxviii]

8. How did Afro-Cubans understand their situation in comparison/contrast to those of Blacks elsewhere?

9. As newly empowered subjects by a social revolution, did these artists, filmmakers, and intellectuals ever face a vital dilemma as a result of their simultaneous commitment to, and endorsement of, class struggle and racial political consciousness?

Embarking upon the topic(s) at hand requires first and foremost a revisionist study of the history of Black thought and interventions in Cuba prior to 1960, particularly from 1912 to 1960,[xxix] as well as an examination of the Black press from the publication of the first Black newspaper by Juan Gualberto Gómez in 1879 until the onset of the Revolution. Before 1959, there was, albeit minute, a class of socially aware intellectuals and professionals, as well as a Black working- and middle-class, many of whom were associated with the *Sociedades de Color* (Black Mutual Aid Societies/) and/or with other Black organizations such as the National Organization for Economic Rehabilitation (Organización Nacional *de Rehabilitación Económica*, O.N.R.E.), and active in the island's urban centers, primarily in Havana, Santiago de Cuba, and Camagüey. By reading the Black press, attending talks, and participating in informal networks of discussion, these people kept themselves relatively well informed of Black cultural, social, and political events in the African diaspora in the Americas, especially in the US; though the same does not hold true for their knowledge of the African continent. There were also Black Cubans who, as merchant marines, athletes, musicians, or as part of a migrant labor force, traveled, and/or lived and worked abroad, primarily in the US, and, in some cases, also in Central America and the Caribbean. Through these geographies of exchange, Black Cubans gained first-hand knowledge of Black diaspora culture, a knowledge that was subsequently shared with family and friends on the island. On the other hand, the degree of knowledge on the part of Afro-Cuban youth prior to the Revolution was questionable and utterly depended, as previously mentioned, upon the degree of knowledge owned by their nuclear and/or extended families. Their awareness was also linked to the degree of involvement of the family with internationally conceived organizations, such as the Communist or Socialist parties.

With noted exceptions, the Cuban national curriculum and its accompanying textbooks made virtually no reference to local, regional (as in Caribbean), or hemispheric Black histories. As in most neo-colonial settings, children were largely taught national history from the vantage point of the former European colonizer and their Creole offspring. Shortly after the onset of the Revolution in 1959, this situation radically changed. At the core of the Revolution's ideological re-engineering of the Cuban people was information technology: the government's principal aim during those first few years was to make Cubans –regardless of colour– cognizant of the decolonizing struggles in Africa and the rest of the so-called Third World, including the struggle of African Americans. It would suffice to browse through key newspapers and some of the illustrated government-sponsored publications from the period or to view some of the newsreels and documentaries produced during the sixties to confirm the detailed attention devoted to the struggles of African and African Americans, and to the ensuing colonial repression and police brutality.[xxx] Without questioning or doubting the existence of white brutality and its attendant system of terror, however, it is important to note that this rather extensive coverage and graphic representations of the violence taking place in Africa and the United States were largely meant to influence matters of domestic policy and race-related internal affairs, by showing Cubans, and particularly Black Cubans, how much better their situation was when compared to that of their Black brothers and sisters in "the land of plenty." Indeed, in Cuba there were no Negro-eating dogs, at least not since the time of the *rancheadores*, nor did the population at large face daily displays of police or state brutality, except perhaps those affected by the numerous and uninhibited public government executions of former assassins, traitors, and counterrevolutionaries (along with a few victims of personal vendettas).[xxxi]

It is fair to say that, at this time, most Afro-Cubans, particularly the youth and those who came from working class backgrounds, considered their situation favorably in comparison with the situation of Blacks elsewhere. They felt empowered by the new government: after all, they were living in a revolutionary context, one in which institutionalized racial discrimination had been abolished. Others, however, particularly those who had been working with Black organizations (such as O.N.R.E), headed by the prominent criminal lawyer, and author, Dr. Juan René Betancourt (1918 – 1976), as well as some of the members and leaders of the more prominent Black Societies, like the Club Atenas or Unión Fraternal] considered that the new political situation placed them, their organizations, and, to some extent, Black Cubans in general, at a *politically* disadvantaged position in comparison to Blacks in the U.S., and, most certainly, in contrast to the situation of the Black middle class prior to 1959. In fact, some of these spokesmen for the Black professional and middle class sectors, like Betancourt, left the country by 1962, after the government permanently closed the Black Societies, dismantled their Federation and all other Black non-governmental organizations existing on the island. At this point, it was clear that their imperative to turn blackness into a legitimate place from which to lobby for political participation in the new society was not compatible with the revolutionary government's agenda, as had been the case with the succession of governments that followed independence from Spain and the founding of the Republic in 1902.

Despite the ideological campaign carried out by the State-controlled media, the very presence of African, and African American intellectuals and militants in Cuba (Amiri Baraka, Ben Bella, Amilcar Cabral, Aimé Cesaire, Eldridge Cleaver, Angela Davis, Huey Newton, Seiko Touré, and Robert F. Williams) during the 1960s and early 1970s, as well as the publication, in Spanish, of the writings of Fanon, Cesaire, and others, including the "explosive," if virtually forgotten anthology of writings by African Americans edited by Edmundo Desnoes in 1967 entitled *Now, el movimiento negro en los Estados Unidos* (*Now; the Black Movement in the United States*), spurred grass-roots discussions among Black Cuban intellectuals and artists. The reflexive process that followed from the often informal discussions of these and other works (together with some of the events previously mentioned earlier in this introduction), led to the conceptualization in 1968 of what has been referred to as a "Black Manifesto" (a document whose very existence has been disclaimed by some of the people said to have been involved in its conceptualization)[xxxii] and to the formation of study groups that were to follow in the late sixties and early seventies (Moore, Howe, Luis). A decade before the study groups, however, Walterio Carbonell's groundbreaking study, *Crítica. Cómo surgió la cultura nacional* (1961), and six years later Manuel Granados' award winning novel, *Adire y el tiempo roto* (1967), stand as piercing and uncompromising critiques of the dangerous persistence of the ideology of whiteness and of white superiority even amidst a Socialist revolution.

Nevertheless, the question remains as to whether or not this first generation of artists, filmmakers, and intellectuals ever faced a vital dilemma when it came to their artistic or intellectual production, as a result of their simultaneous commitment to, and endorsement of, class struggle and racial political consciousness, in a society that deemed "race," on the one hand, an empty signifier, a non-topic, and, on the other, a seditious weapon, particularly in Afro-Cuban hands. I would like to suggest that they did, although it is also possible to observe a degree of difference in the way those belonging to slightly older age-groups responded to the predicament(s) posed by the various instantiations of the Cuban 1960s.[xxxiii] How did they navigate and/or negotiate their collective and individual predicaments in the face of official dictates and of the putative trials resulting from their transgression? Did they voice their dissent or embrace the official pronouncements? Did they make the necessary adjustment in their works and behaviour to conform to officially sanctioned forms of expressions and representation? And if so, were those adjustments an act of political "conversion," or do they attest to what Josefina Ludmer has labeled "*las tretas del debil*" (the tricks of the weak), in reference to the 18th century Mexican nun Sor Juana Inés de la Cruz's response to ecclesiastic officialdom?[xxxiv] Clearly, a close reading of some of the works produced by this generation, of the secondary sources discussing these works, as well as an exploration of the individual and collective histories of its members, is of utmost importance to examine the ways Afro Cuban artists individually and as a generation navigated through the turbulence of those significant years.

So far I have interchangeably referred to people of *noticeable* African descent in Cuba as either Black Cubans or Afro Cubans or both. Perhaps, it is time to say a few words about the bearing the discourse of *cubanía* and *cubanidad* had upon Black subjectivities and identities in 20th century Cuba. In Cuba, as in the rest of the globe where people have tried to make political claims based on race, ethnicity, or religion, the question of terminology and its deployment is an exceedingly political one; and more so when discussing those "new" subjectivities that emerged and were legitimized during the 1960s.

Today is it widely accepted that subjects and subjectivities, like nations, are constituted discursively. In this regard, the discourse of *cubanidad* and *cubanía* –one whose initial bourgeois-humanist conceptualization we owe to the poet-politician José Martí, and his generation of insurgent — intellectuals, and its later institutionalization to Fernando Ortiz — has been a tremendous burden on the ways those who are distinctively non-white Cubans have grappled with their difference, and, consequently, with their personal, social, and political, loyalties and affiliations. Similarly, the discourse of cubanidad has come to bear on the ways so-called white Cubans consistently viewed those who were not like them in terms of color and social status. Martí envisioned a nation "con todos y para el bien de todos" ("for all, and for the good of all"). Later, the Republic (1902 - 1958) conveniently embraced the dream as its goal. But, as is virtually always the case, dreams are typically deferred, making them into the perfect figurations of what nations and social relations strive to be, but are not - not yet, that is. Meanwhile, dreamers perish, and once they do, the state, through the strategic enshrinement of their dreams, perpetuates the spectre of the dreamer and of his/her dream, on the very promise of its deliverance. In Cuba the promise of equality, of "a nation for all," which lies at the core of the discourse of cubanidad, has prevented Black Cubans from attaining full citizenship even after the 1959 Revolution, which, like previous regimes, claimed to have fulfilled the Republic envisioned or dreamed by José Martí.

Of course, this is a jaded and highly controversial issue. For one, Martí died prematurely, thus we lack his opinion on the subject, and thus no one can really predict how Martí and his doctrine/programme conceived in times of war (the anticolonial struggle against Spain) would have fared in *special periods* of peace (after 1902, and particularly after 1989). But also, nationalism as the philosophical and political principle of modernity and of the (aspiring) modern nation-states has lost its lustre, theoretically, at least.

Appendix 1

The following chronology emanates from my idea that the *concept* of the 1960s emerges in relation, and/or in response, to pivotal events taking place in the 1950s. For instance, in my reading, two disparate events such as the Algerian Revolution, and the end of the McCarthy era, created the conditions of possibility for "the 1960s" to emerge.

- 1952 – Batista military *coup* on March 10.
- 1952 – The Mau Mau Rebellion in Kenya.
- 1954 – The end of the McCarthy era.
- 1954 – The beginning of the Algerian war (1954 – 1962).
- 1954 – Brown vs. Board of Education.
- 1955 – The beginning of the non-violent resistance movement led by Martin Luther King JR in the U.S.
- 1957 – Ghana becomes a Republic and Nkrumah its first President.

- 1959 – The triumph of the rebel army led by Fidel Castro in Cuba.
- 1960 – The 'vintage' year of African Independence.
- 1960 – Fidel Castro stays in Harlem, NYC, and his meeting with Malcolm X.
- 1960 – The beginning of inconspicuous Cuban presence in Africa.
- 1961 The Bay of Pigs invasion.
- 1961 The creation of OSPAAL (Organization of Solidarity of the People of Africa, Asia, and Latin America), a tri-continental organization committed to national liberation, anti-imperialist, and antiracist struggles around the globe.
- 1962 – The Cuban missile crisis.
- 1963 Johnson emerges as a leader in domestic civil rights and, ironically, as the US president responsible for the escalation of US involvement in North Vietnam.
- 1963 –U.S. President John F. Kennedy is assassinated.
- 1964 – Martin Luther King is awarded the Nobel Prize for peace.
- 1965 – The Watts' riot. Beginning of Black decolonization in the USA.
- 1965 – Malcolm X is assassinated.
- 1966 – Stokely Carmichael coins the slogan "Black Power" at a rally in Jackson, Mississippi.
- 1966 – Birth of the Black Panther Party in Oakland, CA.
- 1966 –Ché Guevara is killed in Bolivia.
- 1967 – 26 armed Panther members enter the State Capitol in Sacramento.
- 1968 – Martin Luther King Jr. is assassinated.
- 1968 – The Soviet invasion of Czechoslovakia.
- 1968 – Students take to the streets in Paris and, among other things, occupy the Sorbonne and other institutions of higher learning.
- 1968 – "The massacre of Tlatelolco," in Mexico City.
- 1968 – First Congress of Education and Culture in Havana, Cuba.

References

Arenas, Reynaldo. *Before Night Falls.* 1992. New York: Viking, 1993.

Brock, Lisa and Otis Cunningham. "Race and the Cuban Revolution: A Critique of Carlos Moore's "Castro, the Blacks, and Africa." *Cuban* Studies 21 (1991). Reprinted in: http://www.afrocubaweb.com/brock2.htm 13 pp.

Brock, Lisa and Digna Castañeda Fuertes. *Between Race and Empire.* Philadelphia: Temple University Press, 1998

Bronfma, Alejandra. "'Unsettled and Nomadic'" Law, Anthropology and Race in Early Twentieth-Century Cuba." Maryland: Latin American Studies Center. Working Paper #9. University of Maryland, College Park, 2002

-----. *Measure of Equality.* Chapel Hill: University of North Caroline Press, 2004.

Carbonell, Walterio. Crítica: cómo surgió la cultura nacional. La Habana: Ediciones Yaka, 1961.

Casanova, Manuel. Telephone Interview, March 24, 2003.

De la Fuente, Alejandro. *A Nation for All. Race, Inequality and Politics in Twentieth Century Cuba.* Chapel Hill, NC: University of North Carolina Press, 2001.

Desiderio Navarro. "In *Medias Res Publicas*: On Intellectuals and Social Criticism in the Cuban Public Sphere." *From Cuba. boundary 2* 29:3 (2002): 18 - 203.

Desnoes, Edmundo. *Now. El movimiento negro en los Estados Unidos.* La Habana: Instituto del Libro, 1967.

Díaz, Jesús. *Los años duros.* La Habana: Casa de las Américas, 1966.

Domínguez, Jorge. "Foreword." *Castro, the Blacks, and Africa.* Carlos Moore. Los Angeles, California: Center for Afro American Studies, University of California, 1988.

Fanon Franz. *L'an cinq de la revolution algerienne.* Paris: F. Maspero, 1959.

-----. *Les damnes de la terre.* Paris: F. Maspero, 1959.

-----. *Peau noire, masques blanc.* Paris: Editions du Seuil, 1952.

-----. *Pour la revolution africaine; ecrits politiques.* Paris: F. Maspero, 1964.

Fernández Robaina, Tomás. El negro en Cuba, 1902-1958: apuntes para la historia de la lucha contra la discriminación. La Habana: Editorial de Ciencias Sociales, 1990.

Fulleda-León, Gerardo. *Algo en la nada*. La Habana: Ediciones El Puente, 1961.

Giral, Sergio. "La muerte de Joe J. Jones." La Habana: Instituto Cubano del Arte y la Industria Cinematográfica, 1967.

-----. "Cimarrón." La Habana: Instituto Cubano del Arte y la Industria Cinematográfica, 1967.

-----. "El otro Francisco" (The Other Francisco"). La Habana: Instituto Cubano del Arte y la Industria Cinematográfica, 1974.

-----. "Rancheador." La Habana: Instituto Cubano del Arte y la Industria Cinematográfica, 1977.

-----. "María Antonia." La Habana: Instituto Cubano del Arte y la Industria Cinematográfica, 1990.

-----. "Placido la sangre del poeta" (Placido, the Blood of the Poet"). La Habana: Instituto Cubano del Arte y la Industria Cinematográfica, 1986.

Gleijeses, Piero. *Conflicting Missions. Havana, Washington, and Africa, 1959-1976*. Chapel Hill, NC: University of North Carolina Press, 2002.

Gosse, Van. *Where the Boys Are. Cuba, Cold War American and the Making of a New Left*. London: Verso, 1993.

Granados, Manolo. *El orden presentido*. La Habana: Ediciones el Puente, 1962.

-----. *Adire y el tiempo roto*. La Habana: Casa de las Américas, 1967.

-----. *El viento en la casa-sol* La Habana: Union de Escritores y Artistas de Cuba, 1970.

Halperin, Maurice. *Return to Havana*. Nashville: Vanderbilt University Press, 1994.

Hernández, Eugenio. *María Antonia*. La Habana: Editorial Letras Cubanas, 1979.

Herrera, Georgina. *GH*. La Habana: Editorial El Puente, 1963.

-----. *Gentes y cosas*. La Habana: Unión de Escritores y Artistas de Cuba, 1974.

-----. *Granos de sol y luna*. La Habana: 1978.

-----. *Grande es el tiempo*.

-----. *Gustadas sensasiones*. La Habana, 1997.

Howe, Linda S. *Transgression and Conformity: Cuban Writers and Artists After the Revolution.* Madison: University of Wisconsin Press, 2004.

Jameson, Fredric. "Periodizing the 60s." *The 60s Without Apology.* Ed. Sohnya Sayres, et al. Minneapolis: University of Minnesota Press in cooperation with *Social Text*, 1984

Justina, Ana. *Silencio.* La Habana: Ediciones El Puente, 1961.

Ludmer, Josefina. "Las tretas del débil." *La sartén por el mango.* Eds. Patricia Elena González and Eliana Ortega. Puerto Rico: Ediciones Huracán, 1985

Luis, William. *Lunes de Revolución: literatura y cultura en los primeros años de la revolución cubana.* Madrid: Editorial Verbum, 2003

Carlos A. Jáuregui and Dabove, Juan Pablo. 2003. *Heterotropías: Narrativas de identidad y alteridad latinoamericana.* Pittsburgh: Instituto Internacional de Literatura Iberoamericana, University of Pittsburgh, 391-415.

Mañach, Jorge. "El problema negro." La Habana: Editorial Trópico, 1938.

Martí, José. "Mi raza." *The America of José Martí.* Trans. Juan de Onís. New York: Funk & Wagnalls, 1968. 308-312.

Martínez-Echazábal, Lourdes. "*Mestizaje* and the Discourse of National/Cultural Identity in Latin America, 1845-1959." *Latin American Perspectives*, Vol. 25.3 (1998): 21-42.

Martínez Furé, Rogelio. *Poesía yoruba.* La Habana: Ediciones El Puente, 1963.

-----. *Poesia anónima africana.* La Habana: Instituto del Libro, 1968.

-----. *Diálogos imaginarios.* 1979. La Habana: Editorial Letras Cubanas, 1997.

Moore, Carlos. *Castro, the Blacks, and Africa.* Los Angeles: Center for Afro-American Studies, University of California, 1988.

Morejón, Nancy. *Mutismos.* La Habana: Ediciones el Puente, 1962.

-----. *Amor, ciudad atribuida.* La Habana: Ediciones el Puente, 1964.

-----. *Richard trajo su flauta y otros argumentos.* La Habana: Unión Nacional de Escritores y Artistas de Cuba, 1967.

Pérez Sarduy, Pedro. "An Open Letter to Carlos Moore." *Cuba Update* (1990): 34 - 36. Reprinted in: http://www.afrocubaweb.com/lettertocarlos.htm 5 pp.

Pérez Sarduy, Pedro & Jean Stubbs. *AfroCuba*. New York: Center for Cuban Studies & Ocean Press, 1993.

-----. *Afro-Cuban Voices. On Race and Identity in Contemporary Cuba*. Gainsville: University of Florida Press, 2000.

Saldaña, Excilia. "Mi nombre". La Habana: Ediciones Unión, 2003.

-----. *In the vortex of the cyclone: selected poems by Excilia Saldaña*. Edited and translated by Flora M. González Mandri and Rosamond Rosenmeier. Gainesville: University Press of Florida, 2002

Quarles, Benjamin. *The Negro in the Making of America*. 1964. New York: Simon & Schuster, 1996.

Quiroga, José. *Cuban Palimpsests*. Minneapolis: University of Minnesota Press, 2005.

---

[i] Several friends and colleagues have contributed with their comments, suggestions, and enthusiasm, to the intellectual development of this piece. Jose Quiroga (Emory University) and Anani Dzidzienyo (Brown University), both read and enthusiastically commented a much earlier version of this essay. At Santa Cruz, I have has benefited from the many evening conversations with my dear friend and colleague Karen Yamashita whose forthcoming novel also revisits the period. Similarly, I am thankful to Daniel Linger and Mari Paz Balibrea, my former colleague at UCSC, for their thoughtful reading of an earlier version of this essay. And, of course, to Conrad James, whose editorial work has added to the readability of the piece. Similarly, I would like to acknowledge the Institute for Humanities Research and the Chicano / Latino Research Center at the University of California Santa Cruz, my home campus. Their financial support made possible for me to conduct research in Cuba, including personal interviews, which have been pivotal for the elaboration of this piece.

[ii] See Jameson's 1984 article for a discussion of the "Green Revolution" and its relation to the advent of late capitalism and its logic.

[iii] The list is by no means exhaustive, but rather, as a composite of events that have had the most ideological, political, and cultural relevance for Africa and the so-called Third World (including Cuba).

[iv] Born in Maghnia, Algeria in 1916, Ahmed Ben Bella served in the French army during World War II, became active in the Algerian struggle for independence, and was one of the nine members of the revolutionary committee that developed into the FLN (National Liberation Front). Ben Bella was the first president of Algeria, in office from 1963 until he was overthrow by a *coup* in October of 1965.

---

[v] Robert Williams was born in North Carolina, U.S. in 1925, He is best known for his militant leadership of the Civil Rights Movement in the U.S. South and organizing Black people to take up armed self-defense against the Ku Klux Klan. Williams spent time as an exile in Cuba, where he organized "Radio Free Dixie," a clandestine radio station broadcasting to the US-South, From Cuba he went to live in China. Williams died in Michigan, U.S. in 1996.

[vi] Unlike previous forms of Black activism in the US that focused their attention exclusively on people of African descent, the BPP viewed racial discrimination and oppression as affecting not only Black people but also people of color and other oppressed people in the US and elsewhere. By identifying with the struggles of other Black and brown people around the world, theirs was a form of transnational logic that incorporated (and to a certain extent reconciled) the basic tenets of Du Bois' Pan-Africanism, and of Dialectical Materialism, with a thrust to break away from colonial bondage not only in Africa, and the Caribbean, but also in any part of the globe under colonial rule, including the US.

[vii] For a provocative and more extensive discussion of this event, the section entitled "Celluloid Dreams" from José Quiroga's *Cuban Palimpsests*, pages 33 – 47.

[viii] However, there seemed to have been a problem with such deployment: the troops were under the unexpected leadership of a white man: Ernesto "Che" Guevara. A miscalculated decision that betrayed the lack of clear understanding (on the part of the Cubans) about the psychological and postcolonial ramifications of endemic racial oppression in Sub-Saharan Africa,

[ix] The cited text has been excerpted from the book's back cover.

[x] The dates indicate the year of initial aid to those countries.

[xi] According to Gleijeses, after the fall of Ben Bella, Brazzaville, the capital of the (former French) Congo, and Dar-es-Saalam, in Tanzania, would replace Algeria as "the center of Cuban activities on the continent" (160).

[xii] It is worth remembering that Nixon was elected in 1968 – however, those Nixon voters were presumably living a 1960s that had little to do with the ones I describe in this paper. In the US, there was Vietnam and the Civil Rights movement, which actually came together somewhat fortuitously; elsewhere there were other things (the dictatorship in Brazil and then in Chile, the Cultural Revolution in China, the other side of the Vietnam War in North Vietnam, and so on). Thus, I fully agree with my colleague Daniel Linger, that "[t]hese events were not part of one big movement; rather they borrowed (mostly rhetorically) themes from one another and brought them to bear on local issues (Electronic communication, June 18, 2003)

[xiii] I wish Navarro would have opted for a different qualifier to describe the quinquenio gris, since the use of "black" so obviously correlates with a value-laden race discourse.

[xiv] I am borrowing this phrase from the homonymous title of the 1966 award-winning novel by the late Jesús Díaz.
[xv] See *Animal Tropical.*
[xvi] *Casa de las Américas* is a landmark cultural institution in Latin America founded in 1960.
[xvii] Brock & Cunningham, for instance, characterize the book as "basically a series of far-reaching generalizations embellished with isolated stories and heavily suggestive language (8);" while Pérez-Sarduy considers it "an irrational diatribe" (3), "governed less by reason than by passion" (2).
[xviii] The response of the Cuban Revolution, however, is not unique. As my colleague Mark Anderson pointed out to me, "most, if not all, leftist revolutions of the 20th century [have] reproduced forms of racial, ethnic, gender and/or sexual oppression" (Electronic correspondence, Tuesday, May 13, 2004). See, for instance, Charles Hale's study of the Sandinistas and Miskitu in his book *Resistance and Contradiction: Miskitu Indians and the Nicaragua State, 1894-1987.*
[xix] Juan Gualberto Gómez founded the newspaper *La fraternidad* in 1879, and the Directorio Central de Sociedades de Color (the Central Directory of Black Societies) in 1890. Later, during the Republic, he became a senator for the Liberal Party.
[xx] The term *jabao* is used to refer to a person with Negroid features, but with a light freckled complexion and blondish or reddish hair.
[xxi] The efforts were concentrated primarily in the labor market, and in the recreational sectors. Prejudice and racism, however, continued to exist and thrive in the private spheres.
[xxii] The complexities and contradictions of that foundational story are brilliantly illustrate by Jesús Masdeu in his novel *La raza triste*, 1923
[xxiii]For a recent example (September 2007) of this type of logic see the essay published in *La Jiribilla, "El tema racial y la subversion anticubana." In this piece, the author generally* considers US-based academic critiques of the "racial question" in the island as "anti-Cuban subversion," a form of imperialist attack against the "socialist regime" (1). Similarly, those scholars working on the topic of race in Latin America are often forced to address what is generally referred to as the "imposition" trope, whereby one is accused of imposing the US-based system of racial hermeneutics into a context where race is said to be irrelevant when placed against class, and other social markers of segregation and discrimination.
[xxiv] In a critique of Manolo Granados award-winning novel, *Adire y el tiempo roto*, 1967, critic and current Dean of the School of Letter at the University of Havana, Rogelio Rodríguez Coronel, considered the novel to be flawed as a result of the prevalence of ideological tendencies, such as *negritude*, that over-estimate the role of race, which is only one of the factors to consider within class struggle (*La Novela de la Revolución Cubana* 154). Moreover, he characterizes the story of the protagonist, Julián, as a "pathological case within the Revolution" (155).

[xxv] In this respect the publication in 1996 of a special issue of *Temas* dedicated to Black contemporary issues on the island is a landmark amongst recent scholarship on the subject.

[xxvi] Perhaps a way to tackle this contradiction is to conclude that all governments are basically conservative at home, that is, support for innovative/revolutionary measures "abroad" cannot translate to the home front.

[xxvii] In his controversial study, *Castro, the Blacks and Africa* (1988), Carlos Moore refers to the domestic policies enacted by the Cuban government as "Negrophobic."

[xxviii] It should be noted that this reception is made possible by two interrelated factors: first, the avowed internationalist profile of the Cuban revolution that, among other things, promoted the translation and publication of writings by Black revolutionary, anti-colonialist, and anti-imperialist authors such as Franz Fanon, Angela Davis, and Aimé Cesaire, amongst others, and, second, by the island's privileged location at the crossroad of Black trans-Atlantic affairs.

[xxix] 1960 marks the end of the Black Mutual Aid and Recreational Societies in Cuba.

[xxx] Some examples are the politically sharp documentaries "Now," and "LBJ," produced by *Noticiero ICAIC*, and directed by Santiago Alvarez in 1965 and 1967, respectively.

[xxxi] These public spectacles of violence that took place during the purging of political enemies carried by the revolutionary government during the first two years of its rule, however, were popularly hailed by the chilling cries of a thrilled, revenge-craving population: "*¡paredón, paredón, paredón*!"

[xxxii] For instance Nancy Morejón. Personal Interview, December 20, 2004.

[xxxiii] When speaking of the 1960s in Cuba, the following periodization is in order: 1959 - 1961, 1962 - 1964, 1965 - 1968, and 1969 - 1971.

[xxxiv] In the homonymous article, Josefina Ludmer carries out an illuminating study of, Sor Juana Inés de la Cruz – the 17th century Mexican nun – response to ecclesiastic officialdom. According to Ludmer, in her response, Sor Juana displays "las tretas del débil."

Chapter 7

Cultural Trans-nationalism and Contemporary Afro-Caribbean Poetry: The Case of Blas Jiméncz and Nancy Morejón

Antonio Tillis

Undoubtedly, the history of "Blacks" in the Americas, and arguably beyond, is one steeped in generational migration whether forced, mitigated, or explorative. This trans- and intercontinental shifting from localized spaces of "home" represent Black globalization, which today, spans over five centuries, creating amalgams and reconfigurations of defined and imagined "home-spaces," identities and world economies. Africans, and subsequently Africa-descended peoples, like many Nordic, Western and Eastern Europeans, have engaged in cross-cultural and cross-territorial expansion for centuries leaving behind a contiguous cultural heritage that has its etiological ontology in etched cartographies that navigate multifarious waters connecting to tributaries that collide and converge into and from the expanse shores of the western cape of Africa. Additionally, this collision has created a milieu of typologies that have been used to identify miscegenated bodies. An important territorial component of Africa's cartographical global landscape is the Caribbean islands. In as much, this paper purposes to explore issue relating to cultural transnationalism in the works of two Spanish-American/Caribbean poets of African ancestry, Blas Jímenez (Dominican Republic) and Nancy Morejón (Cuba). Specifically, the poetics of each author will be analyzed in order to interrogate the author's location of "home" (national and ethnic) and identity (national and racial/ethnic) using the gaze of cultural transnational discourse as a theoretical paradigm. Cultural capitalism will be discussed with regard to the ways in which each author poetically views the notion(s) of culture as an exportable and importable commodity in the economy of cultural exchange, and the ramifications of such exchanges on citizenship and identity formation. Specifically, interrogated in this analysis are poetic inquiries into the definitions of "home" in terms of Cuba and the Dominican Republic (DR) and the effect of ideological transnationalism on citizenship and identity formation.

In *Imaginary States: Studies in Cultural Transnationalism*, Peter Hitchcock states that "(m) ultiple and disjunctive identities – gendered, raced, located, classed, sexed, etc. – certainly challenge in profound ways many treasured and normative notions of self, but it is not hybridity itself that guarantees this challenge, in the same way that a unified subject cannot ineluctably express perspicacity" (6). He continues by adding, "(t) o this extent, cultural transnationalism is not about hybridity per se, but is first and foremost about the experience of globality"(7). Deduced from Hitchcock's statement, cultural transnationalism takes into consideration the contestatory and limited nature of viewing "culture" solely within the normative understanding and framework of a hegemonically defined nation. The implication here is that, in terms of home and identity, they represent decentered, deconstructed, reconstructed and abstract populisms that are shaped and defined by cultural contact and the importation and exportation of ideologies relating to the home-space (nation) and identity (nationality) therein. Noting the connectedness between global contact and transnational discourse, Hitchcock challenges contemporary cultural and transnational scholars to re-think the global in terms of its fluidity, complex configurations and intersecting histories, venturing ideologically and culturally beyond the ramifications of mere locality vis-à-vis a territorially bound local space. In continuing, Hitchcock offers the following as a tripartite rubric for the schematization of cultural transnationalism:

> ...(cultural transnationalism) might be schematized as follow:
> (1) it represents any array of critical methodologies broadly associated with cultural studies that are attempting to rethink culture as an object of knowledge beyond its strict and restricting national base;
> (2) it refers to modes of artistic and imaginative expressions that give vent to supra-national and transnational yearnings; and
> (3) it connotes various ways of being transnational that as yet have no viable political, economic, and social framework to sustain adequately the possibilities they might embrace. (2-3)

As proprietors of a multi-nationally stamped passport, Blas Jiménez and Nancy Morejón represent two Spanish-speaking contemporary Caribbean poets of African descent that have utilized their lyric voices to challenge the definitive national delineations of culture and race/ethnicity in Cuba and the Dominican Republic. Born in the 1940s, they emerge as chronological literary contemporaries as their first published volumes of poetry reflect ideological inquiries into the questioning of culture in terms of identity, nation, Blackness, and cultural commodity. In so doing, "home" for both poets represents that imagined space replete with its history of forced migration from Africa, slavery in the Americas, disenfranchisement, alienation, contradiction, contestation and reconciliation. For Morejón, the aforementioned is evident in many works such as in what has come to be her "signature" poetic piece, "Mujer negra" (Black Woman) and in "Negro" (Black Man). For the Dominican Jiménez, it is his "Asustando el tiempo" (Frightening the Time), "Ser negro en el Caribe Es" (Being Black in the Caribbean Means) among others that challenge the geographical borders that manipulatively define home and identity, while re-creating malleable definitions used as a collective signifier for cultural difference and commonality in Caribbean nation-islands.

The editors of *Approaching Transnationalism* are mindful of the slippery slope that exists between transnationalism and appropriations of identity with regard to transnational subjects. They assert:

> It is important to see transnational subjects as embodied beings, as bearers of gender, ethnicity, class, race, nationality, and at the same time agents constantly negotiating these self-identities *vis-à-vis* others in transnational spaces. It should also be noted that transnational identities, while fluid and flexible, are at the same time grounded in particular places at particular times. As transnationality becomes the way of life for many, the maxim of, 'no one can have two countries' (Murphy, 1988: 369) is no longer true. Although identities, whether ethnic, racial, social or national, are traditionally said to be 'localised' (Rouse, 1995: 353) and derived in relation to the specific contexts of a particular space, transnational subjects obviously play by a different set of rules since they live in, or connect with, several communities simultaneously. Their identities, behaviors and values are not limited by location; instead, they construct and utilize flexible personal and national identities. (2-3)

Morejón and Jiménez, both of whom represent transnational subjects, reflect bartered identities that are influenced by contested ideologies that are challenged in space, time, language, and place. Jiménez, who was formally educated in the United States (in Texas during the 1960s) and Morejón who has lived, studied, lectured in the US, France and the former Soviet Union become tangible re-pressentations of Africa-descended globe-trotters whose definitions of self, racially/ethnic/and national, have been formalized through contact with sets of normativity within and beyond the limited borders of Cuba and the Dominican Republic. And, their poetry represents immortal testaments of evolutionary transnationality that links Africa, the Americas and beyond in cultural contestation, reconfiguration, reconciliation, and bartering.

Blas Jiménez is recognized by many scholars of the Afro-Hispanic literary tradition as one of the first, if not the first, 20th century Dominican poet to self-identify as Black and to expose the complexities of race in the Dominican Republic. These "complexities" are rooted in the long, historical denial of an African heritage in the Dominican "home-space" and elsewhere in the Caribbean. In his work, Jiménez confronts the denial of a place for African heritage and identification within the imagined construct of Dominican/Caribbean national identity. His poetry is critical of those Dominican/Caribbean citizens who try to mask their Blackness in their privileging of indigenous or European traditions in an attempt to define racially and/or ethnically self, nation or the imagined home space. Jiménez's work challenges the nation and the self to acknowledge the racial underpinning that emerge as a bi-product of adopting transnational cultural idioms regarding Blackness. His effort to reconcile the collision is a poetic voice that, paraphrasing Hitchcock, expresses globality in terms of its damaging effect on defining normative constructions of self and home based on those imported from transnational spaces, historically Spain and the United States. Cultural transnationality is expressed in the historical moments of global contact during colonization, the forced migration of Africans to the nation-island for the slave trade, the migration of Haitians, Cubans and other Caribbean-blacks for political and socio-economic purposes post-slavery. The author, in many published interviews, recalls his definition of self in the home/nation-space prior to reconciling his Blackness in the transnational space, upon arriving to the United States for post-secondary studies. As a result of his "awakening" in the transnational, the poet poetically advocates a cathartic awakening in the national, as evinced in his poem "Asustando el tiempo", (Frightening the Time). From the first stanza, the poetic voice presents a Caribbean that is challenged by the national ideologies that define home, the racial/ethnic self, and cultural traditions. It states:

Caribe
Muere tu juventud
Por ideales revolucionarios
En tradiciones importadas

(Caribbean
your youth die
from revolutionary ideals
in imported traditions)[i]

In the form of a poetic apostrophe directed to imagined-home spaces and the inhabitants therein, the poetic voice addresses the residual, contestatory effects of the transferal regarding ideological transnational thought. Stating that that which represents the future of national identity, thus home, dies as a result of imported traditions, the poetic voice addresses directly the potential danger of transnational thought as it relates to definitions of nation, national culture and self. Implied is the effect of adopting definitions that are steeped in imported racist ideologies of the Unites States and Europe into the Caribbean home space. Thus, the Caribbean becomes a representation of "home" that localizes Blackness within a disjuncture that historically contests/denies/ subjugates /vilifies its visibility and importance within the defined nation. The poem continues:

El hombre
Sentado sobre su historia
Sueña con futuros europeos
Al ritmo enloquecedor de las esquinas calientes

Mujer
Atada a la mediocridad
Cae abatida por el canto del poeta
Se observa divinia y se entrega por el oro

El niño
Sin mañana y sin historia
Con su llanto
Asustando el tiempo. (11)

(Man
seated upon his history
dreams about European futures
to the maddening rhythms on hot street corners

Woman
Bound to mediocrity
Falls dejected by the poet's song
Observes herself divine and exchanges it for gold
Child
Tomorrow-less and history-less
With its cry
Frightening the time.)

Noted Afro-Hispanic scholar, Marvin Lewis, in his analysis of these last stanzas, states that they address the lack of history and identity due to purposed historical erasure of and deliberate self-hatred among Blacks in the Dominican Republic and other Caribbean nations. Manifested is an imported and embraced view of self and consequently home, that is imbued with falsified notions of what Blackness is/ "aint" and how it relates to a constructed national identity in the home/nation space that is packaged and sold for global consumption. However, that which is centric to the erasure and self-hatred is the imported/adopted ideals of the Eurocentric appeal in the Caribbean. Man, woman and child become symbolic metaphors for historical lineage and continuance of the global view of Blackness that has its beginning in the New World encounter and consequently, slavery in the Americas. The residual is a present-day people whose knowledge of and regard for self reflect this psychologically violent history, as they too, engage in the erasure of a racial self from the configuration of national identity. Hence, there are no Blacks in the Dominican Republic, only whites and variation of "indio." In the final poetic analysis, that which remains is a national entity, the Dominican of African ancestry, that is seem to be void of a tomorrow and history.

Similarly, Jiménez continues his poetic query into cultural transnational discourse in the introductory poem to the second book in the collection *Caribe africano en despertar*. "Ser negro en el Caribe es" begins book two, *Africano*, with a poetic questioning of Caribbean identity in terms of blackness. Interrogated is the ontological essence of all that connotes ones "Caribbeanness." Arguably, this notion of spatial, yet cartographical affinity and inscription to place is the underpinning of a transnational interpretation of this poem. The poem reads thus:

Dejar que tus ritmos te guíen
conocer tus verdades
crearte con los sonidos de tu alma
es vivr en ti
es ser
existir en un mundo ya muerto
y renacer
en tu lucha anónima
una rebeldía constante
al describrir que los dioses han muerto
porque solo creces
gritando por tus derechos
sudando por los alimentos
como la vida en ti
vida de negro
al escapar y encontrarte (39)

(Letting your rhythms guide you
Getting to know your truths
Creating yourself with the sounds of your soul
It is living within yourself
It is being
Existing in a world already dead
and being reborn
in your anonymous fight
a constant state of rebelliousness
upon discovering that the gods have died
because you grow alone
shouting for your rights
sweating for nourishment
like the life within you
Black life
upon escaping and finding yourself.)

In "Ser negro," Jiménez tackles a major backlash that is associated with transnational subjecthood: the malleable nature of identity and dislocation of the same. Thus, for the transnational poetic receptor, the epistemological quest becomes one marred in historical revisionist ideology linked to questions of race, nationality and belonging, which dominates the personal discourse and presupposes an inherent transnational composition for Caribbean peoples. And, a contemporary understanding of the present-day ramifications of the consequence of transnational movement in the Caribbean requires a historical "connecting of the ideological dots." The poetic voice begins suggesting that the "rhythms," "truths," and "sounds" of the soul will guide the Caribbean subject toward a state of "being," or assured existence. Poetically begged is the notion that self- empowerment is the by-product of a knowledge/affirmation of the historically contested self. In terms of material culture, the poetic references implicate cultural traditions of transplanted transnationals whose histories are embedded in migratory patterns that connect Africa, Europe and other nation-islands, as the "rhythms" about which the poetic voice speaks can be interpreted as musical instrument endemic to cultures, peoples, and specified locations. Thus, the cross-cultural contact becomes, as Hitchcock states "an episteme, a functional knowledge of rational attachment, and that Kantian aesthetic of excessive identification, an overreaching of the symbolic by the affective embrace of the imaginary" (165). Suffice it to say, the symbolism present in the poem relates to the embracing of the imaginary aesthetic associated with identification markers that define ones blackness and Caribbeanness, replete with the travail connected to both identity markers. Jiménez semiotically manipulates the existential, ontological query of the poetic voice through references that symbolize vestiges of material culture, as alluded to earlier. In "Letting your rhythms guide you," an understanding is that the "rhythms" that "guide" toward "being" symbolically represent material attributes associated with what it means to be a Caribbean subject. The bongo drum, conga drums, steel drums, timbales, guiro, maracas, claves and tambourines collectively evoke "rhythms" that manifest themselves corporally in calypso, reggae, salsa, merengue, dance hall and rumba – all representative of an imagined culture that defines a people in terms of race, nationality and locality. As the poem continues, the lines "existing in a world already dead / and being reborn / in a constant state of rebelliousness" speak to the constant negotiation of self, experienced through cultural/transnational critique and contact. Implied is the continual dismantling of the daunting identity palimpsest as superimposed identities are challenged, giving way to new expressions of Caribbean personhood. The hope is to render void the hegemonic definitions of what it means to be Black/Caribbean in an attempt to celebrate the "true" understanding of the struggle for emancipation of the mind; an understanding that would situate blackness in the center of the reflexive discourse as Caribbean subjects engaged in automatic and involuntary "unthinking" in order to "rethink" themselves. The concluding tone of conciliatory hope rests in the understanding that the fight (the contestatory challenge of "unthinking" and "rethinking") will and must continue until there is total emancipation of the "life within you / Black life" and an understanding that the symbolic "Black life" (replete with its cultural transnational understanding) is that which defines, as it is "located" intrinsically within people, place, and space in Caribbean nation-islands.

"Asustando el tiempo" and "Ser negro en el Caribe es" are but two examples of the manner in which this Dominican-poet transnational uses his craft to position the intersections of race, identity and space. In many of his poems, like "Asustando", Jiménez challenges the globality of the vilification of Blackness and the adoption of such a world-view in localized spaces. Additionally, in "Ser negro" Jiménez's interrogation of citizenship for Caribbean subjects, principally those of visible African ancestry, rises to the thematic fore of the creative piece. His use of the Caribbean as an example of a transnational space demonstrates how imported ideologies into the national islands resulting from various means of human migration have resulted in cultural collision, definition, redefinition, challenge and compromise. His work calls into question cultural transnationality and the notion of Blackness in global spaces. Like Jiménez, contemporary Cuban national poet Nancy Morejón utilizes the history of transnational migration in the Caribbean to reveal its impact on issues of race, gender and identity in her native Cuba.

This 2001 recipient of the national prize for literature is one of the most celebrated voices in post-revolutionary Cuban poetry. Nancy Morejón's work is noted for the richness of interwoven histories that are embedded within manipulated multiple lyric voices that transverse space, place, and time. Mariela Gutiérrez states: "Nancy Morejón's poetry should be seen as the poet's innermost journey into the roots of Cuba's African ancestry" (209). Gutierrez's critical comment echoes Hitchcock's notion of people as trade, human capital, within the framework of cultural capitalism and transnationality. For it is understood that the forced migration of Africans into the human slave trade created a conduit for transnational cultural capitalism in the Americas, as African were forced into an economic market that became dependent on human trade and cultural skill sets honed and perfected in ancient West African civilizations such as in agriculture, mining, etc. The first stanza of Morejón's "Mujer negra" poetically recreates this history as the lyric voice states:

> Todovía huelo la espuma del mar que me hicieron atravesar.
> La noche, no puedo recordarla.
> Ni el océano podría recordarla.
> Pero no olvido al primer alcatraz que divisé.
> Atlas, las nubes, como inocentes testigos presenciales.
> Acaso no he olvidado ni mi costa perdida, ni mi lengua ancestral.
> Me dejaron aquí y aquí he vivido.
>
> (I still smell the foam of the sea they made me cross.
> The night, I can't remember it.
> The ocean itself could not remember that.
> But I cannot forget the first gull I made out in the distance.
> High, the clouds, like innocent eyewitnesses.
> Perhaps I haven't forgotten my lost coast,
> Nor my ancestral language.
> They left me here and here I've lived.)

Introduced in the first stanza is the concatenation of geographical spaces for economic gain as Western Europe, in the case of Cuba, Spain, initiates the process of the transferal of people and cultural normativity into the New World. Such alteration of place forged collisions as new cultures and peoples were created via the transatlantic contact. The reference to memory in Morejon's work can be interpreted within the transnational as the beginning of the process of producing "multiple disjunct identities" as the concluding lines of the aforementioned stanza allude to contestation in "perhaps I haven't forgotten my lost coast nor my ancestral language." Woven in the lines is the space where national, ethnic, and later on gender identities are negotiated. Cognizant of Africa and her African heritage, the poetic voice recreates a sense of "home" in the transnational space as the poem continues:

> Y porque trabajé como una bestia,
> Aquí volví a nacer.
> A cuánta epopeya mandinga intenté recurrir.
> Me rebelé.
> Su Merced me compró en una plaza
> Bordé la casaca de Su Merced y un hijo macho le parí.
> Mi hijo no tuvo nombre.
>
> (And, because I worked like a beast,
> here I came to be born.
> How many Mandinga epics did I turn to for strength.
> I rebelled.
>
> His Lordship bought me in a public square.
> I embroidered His Lordship's coat and bore him a male child.
> My son had no name.)

Realizing that the imaginary boarders of Africa, representative of nation, have been broadened as a result of the trans-Atlantic slave trade, there exists an acknowledgement of a shifting identity and national space. The verse "here I came to be born" reconfigures the traditional interpretation of the transnational subject through expounding on the collision of culture and identity producing a new transnational subject whose sense of self and nation are compromised as a result of the forced geographical shift. Later, substantiation of the transnational as a vehicle for cultural commodity and human trade is addressed. The voice states that she was purchased, performed a foreign cultural assignment, was violated, produced a son out of the transcultural attack, and has no identity marker for the "child" she claims as her own, who was presumably sold as human capital.

As the epic-like poem continues, it address issues related to conflict and resolution in the transnational space as they point to national identity. Within the poem, there is a shift from ambivalence, rejection, and reconfiguration to reconciliation for the transnational subject. The poem concludes with an acceptance of an understanding of nation and Afro-Cuban identity resulting from the process of cultural transnational negotiation spatially and ideologically. The poetic voice maintains that:

Esta es la tierra donde padecí bocabajos y azotes…
En esta misma tierra toqué la sangre húmeda
y los huesos podridos de muchos otros,
traídos a ella, o no, igual que yo.
Ya nunca más imaginé el camino a Guinea.

(This is the land where I suffered mouth-in-the-dust and lashes…
In this same land I touched the fresh blood
And decayed bones of many others,
Brought to this land or not, just like me.
I no longer dreamt of the road to Guinea.)

Final verses of the poem culminate in the reconciliation of the transnational identity as the poetic voice lays claim to place and identity:

Nada nos es ajeno.
Nuestra la tierra.
Nuestros el mar y el cielo.
Nuestra la magia y la quimera.

(Nothing is foreign to us.
The land is ours.
Ours the sea and the sky,
The magic and the vision.)

As Morejón references the oncoming of communism in Cuba, her poetic voice, representative of a gendered transnational subject, affirms an identity, collective and national, that is born out of cross-national and cross-cultural contact. The result is an articulation of "home" and "identity" that have been challenged and reconfigured by the physical and ideological movement from one "place" to another.

Similarly, Morejón's "Negro" can be read as an exaltation of corporal blackness, as she centers the historical vilification of blackness, implicated in the poem through the symbolic use of the black male, in order to deconstruct the vile characterization of personhood for the purpose of reconstruction in the home space.

The transnational implication is lodged in the temporal locality referenced in the poem, spanning from the colonial period, progressing through slavery, emancipation and Cuban independence. In "Negro," Morejón positions the black male as a collective transnational subject replete with historic negotiations in terms of gender, ethnicity, race, and nationality in the Cuban national space. The inference is that, although these Black male bodies are inherently "Cuban," questioned is their "Cubanness" in a national space that privileges skin tones and hues that are at the lighter end of the color spectrum bordering the ideal white, or slightly "off-white." The poem begins:

> Tu pelo,
> para algunos,
> era diablura del infierno;
> pero el zunzún allí
> puso su nido, sin reparos,
> cuando pendías en lo alto del horcón,
> frene al palacio
> de los capitanes.
> (Some thought your hair
> the devil's own hell;
> but the tiny *zunzun*
> built its nest there, heedless,
> while you hung high on the scaffold
> before the Palace
> of the Spanish Capitains.)

In the first stanza, the poetic voice recounts the social positioning of Africans as they are introduced into the transnational space for the purpose of involuntary labor initiating the subsequent (dis) regard of blackness in discourses on Cuba nationalism. The voice speaks to the juxtaposition of "self" verses "other" as this "body" has been codified in terms of a European concept of beauty. However, an immediate "natural" acceptance/ adaptation to the transnational space is evoked as a semiotic representation of place/nation, the *zunzún*, embraces, or "locates" this dislocated subject. What is meant is that nature signifies an act of reclamation through the poetic performance of the *zunzun*, as its "home" is made in the dejected hair of the black man. Immediately, the poetic voice presents a binary that represents the contestatory trajectory of transnational subjects with regard to nation. Implied is the rejection of the symbolic black man and his "natural" acceptance within the same space. The broader inference is the question of national identity for many Blacks who migrated to Cuba and now call this nation-island their home. Issues of nation are complicated by those surrounding gender in the poem as the second stanza presents a poetic questioning of the usefulness of black male genitalia.

> Dijeron, sí, que el polvo del camino
> te hizo infiel y violáceo,
> como esas flores invernales
> del trópico, siempre
> tan asombrosas y arrogantes.
> Ya moribundo,
> sospechan que tu sonrisa era salobre
> y tu musgo impalpable para el encuentro del amor (72)
>
> (They said the dust of the road
> had made you disloyal and purplish
> like those tropical winter
> flowers, so stunning and
> arrogant always.
> Your agonized smile-
> they guessed it must have been brackish.
> and your soft moss never meant for the act of love.)

Continued is the poetic manipulation of nature in order to render transnational implications. The physical present of the black body in the transnational locale is compared to the arrogance of the tropic winter flower, whose radiance is brilliant in a "season" that discourages nature's display of aromatic blossoms. Yet, the tropical winter flower appears, full of arrogance and pleasing to sight of the gaze in the public sphere, which equates to ownership of place. The smile of this subject is described as "brackish." Such a descriptor can de related directly to the ideology of cultural transnationalism. The interpretation is that brackish typifies the nature of salty waters, as fresh and salt water mixes. Thus, the connection lies in the symbolic "mixing" of "waters" as Africa and New World produce a miscegenated subject that encompasses cultural configurations of the both. Yet, somehow this "mixing" implicates the cross-germinated , symbolic "stalk" of this arrogantly stunning winter flower. A black-male genitalia is presented amidst a questioning of its purpose and function. The purpose and function of his "soft moss" is presented impotently, which speaks directly to the disregard of his transnational, transcultural self. The poetic voice in following stanza is reminiscent to that of Blas Jiménez.

> Otros afirman que tus palos de monte
> nos trajeron ese daño sombrío
> que no nos deja relucir ante Europa
> y que nos lanza, en la vorágine ritual,
> a ese ritmo imposible
> de los tambores innombrables.
>
> (Others say the rugged sticks you cut
> brought us that black stain
> that refuses to let us shine before Europe
> and which hurls us into rival vortex,
> that furious rite of nameless drums.)

Like the countless drums that guide the "rhythms" of those presented in Jiménez' "Ser negro," the conga, bongo and others surface nameless as they intertwine in the vortex of whirling nameless cultural commodities, centering them for the purpose of recognition. The contestations created in the stanza represent binary oppositionality relating to location/dislocation, national/alien, in an attempt to reconcile the "nameless parts" that are culturally and biologically whirled in the symbolic vortex, or Cuba. Additionally, those black transnationals are unrecognized by "Europe" as their "black stain" has rendered them visually different. Taking this analogy to next level of interpretation, "black stain" and "invisibility" correlate to the plight of many transnationals as their cultural vestiges are marginalized in the discourse of national culture and identity. However, in the concluding stanza, the poetic voice broaches the idea of reclamation and reconciliation of the constituent parts.

> Nosotros amaremos por siempre
> Tus huellas y tu ánimo de bronce
> Porque has traído esa luz viva del pasado
> Fluyente,
> Ese dolor de haber entrado limpio a la batalla,
> Ese afecto sencillo por las campanas y los ríos,
> Ese rumor de aliento libre en primavera
> Que corre al mar para volver y volver a partir.

(Forever, we will love your footprints
and your bronze spirit.
for you have brought that living light
of the fluid past,
that pain of entering cleanly into battle,
your simple affection for bells and rivers,
that whisper of the free breath of spring
that flows seaward only to return
returning only to depart again.)

In the final poetic analysis, the transnational black male body, symbolic of a collective whole, reaffirmed as the use of the first person and second familiar sound the clarion call for reclamation. Additionally, the "living light / of the fluid past" connects people to territorial spaces rendering an articulation of the home space and national identity that is ephemeral, as allusions to further (re) configurations, contestation, struggle are symbolically afloat on the waters that border nation as they " return / returning only to depart again," and ultimately returning and departing with the ebbs and flows of "others" that transnationally enter into Cuba's territorial space.

As Hitchcock asserts in the conclusion of *Imaginary States*: "...the prospect of cultural transnationalism, a collocation of theoretical tools with which one may broaden yet complicate our approaches to the myths and material realities of cultural integration on a world scale" (187). Hitchcock and other scholars delving into the theoretical domain of the transnational assert that issues unearthed as a result of global, transnational inquiry are not unproblematic and easy resolvable. In transnational spaces such as Cuba and the Dominican Republic, the collocation of binaries such as black/white, Cuban/Dominican/Other, locate/dislocate represents by-products of the transnational encounter. And, as societies try to "sift" for understandings, the contestatory and historical nature of the development of the ideologies and their positioning are addressed. Morejón's "Negro" concludes with a reconciliation, similar to that experiences by transnational subjects as they try to situate "self" in the midst of competing comodifications in an attempt to locate the dislocated markers for race, nationality, and subjecthood in spaces where these issues have been wrought with historical debate and (mis) understandings.

In conclusion, cultural transnationalism as a theoretical discourse is accompanied with implications of redefining and challenging nationally accepted identifiers of self and others. As presented in this brief analysis on the appropriation of cultural transnationalism in Caribbean poetry, it was the goal to demonstrate how cultural ideology can be viewed as an importable commodity that codifies transnationality; in so doing, creating points of contestation and reconciliation of defining the self, the nation, and beyond. Blas Jiménez and Nancy Morejón are but two contemporary examples of Caribbean transnational subjects, who use the power of their poetry to demonstrate the many complexities of transnational ideology as it is packaged, imported and sold in national home spaces and beyond. Additionally, poetry for the both becomes the creative space where their personal reconciliations of the national and transnational are placed in dialogue in an attempt to understand the impact that one has on the other in terms of defining the self and nation, regarding race, ethnicity, gender and national culture, transnationally.

References

Appadurai, Arjun. *Modernity at Large*. Minneapolis: University of Minnesota Press, 1996.

Davis, James. "On Black Poetry in the Dominican Republic." *Afro-Hispanic Review* 1.3 (1982): 27-30.

DeCosta-Willis, Miriam, ed. *Singular Like a Bird.* Washington, DC: Howard University Press, 1999.

Gilroy, Paul. *The Black Atlantic*. Cambridge, Mass.: Harvard University Press, 1993.

Gutiérrez, Mariela. "Nancy Morejón's Avenging Resistance in 'Black Woman' and 'I Love My Master': Examples of a Black Slave Woman's Path to Freedom." *Singular Like a Bird.* Ed. Miriam DeCosta-Willis. Washington, DC: Howard University Press, 1999. 209-219.

Hitchcock, Peter. *Imaginary State: Studies in Cultural Transnationalism.* Urbana- Champagne: University of Illinois Press, 2003.

Jiménez, Blas. *Caribe africano en despertar*. Colección Cimarrones, Santo Domingo: Editora Nuevas Rutas, 1984.

Lewis, Marvin. "Contemporary Afro-Dominican Poetry." *CLA Journal* 34.3 (1991): 301- 316.

Morejón, Nancy. *Singular Like a Bird:Selected Poetry by Nancy Morejón*. Trans. Kathleen Weaver. Yari Yari Conference. New York: Black Scholars Press, 1997.

Morley, David and Kuan-Hsing Ghen editors. *Stuart Hall: Critical Dialogues in Cultural Studies*. London: Routledge, 1996.

Ong, Aihwa. *Flexible Citizenship: The Cultural Logics of Transnationality*. Durham: Duke University Press, 1999.

Sagás, Ernesto. *Race and Politics in the Dominican Republic*. Gainesville: University of Florida Press, 2000.

Tillis, Antonio. "Nancy Morejón's 'Mujer negra': An Africana Womanist Reading." *Hispanic Journal* 22.2 (Fall 2001): 483-493.

________. "Awakening the Caribbeab African: The Socio-Political Poetics of Blas Jiménez." *Afro-Hispanic Review* 22.2 (Fall 2003): 29-38.

________. "Postcolonial Pilgrimage: Toward an Afro-Cuban Identity in the Poetry of Nancy Morejón." *Mosaic, a Journal for the Interdisciplinary Study of Literature* 36.4 (December 2003): 65-79.

Yeoh, Brenda et al, eds. *Approaching Transnationalisms: Studies on Transnational Societies, Multicultural Contacts, and Imaginings of Home*. New York: Springer Publishing, 2003.

---

[i] Translations of Jiménez's poems are my own.

Chapter 8

Cocolos, Emigration and Dominican Narrative[i]

Lancelot Cowie

With the scarcity of manpower in the cane fields of the Dominican Republic, a drive to recruit labourers from the Lesser Antilles was started at the end of the 18th Century and reached its zenith at the beginning of the 19th Century. The majority of workers came from St. Kitts, Nevis and Anguilla and their principal destination was the sugar factories of San Pedro de Macorís,[ii] Santo Domingo, Puerto Plata and La Romana, where they arrived with grand dreams of improving their economic condition and then returning to their native countries. Those dreams soon became an illusion. That group of black immigrant labourers, discriminated against and isolated within the host society, was soon given the contemptuous nickname "Cocolos". The origin of this word is uncertain. The most common view holds that the word results from an error in the pronunciation of the name of the island Tortola. For his part, the historian Frank Moya Pons explains it as a "modification of the word 'congolo', which means 'from the Congo', in the same way that people from Angola were called 'Angolos' and some African slaves and their descendents were called 'Negrolos'". Other opinions emphasize the Portuguese origin of the word, "'o coco' being the term used in Portuguese to refer to blacks from Africa", a term the Spaniards incorporated into their lexicon when they became involved in the slave trade.[iii] Nevertheless, the lyrical definition of Antonio Frías Gálvez in his poem "Cocolo de Cocolandia" (Cocolos from Cocoland) captures the true essence of the spirit of the Cocolo, which is quite different from the inappropriate terms that do not properly describe them:

Los Cocolos son aquellos
negros que vinieron
de sus islas tropicales
con banderas de hermandades
con trajes oscuros, de luto y domingueros,
respeto, mutualismo y sociedades.

Los Cocolos son aquellos

negros que vinieron
de sus islas tropicales
con espejos, flautas y tambores,
alegrando las calles soñolientas,
en cadencia de trémulos sudores,
en torbellinos de huracanes.

Los Cocolos son aquellos
negros que vinieron
de sus islas tropicales,
collar de esmeralda
a oriente del Caribe
mar de los conquistadores
de la madre España.

Los Cocolos ya no vienen,
los Guloyas son ya abuelos,
de pasos lentos en sus bailes
de fatiga en los saltos
de tambores destemplados
de sonidos bajos en la flauta
de miradas que sembró el tiempo
de pelos canosos
sobre sus lienzos negros...

Cocolos are those Negroes
who came
from their tropical islands
with flags of fraternities
with dark Sunday suits,
respect, friendly societies and associations

Cocolos are those Negroes
who came
from their tropical islands
with mirrors, flutes and drums,
livening up the sleepy streets
with cadences of shivering toil,
with hurricane-like whirlwinds

Cocolos are those Negroes
who came
from their tropical islands
emerald necklace
from the Caribbean,
sea of the conquistadores
from Mother Spain

The Cocolos now come no more,
the guloyas dancers are now grandfathers,
their steps slow in the dances,
tired in their jumps,
their drums out of tune,
the sound of their flutes low,
with looks blurred by time,
white hair
on their black faces

This article will examine the vindication of the Cocolo group— the celebration of their virtues, their resistance, their way of thinking and their cultural life — as portrayed in a selection of Dominican novels. These are Fracisco E. Moscoso Puello's *Cañas y Bueyes* (1936), *Over* by Ramón Marrero Aristy (1940), *Jengibre* by Pedro Andrés Pérez Cabral (1940), *Batey* by Tarquino Donastorg (1972), Diógenes Valdez's *Retrato de dinosaurios en la era de Trujillo* (1997), *Tiempo muerto* by Avelino Stanley (1998), and *El personero* by Efraim Castillo (1999). Together these works trace the life of the Cocolos, specifically, the hazardous voyage, their introduction to a strange land, the transfer to the awful quarters where they would live during the sugar cane harvest, their adjustment to the back-breaking work, the abuse and discrimination, the disillusionment and the frustrated dream of return to their homeland and their culture.

Marrero Aristy and Stanley portray the voyage so reminiscent of the slave crossings, focussing specifically on the inhuman conditions to which the immigrants were subjected. In the words of the former:

> En el vientre de un buque de carga, meten generalmente una cantidad de hombres dos o tres veces mayor que la prudente. Allí los negros pasan días y noches, los unos encima de los otros, alimentándose con pan y sardinas de latas que les son suministrados por los que el central envía a reclutar hombres a Haití y las islas inglesas. Gentes no acostumbradas a navegar, vomitan con frecuencia encima de sus compañeros. (Marrero Aristy, 1981:79)

> (In the bowels of a cargo ship, they usually put two or three times the number of men than they should. There, the blacks spend the days and nights, on top of each other, eating the bread and tinned sardines given

them by the men sent to recruit them in Haiti and the British islands. People not accustomed to travelling by sea frequently vomit on their companions.)

Stanley, for his part, describes the same problems in a more measured, yet more expressive manner, while he draws attention to the strong physical constitution of the Negro in the face of all adversities, especially hunger:

> Prácticamente parecíamos momias negras. Fueron once días comiendo mal y durmiendo peor, cuando acertábamos a dormir. La comida que llevábamos nos la comimos en los primeros cinco días pensando que íbamos a llegar en el tiempo normal. Pero nos demoramos tanto que el hambre no nos mató porque éramos negros. Y el negro pasa tanta hambre durante su vida que puede morir sin comer; pero no muere de hambre. (Stanley, 1999:13)
>
> (We practically seemed like black zombies. We spent eleven days eating badly and sleeping worse, when we did manage to sleep. We ate the food we had in the first five days, thinking that we would arrive within the normal time. But we were delayed so much that it is only because we are black that we did not die of starvation. The black man experiences so much hunger in his life that even though he may die if he does not eat, he will not die of hunger.)

Moscoso Puello's account differs from those just mentioned, not in substance, but because he romanticizes the voyage of the Cocolos on the Caribbean sea:

> Llegan por el mar. Una mañana amanece un balandro en el puerto. Desde el muelle se alcanzan a ver como náufragos recogidos en el mar. Se baldea la cubierta sucia y hedionda. Es un espectáculo que hace pensar en los tiempos de la trata. Son estos barcos de ahora una miniatura de los galeones. Pero no tienen cepo, ni hay esposas, ni ningún instrumento de tortura. A bordo han hecho una travesía alegre, feliz, llena de satisfacción. Han pasado sus noches, contemplando el bello cielo del Caribe, sin sentir el dolor de sus abuelos. Y ahora en el puerto, enseñan su dentadura blanca, como pulpa de coco, para mostrar alegría. Se oye un vocerío. Dos o tres yolas se acercan ala embarcación. Y después de pasar una o dos horas en el muelle, por delante de sus equipajes, cajas, canastas y macutos, abrazan y saludan a sus conocidos. Desembarcan al mismo tiempo, dos o tres cerdos. En ocasiones, un par de monos *tities*. (Moscoso Puello, 1975:109)

(They come by sea. One morning, a ship appears in the port. From the pier, one can see them like shipwrecked people rescued from the sea. The dirty, smelly deck is washed down with water. It is a sight that reminds you of the days of the slave trade. These ships are miniatures of the galleons. But they have no stocks, or handcuffs or any instruments of torture. The travellers have had a happy, enjoyable and very satisfying crossing on the ship. They have spent the nights contemplating the beautiful Caribbean sky, without feeling the pain their grandfathers did. And now, in the port, they show off their white teeth, like the flesh of coconuts as they express their happiness. You can hear the commotion. Two or three sailboats draw near to the ship. And after spending one or two hours on the pier with their luggage, boxes, baskets and sachets in front of them, they embrace and greet their acquaintances. At the same time, two or three pigs are taken off. Sometimes, a couple of capuchins.)

Living conditions in the *batey*, "which was more suited to animals than to people" constitute an additional form of hardship which, along with the paltry ration, became a permanent aspect of the suffering portrayed in the majority of novels under discussion. *Over*, for example, presents a sociological view of this heterogeneous group of workers, emphasizing the overcrowded conditions in which they lived (Marrero Aristy, 1981: 83–84). Stanley stands out along with Marrero Aristy for his very graphic descriptions of the deplorable conditions endured during the harvest. In *El tiempo muerto*, there is a first person account by a Cocolo of the harshness of the toil in the cane fields: oxen and carts bogged down in the mud,[iv] the broiling sun beating down, the gruelling work in the bagasse dumps. These conditions are captured also by Francisco García Moreira in *Tiempo muerto: memorias de un trabajador azucarero* (1969). In *Tiempo muerto*, Avelino Stanley establishes a definite relationship with this novel and his account of the bagasse scene contrasts with the laconic style of the Cuban author. Both succeed in conveying to the reader a sense of the tragedy that this new form of slavery represents, although García Moreira's account achieves a greater level of realism:

Las condiciones ahora eran más duras. El trabajo mayor. Siembra, resiembra, limpieza, abonado, virado de la paja..., todo a la intemperie. Por las mañanas había siempre un frío y un rocío que me empapaba de pies a cabeza. Después el sol implacable que me deshidrataba. Tanto era su rigor que llegó un momento en que me provocó hemorragia por la nariz. Con un poco de agua por la cabeza me la contenía. Y para que no volviera, ponía hojas verdes de los árboles bajo el sombrero y la camisa. Por las tardes llegaban las lluvias, las que después de haber sufrido un sol abrasador me dejaban tiritando, hasta que la ropa toda se me secaba encima. [...] Los arados rompían las cuevas de insectos venenosos: arañas, alacranes, ciempiés, etcétera, cuyas picadas me tenían varias horas sufriendo. [...] La pila de bagazo estaba a la intemperie y como éste venía caliente por la presión de los molinos, al apilarse, el calor se conservaba debajo y por arriba la calentaba el sol, haciendo de aquello un verdadero infierno. En los pies se me hacían ampollas y cuarteaduras, y mi madre me tenía que poner fomentos fríos. Los días de limpieza eran los más fuertes. Era necesario correr mucho bagazo para mantener el fuego de los hornos. Los hombres mismos teníamos que compensar el bagazo a mano porque los molinos a veces no mandaban lo suficiente. Al ir bajando la pila el calor aumentaba. Por las tardes aquello era humanamente irresistible. (García Moreira, 1969: 18, 26. Cf. Stanley, 1999: 144–45)

(The conditions now were harsher. The work load heavier. Sowing, re-seeding, cleaning, fertilizing, turning the straw— all at the mercy of the elements. In the morning, there was always coldness and dew which soaked me from head to foot. Afterwards, the relentless heat of the sun dehydrated me. It was so oppressive that there was a time when it brought on a nosebleed. I was able to control it by pouring some water on my head. And to prevent it from recurring, I put green tree leaves under my hat and shirt. In the afternoons, the rains came and since I had endured the scorching sun, they left me shivering, until my clothes became dry on my back [...]. The ploughs would break up the nests of the poisonous insects: spiders, scorpions, centipedes etc. whose bites left me in pain for several hours [...]. The pile of bagasse was in the open air and since it was hot as a result of the pressure from the mills, when it was piled up the heat was trapped at the bottom and the top part was heated up by the sun, making the whole pile a veritable hell. I got cuts and blisters on my feet and my mother had to treat them with cold poultices. The cleaning days were the toughest. You had to carry a lot of bagasse to keep the ovens going. The men had to gather the bagasse by hand because sometimes the mills did not supply enough. And as the pile got lower and lower, the heat increased. In the afternoons, it was humanly impossible to cope with it.)

Salaries were paid in vouchers, making it difficult to accumulate savings, which was really the primary purpose for the Cocolo migration to the Dominican Republic. All the novelists focus on this traditional type of injustice since "with the little piece of paper you could not buy anything except in the factory store". There, purchases could be made only with vouchers. You could buy only what they sold there. If you did not use up the full value of the voucher, you did not receive money back. They would give you another voucher" (Stanley, 199:88. Cf. Marrero Aristy, 1981:69 and García Moreira, 1969:31). Undoubtedly, the title *Tiempo muerto* is a symbol of the suffering of the immigrant worker after the harvest is over and he has to try to survive by finding jobs that pay badly wherever he can, as well as suffer persistent hunger (Stanley, 1999:90. García Moreira, 1969:34–35. Marrero Aristy, 1981:153–56).

As reflected in the texts under discussion, working conditions and other adverse circumstances gave scope for the strong character of the Cocolos to show itself: the greater the difficulty, the greater their capacity to cope, according to sayings such as "We blacks are stronger than a bad head of cattle" (Stanley, 1999: 87). However, this zeal sometimes disappeared when the Cocolo had to face oppressive conditions on the job, such as when a cane fire occurred:

> Escalante y el mayordomo espolearon sus caballos y se encaminaron hacia el fuego, en tanto que el jefe, machete en mano, arengaba a unos cuantos trabajadores que estaban en la bodega comprando algo para comer. La mayoría del personal estaba en los cortes. Un *cocolito* que trató de ocultarse en el cuarto de un barracón, fue sacado a planazos por el jefe. Acudir al fuego era un deber, y nadie podía ni debía eludirlo.
> Todos los hombres, mocha en mano, corrieron al siniestro. El jefe cruzaba carriles y, haciendo atajos, exhortaba a los braceros dispersos, acudir a la candela. Ya Escalante, a quien todos respetaban, con una veintena de hombres, ordenaba:
> —¡Aquí, muchachos!... ¡Una trocha! ¡Arriba!
> Con rapidez no usada, el personal le entró como fieras al ardiente cañaveral. (Donastorg, 1972: 63–64)
>
> (Escalante and the foreman spurred on their horses and headed for the fire, while the manager, with machete in hand, castigated some of the workers who were in the store buying something to eat. The majority of the workers were out reaping. A little Cocolo boy who tried his best to hide in the bedroom of the hut was removed with a few shovel blows by the manager. Going to the fire was a duty, and no one could or should avoid it.
> All the men, *machetes* in hand, ran towards the disaster. The manager crossed railway tracks and exhorted the scattered labourers to go to the fire. Already, Escalante (who was respected by all) along with about 20 men, was giving orders:
> "Here, we got a trail, up, up!"

With unaccustomed speed, the men rushed on to the trail and entered the burning cane field like wild beasts.)

Within the Cocolo household, the mother does not tolerate disobedience from the children and "when a Cocolo says 'that's enough', it must be 'that's enough'" (Stanley, 1999: 93). Arrogance ("Cocolos, with their broken English, seem to consider themselves superior" Marrero Aristy, 1981:84) and assertiveness are outstanding characteristics of the Cocolos:

> Son menos dóciles que los haitianos. A menudo hace Chencho *mala sangre* con Blakis, el maquinista de la No.3. Este hombre es muy testarudo. Siempre quiere hacer lo que le da la gana. Le llama la atención sobre la manera de colocar los vagones en el chucho, le pide que no los deje tan lejos del cargadero.
> Blakis sonríe maliciosamente. Le enseña los dientes como pulpa de cajuil y finge no entender. Ese es el recurso supremo de los *Cocolos.*
> —Mi no comprendi, Chencho!
> Cuando dice esto es para hacer su voluntad. Para no obedecer. Cuando un *Cocolo* termina por no entender lo que se le está diciendo, cuando olvida el español, hay que dejarlo. (Moscoso Puello, 1975:110)
>
> (They are less docile than the Haitians. Chencho often gets annoyed with Blakis, the driver of engine N° 3. This man is very stubborn. He always wants to have his own way. They talk to him about the way he positions the wagons on the switch, asking him not to leave them far from the loaders.
> Blakis smiles mischievously. He shows his teeth like cashew pulp and pretends not to understand. That is the ultimate strategy of the Cocolos.
> "Ah doan understan, Chencho".
> He does this when he wants to have his own way. To avoid obeying. When a *Cocolo* does not understand what you are saying to him, when he forgets Spanish, you have to leave him alone.)

In addition, resistance took the form of the creation of trade unions, whose revolutionary zeal was squelched by the exile of the leaders. In *Jengibre*, Charlie Prandy and Taringo, both with experience in organizing strikes, harangue the Cocolos, encouraging them to unite. What is unusual is the fact that Pérez Cabral incorporates much dialogue, transcribing the broken language of the trade unionists (Pérez Cabral: 97). Language takes on a new dimension in Avelino Stanley's *Tiempo muerto* because the protagonist sees it as a form of protection:

> Tomé el periódico y, de tanto leerlo y releerlo, como no tenía otra cosa que hacer, terminé aprendiendo esa lengua en la que, al principio, se me hacía todo tan difícil. No quiero decir que la leía con toda la soltura requerida. Pero al poco tiempo sí lo logré porque siempre leía los pedazos de periódicos en los que el vendedor de pescado envolvía su mercancía todos los sábados. Saber leer me ayudó a aprender una forma de defensa. (Stanley, 1999:109)
>
> (I took the newspaper and from reading and re-reading it, as if I had nothing else to do, I ended up learning that language which, at the beginning, was so difficult for me. Not that I read it with complete fluency. But in a short time I did succeed because I would always read those pieces of the newspaper in which the fish-seller wrapped the merchandise every Saturday. Learning to read provided me with a form of defence.)

In *Retrato de dinosaurios en la Era de Trujillo*, Diógenes Valdez highlights the rich vocabulary and the picturesque speech of the Cocolos of San Pedro Macorís:

> Entre los 'macorisanos', existe una forma de hablar muy pintoresca, en ocasiones, todo lo dicen mitad en un creole inglés y la otra mitad en un castellano demasiado folclórico. Las viejas iglesias, llamadas 'chorchas' — corruptela de la palabra inglesa, *church*— de estilo victoriano, abundan por doquiera. Las logias son más bien refugios donde los negros de origen inglés encuentran entre ellos mismos la comprensión que otros les niegan. (Valdez, 1997: 8)
>
> (The "Macorisians" have a very unusual manner of speaking. Sometimes half of what they are saying is said in creole English and the other half in a very folkloric Spanish. The old Victorian-style churches, or "chorches" as they are called, are everywhere. The lodges are really places of refuge where Negroes from the British islands are able to find among their own the understanding they do not receive from others.)

The Cocolos were active in Masonic life and founded the "Estrella de Puerto Plata" lodge (1899) and the "Loyal Lux Dominicana" (1896). But they also brought with them a rich Caribbean gastronomy to Dominican society: "yanikeke", "dumpling", "fungi", "mauby" and "guavaberry", the Christmas drink (Stanley, 1999: 145. Castillo, 1981: 169–210).

From the works discussed, there is clear evidence of the blatant racism that immigrants in Santo Domingo have to endure. In *Jengibre*, Pérez Cabral projects the scorn of Dominicans towards black workers, especially Haitians. His perspective on the matter has incurred strong criticisms from those who see him as racist and prejudiced (Nadal, 1985:14–15). One must remember the racist ideology of Rafael Leónidas Trujillo (1930–1961) which resulted in the rabid anti-Haitian activity, culminating in the massacre of 1937. Efraim Castillo, in *El personero*, develops a new perspective on the theme when he relates the racism towards the Cocolos and Haitians to the sugar economy. In a document purportedly written to Trujillo by Monegal, the ideologue of that era, we find the following explanation:

> ¡Tenga cuidado con la caña, *Jefe*! Deberá Usted siempre recordar, amado, que en las faenas de recolección Haití siempre ha sido un dechado de virtudes y gracias a esas cualidades llegó a ocupar un lugar cimero en el mundo preindustrial. Si damos rienda suelta a una política cañera estaremos afilando el cuchillo para nuestras gargantas. Deberá recordar, amadísimo, que la negritud del Este es una negritud ocasionada por la caña y la contratación de los llamados isleños o *Cocolos*, que llegaron por un periodo determinado de años y se quedaron para siempre. Los braceros haitianos harán lo mismo aunque los contratos se estipulen de gobierno a gobierno. ¿Cómo vería usted que nuestra riqueza cañera, a mediano plazo, se convierta en una dependencia de la mano de obra haitiana? Así el *batey*, Su Excelencia y *Líder*, se convertiría en un microcosmos haitiano, en una célula cultural completa, en donde los odios ancestrales saldrán a flote y la noche de los cuchillos, más tarde que nunca, asolará esta Patria que Usted se ha dignificado a levantar de sus cenizas. (Castillo, 1999: 138–39)

> (Be careful with the sugar cane, C*hief*! You should always remember, beloved, that in the task of reaping, Haiti has always been a shining example and thanks to its strength in this area, it came to occupy a lofty position in the pre-industrial world. If we go headlong into a policy that depends on sugar, we would be sharpening the knives for our own throats. You must remember, most beloved, that the negro population is there because of the sugar industry and the contracting of those referred to as islanders or *Cocolos* who came for a certain number of years and are now staying forever. The Haitian workers will do the same, even if the contracts are arranged between the two governments. Do you see how our wealth gained through sugar cane, in the medium term, could lead to dependency on Haitian labour. In such a case, the *batey*, Your Excellency and *Leader*, will become another Haiti, an entire cultural enclave where ancestral hatreds will manifest themselves and sooner or later the night of the daggers will destroy this Fatherland which you have deigned to raise from its ashes.)

The perspective on the border and the 1937 massacre is rounded out with this quotation from the same novel:

> El 37, contrario a lo que muchos creen, no será recordado como un año de luto y dolor para nuestro país, que prácticamente ha alcanzado la gloria bajo su dirección, sino como una fecha ratificadora de la *Separación* del 44. Esa política del *chapeo*[v] deberá erigirse como una constante necesaria, lógica y nacionalista, si verdaderamente deseamos ser libres como país que respeta y venera sus ancestros. Nunca he dudado de que en algún rincón oscuro de la Patria se anide un *Moisés* que emerja vigoroso para desear reivindicar lo que los haitianos consideran como suya: la isla total. Nuestra frontera no puede convertirse, bajo ningún concepto, queridísimo *Jefe*, en otra Isla de la Tortuga, que nos enajene para siempre. Así, la Frontera deberá ser el lugar para la vigilancia eterna, llevando hasta ella hombres y mujeres puros, que evadan de sus conciencias todas las tentaciones que la corrupción del contrabando puede ofrecer. Estas dos variables enriquecerán robustamente la política intramigratoria y fortalecerán los dos poderosos signos de nuestra nacionalidad: el mulataje y la lengua. (Castillo, 1999:138)
>
> (Nineteen thirty-seven, contrary to what many believe, will not go down in history as a year of mourning and pain for our country, which has for all practical purposes attained a position of glory under your leadership, but as a date that ratified the *Separation* of 1844. That policy of *chapeo* must be maintained as a necessary, permanent cornerstone of national policy, if we truly want to be free as a country that respects and venerates its ancestors. I have never doubted that in some dark corner of the Fatherland, there is a *Moses* waiting to emerge in power to claim what the Haitians consider to be theirs: the whole island. Our border cannot become, under any circumstances, beloved *Chief*, another Tortuga Island, separating us for ever. And so, the Frontier must be a place of eternal vigilance, and we must post there men and women who are pure, who will not yield to the temptation to be corrupted by contraband. These two factors will greatly enhance the policy of internal migration and strengthen the two powerful symbols of our nationality: mulataje and language.)

The many and varied expressions of racism and anti-Haitian feelings are evident in these novels, with the most hurtful and denigrating epithets subtly interspersed throughout and presenting a picture of the foreman, white or black, administrators, those who abuse their authority. The comparison between the characteristics of the Cocolos and of the Haitian workers demonstrates that the former function as a close-knit, unified community, which can adapt to the circumstances and use them to their advantage. The latter, on the other hand, tend to be seen as inferior, with the label of being illiterate practitioners of witchcraft. Nevertheless, Manuel Millares Vázquez gives a detailed description in *Vidas fecundas* of Haitian life on the sugar cane plantations. With the inclusion of the comments of a foreman about a rebellious Haitian, he recognizes that "those uncivilized people do not consider themselves inferior to us". In response to his threat to throw her off the plantation, the woman "showed him the soles of her feet and said, 'you believe that because you are white, you are worth more than I. Look, the soles of my feet are white and I walk on the ground with them'" (Millares Vázquez, 1964: 102). In addition, racial segregation can be seen in the prohibition of the Cocolo from participating in political life during the Trujillo dictatorship, against trade union activity, and in denying them advancement, which was generally blocked by supporters of the government.

The novels analyzed have rescued from official oblivion knowledge of the vicissitudes of Caribbean immigrants, who, like those who participated in the construction of the Panama Canal, have left the imprint of their culture, work ethic and language on the Dominican Republic. What is surprising is the absence of any reference to the artistic legacy of the Cocolos, such as dance, musical instruments and the carnival personalities, especially the *momises* and the *guloyas* brought from St. Kitts, Anguilla, Tortola, Nevis, Barbuda and Antigua. It may be that the writers have focussed their attention more on the vindication of the Cocolo community as exploited subjects. The only novel written from a Cocolo perspective is Avelino Stanley's *Tiempo muerto*. However, it is only in the 15th re-edition of *Tiempo muerto*, that Stanley amplifies chapter 10 to give greater focus on Cocolo culture. Frank Luna's photograph, which adorns the cover of this publication, is an eloquent tribute to the veterans of the Guloya Dance Theatre: Ruddy, Marola and, in particular, the main performer Daniel Henderson, Linda.

The writer seems to adhere to Nadal Walcot's *Los Cocolos*, which details the Caribbean provenance of the dances, supporting the analysis with his riveting etchings.

Tiempo Muerto destroys the stereotyped myth of the Cocolos as being inferior and backward by extolling the talents of Yacob, the

"Cocolo" performer. The Guloya dance is not only emblematic of this migrant culture but constitutes an integral part of Dominican national dance expression; the Guloya dance is the core of the carnival parades. This cultural retention is still being cultivated and promoted by Cocolo descendants today. The novelist assumes the measured distance of a journalist in his projection of the different Cocolo performances. The account by Irma, a non-Cocolo intellectual is bereft of poetic images. Descriptions are limited to the costumes and the resonance of the drums and flutes. The dance of the "Wild Indian" is performed by a group of dancers who wear brightly coloured suits adorned with several mirrors; they don elaborate head pieces made from turkey feathers. A drum, a bamboo flute and an instrument called "tingalín" produce the accompanying music. During the enactment, the dancers simulate a fight with well-measured steps. The "Pick Cook Fighters" is similar to that of the Wild Indian dance. Stanley also gives a vivid picture of the "David and Goliath" drama. Another theatrical piece is the "Donkey or the Bull", where several characters in red costumes represent these animals while parading and simulating battles with the crowd. The dance of the "Zancos" is depicted with several characters dressed in jackets replete with mirrors cavorting on stilts. Woodcutters who return from the forest after several months of hard work act out the dance of the "Momís". They bring presents for their relatives and are dressed in bright colours to revere their king. The "Giant Spire", a heavy drinker decked out in red, carries a whip in his hand to beat his errant wife. When he finds her, in the company of another man, a big fight ensues until he subdues his rival.

Avelino Stanley, like the Dominican documentalist Juan Rodríguez preserve for posterity the rich heritage of Cocolo dance culture and it is not surprising that UNESCO has declared Cocolo Culture, Patrimony of Humanity in 2005. Rodríguez' audiovisual presentation and the pioneering drawings by Adolfo Nadal Walcot are pivotal in comprehending this diasporic culture.

References

Álvarez Santana, Fermín. *San Pedro de Macorís: su historia y desarrollo.* República Dominicana: Comisión Presidencial de Apoyo Desarrollo Provincial, Colección provincial, n° 10, 2000. Capítulo 18, pp.294-299.

Amiama, Manuel Antonio. *El terrateniente.* Santo Domingo, República Dominicana: Impresora Arte y Cine, 1970. [1ª ed., 1960]

Andujar, Carlos. *Identidad cultural y religiosidad popular.* Santo Domingo, República Dominicana: Breve Letra Gráfica, 1ª ed., 2007.

Báez Evertsz, Franc. *Braceros haitianos en la República Dominicana.* Santo Domingo, República Dominicana: Instituto Dominicano de Investigaciones Sociales, 2ª ed., 1986. [1ª ed. 1984]

Bazil, Darío. "Francisco Moscoso Puello" In *Poetas y prosistas dominicanos.* Santo Domingo, República Dominicana: Editora Cosmos, 1978, pp.167-177.

Bazil, Darío. "Ramón Marrero Aristy" In *Poetas y prosistas dominicanos.* Santo Domingo, República Dominicana: Editora Cosmos, 1978, pp.223-235.

Belliard, Basilio. (Comp.) *La narrativa de Avelino Stanley.* Santo Domingo, República Dominicana: Editora Búho, 1ª ed., 2006.

Cansen, Senaida y Cecilia Millán. "Los bateyes en la República Dominicana" In *Género, trabajo y etnia en los bateyes dominicanos.* Santo Domingo, República Dominicana: Instituto Tecnológico de Santo Domingo, Programa de Estudios de la Mujer, 1991, pp.35-42.

Castillo, Efraim. *El Personero.* Santo Domingo, República Dominicana: Editora Taller, 1999.

Castor, Suzy. *Migración y relaciones internacionales. (El caso haitiano-dominicano).* México: Facultad de Ciencias Políticas y Sociales, Universidad Nacional Autónoma de México, Centro de Estudios Latinoamericanos, CELA, 1983.

Céspedes, Diógenes. "El sentido de la responsabilidad social frente a la escritura: un estudio de *Jengibre.*" *Revista de Crítica Literaria Latinoamericana.* Año V, n° 9, Lima, Perú, primer semestre, 1979, pp.33-56.

Chez Checo, José y Refael Peralta Brito. *Azúcar, encomiendas y otros ensayos históricos.* Santo Domingo, República Dominicana: Fundación García Arévalo, 1ª ed., 1979.

Corten, Andrés et al. *Azúcar y política en la República Dominicana.* Santo Domingo, República Dominicana: Ediciones de Taller, 1981. [1ª ed., *Imperialismo y clases sociales en el Caribe,* Buenos Aires: Cuenca Ediciones, 1973; 2ª ed., Santo Domingo, República Dominicana: Editora Taller, 1976]

Del Castillo, José. "Las inmigraciones y su aporte a la cultura dominicana: finales del siglo XIX y principios del siglo XX" In Bernardo Vega et al, *Ensayos sobre cultura dominicana.* Santo Domingo, República Dominicana: Fundación Cultural Dominicana, Museo del Hombre Dominicano, 1988, pp.169-210.

Donastorg, Tarquino. *Batey.* San Pedro de Macorís, República Dominicana: Imprenta Lockhart, 1972.

Emeterio Rondón, Pura. "A propósito de *Tiempo muerto*" In *Estudios críticos de la literatura dominicana contemporánea.* Santo Domingo, República Dominicana: Ediciones Librería La Trinitaria, 2005, pp.57-63.

Enciclopedia Dominicana, Tomo II, Santo Domingo, República Dominicana, 1976, pp.125-126.

Florentino de Nadal, Maritza. "Acerca de Moscoso Puello y su novela *Cañas y bueyes.*" *Isla Abierta,* Suplemento de *Hoy*, Sábado 22 de junio de 1985, pp.14-15.

García Arévalo, Manuel et al. *Presencia étnica en San Pedro de Macorís.* San Pedro de Macorís, República Dominicana: Publicaciones de la Universidad Central del Este. Serie XXX Aniversario de la UCE, 2000.

García Moreira, Francisco. *Tiempo muerto: memorias de un trabajador azucarero.* La Habana, Cuba: Instituto del Libro, Ediciones Huracán, 2ª ed., 1969.

García Muñiz, Humberto y Jorge L. Giovannetti. "Garveyismo y Racismo en el Caribe: El caso de la población cocola en la República Dominicana." *Caribbean Studies.* Vol. 31, No.1, January – June 2003, pp.139-211.

García, Juan Manuel. *La matanza de los haitianos. Genocidio de Trujillo, 1937.* Santo Domingo, República Dominicana: Editora Alfa & Omega, 1ª ed., 1983.

García, Juan Manuel. *La matanza de los haitianos: Genocidio de Trujillo, 1937.* Santo Domingo: Editora Alfa & Omega, 1ª edición, 1983.

González Enriquez, Raúl. *San Antonio S.A.*. México: Editorial América, 1942.

González Herrera, Julio. *Trementina, Clerén i Bongó.* Santo Domingo, República Dominicana, 2ª ed. Facsimil, 1974. [1ª ed., Editorial Pol Hermanos, Ciudad Trujillo, República Dominicana, 1943]

Graciano, Berta. *La novela de la Caña. Estética e Ideología.* Santo Domingo, República Dominicana: Editora Alfa & Omega, 1ª ed., 1990.

Guerrero, José G. "La palabra 'Cocolo'." *Boletín 35. Museo del Hombre Dominicano.* Santo Domingo, República Dominicana: Secretaría de Estado de Cultura, Año XXXI, n° 35, 2004, pp.17-31.

Inoa, Orlando. *Azúcar. Árabes, cocolos y haitianos.* Santo Domingo, República Dominicana: FLACSO, Editora Cole, 1999.

Inoa, Orlando. *Los Cocolos en la sociedad dominicana.* Santo Domingo, República Dominicana: Helvetas, Asociación suiza para la cooperación internacional, 2005.

James, Norberto P. *Denuncia y Complicidad.* Santo Domingo: Editora Taller, 1ª ed., 1997.

Jarvis Luis, Rafael. *La Romana origen y fundación.* Santo Domingo, República Dominicana: Dirección General de la Feria del Libro, 2006.

Lizardo, Fradique. "Cocolo", Suplemento *Listín Diario*, Sábado 15 de enero de 1977, p.13.

Madruga, José Manuel. *Azúcar y haitianos en la República Dominicana.* Santo Domingo, República Dominicana: Ediciones MSC, 1986.

Marrero Aristy, Ramón. *Over.* Santo Domingo: Biblioteca Taller 14, 11ª edición, 1981. [1ª ed., 1940]

Martínez, Héctor Luis. "La fuerza de trabajo inmigrante, 1880-1900" In *San Pedro de Macorís. En el Renacimiento de la Industria Azucarera Dominicana, 1870-1930.* Santo Domingo, República Dominicana: Dirección General de la Feria del Libro, 2006, pp.107-117.

Méndez, Maule Cruz. "Los Cocolos: su incidencia en la vida y la cultura dominicana" In *Cultura e Identidad Dominicana. Una visión histórico-antropológica.* Santo Domingo, República Dominicana: Ciudad Universitaria, 1998. Capítulo VIII, pp.115-129.

Millares Vázquez, Manuel. *Vidas fecundas.* Madrid: Afrodisio Aguado, 1964.

Moquete, Clodomiro. "Entrevista a Avelino Stanley." *Vetas.* Año XIV, n° 78, diciembre de 2006, pp.6-17.

Moscoso Puello, Francisco E.. *Cañas y bueyes.* Santo Domingo, República Dominicana: Amigos del Hogar, 1975. [1ª ed. Santo Domingo: Editorial La Nación, 1936.]

Moscoso Puello, Francisco E.. *Navarijo.* Santo Domingo, República Dominicana: Sociedad Dominicana de Bibliófilos, 2001. [1ª ed. 1956]

Mota Acosta, Julio Cesar. *Los Cocolos en Santo Domingo.* Santo Domingo, República Dominicana: Editorial La Gaviota, 1977.

Moya Pons, Frank. *El batey. Estudio socioeconómico de los bateyes del Consejo Estatal del Azúcar.* Santo Domingo, República Dominicana: Fondo para el Avance de las Ciencias Sociales, 1986.

Navarro, Noel. *Marcial Ponce de Central en Central.* La Habana, Cuba: Unión de Escritores y Artistas de Cuba, 1ª ed., 1977.

Pérez Cabral, Pedro Andrés. *Jengibre.* Santo Domingo, República Dominicana: Editora Alfa & Omega, 1978. [1ª ed., 1940]

Requena, Andrés Francisco. *Los enemigos de la tierra.* Santo Domingo, República Dominicana: Editora de Santo Domingo, 3ª ed., 1976. [1ª ed. Editorial La Nación, Ciudad Trujillo, 1936]

Rodríguez, Juan y José G. Guerrero. "Cultura y política en los Momises de San Pedro de Macorís." *Boletín 28. Museo del Hombre Dominicano.* Santo Domingo, República Dominicana: Secretaría de Estado de Cultura, Año XXVII, n° 28, 2000, pp.227-239.

Sánchez, Juan J. *La caña en Santo Domingo.* Santo Domingo, República Dominicana: Ediciones de Taller, 1972. [1ª ed. Santo Domingo, Imprenta de García Hermanos, 1893]

Sommer, Doris. "*Over*: the contest for populist rhetoric" In *One Master for Another.* University Press of America: Amherst College, 1983, pp.125-159.

Stanley, Avelino. *Danza de las llamaradas.* Santo Domingo, República Dominicana: Cocolo Editorial, 1ª ed., 2001.

Stanley, Avelino. *Tiempo muerto.* Santo Domingo, República Dominicana: Cocolo Editorial, 3ª reimpresión, 1999; 15ª reimpresión, 2006. [1ª ed., 1998]

Stinchcomb, Dawn F. *The Development of Literary Blackness in the Dominican Republic.* University Press of Florida, 2004.

Valdez, Diógenes. *Retrato de dinosaurios en la Era de Trujillo.* Santo Domingo, República Dominicana: Editora Libros, 1997.

Walcot, Nadal. *Los Cocolos.* Santo Domingo, República Dominicana: Consejo Presidencial de Cultura, Instituto Dominicano de Folklore, 1ª ed., 1998.

Webster, Jonny. "'La historia de un negro no le interesa a nadie': el 'Cocolo' en *Tiempo muerto* de Avelino Stanley." *Afro-Hispanic Review.* Vol.22, n° 2, Fall 2003, pp.20-28.

Wheaton, Philip E. *Triunfando sobre las tragedias. Historia centenaria de la Iglesia Episcopal Dominicana 1897-1997.* Santo Domingo, República Dominicana: Iglesia Episcopal Dominicana, 1997.

Zakrzewski Brown, Isabel. *Culture and Customs of the Dominican Republic.* London: Greenwood Press, 1999, p.54.

Documentary

Cocolo Dancing. Drama Tradition. Director, Script Writer and Producer Juan Rodríguez. República Dominicana: Secretaría de Estado de la Cultura, Museo del Hombre Dominicano.

---

[i] Translated from Spanish by Victor Simpson PhD.

[ii] For a complete description of the Cocolo community in San Pedro de Macorís, see the quotation from the novel *Navarijo* by Francisco E. Moscoso Puello in the detailed research of Humberto García Muñiz and Jorge L. Giovannetti. "Garveyismo y racismo en el caribe: El caso de la población cocola en la República Dominica". January-June 2003: 151. *Caribbean Studies*, Vol. 31, no. 1.

[iii] Quotation and definitions taken from Fermín Álvarez Santana. *San Pedro de Macorís: su historia y desarrollo.* 2000, Dominican Republic, Presidential Commission for Development Assistance to the Provinces, Provincial Collection no. 10, ch. 18:298–99. Cf. Fradique Lizardo, "Cocolo". 1977. *Listín Diario*, "Supplement", Saturday 15 January: 13 which includes the word "cocolis", the name of an ancient Sudanese tribe.

[iv] Cf. Raúl González Enriquez, *San Antonio S.A.* 1942:45. México, where the Mexican author describes a similar effect of the rains on the sugar cane harvest in Veracruz; Pérez Cabral: 133–35; Moscoso Puello: 126 and Marrero Aristy: 127–28, who describes it with greater lyricism. Sometimes it rains torrents. The

railway lines become impassible. Men go in and come out of the fields, soaked like a guabina, bent over with the cutlass under their arm, shivering from the cold, half naked. [. . .] The axle of the cart complains like a sick person [. . .] The torrents of rain fall on the men whose lives are being ruined in the cane fields. Incidences of malaria increase throughout the plantation. . . The days are grey, as life itself.

[v] *Chapeo:* a kind of "ethnic cleansing".

Chapter 9

Exploitation and Survival: The Black Experience in Díaz Alfaro's Terrazo

Victor C. Simpson

The 1947 publication of *Terrazo*, the first collection of short stories by Abelardo Díaz Alfaro, was greeted with enthusiasm by Puerto Rican critics. From a thematic perspective, the interest of critics lay in two main areas. First is the very strong tone of denunciation of the appalling conditions in which the rural peasant existed and the systematic exploitation of which he was the victim. The second element of significance is the perception that Díaz Alfaro was using this collection of short narratives to project Puerto Rican resistance to the pervasive American influence over the island at a time when there was serious concern regarding the threat posed to the local culture by a different and, presumably, more powerful one. The comments of Margot Arce de Vásquez seem to encapsulate the interests of these critics:

> Díaz Alfaro nos ha dado toda la intensidad del drama puertorriqueño: la esclavitud colonial, la inhumana explotación económica, los males del hambre, el desempleo, la miseria y la enfermedad. Pero sobre todo, ha registrado el dramático choque de las dos culturas y de las dos lenguas, la importación viciosa de un sistema de valores extraños y sin sentido para la sensibilidad criolla. (Díaz Alfaro 109)

Beyond these general preoccupations, *Terrazo* addresses in two of its narratives—"Bagazo" and "El cuento del baquiné"—the subject of the black experience. So, while the quoted comments demonstrate an interest in the exploitation of the "jíbaro" and are concerned with the perceived negative impact of foreign influence on the local culture, this article will explore some aspects of the reality experience by Blacks which, at the time the volume appeared, was still being generally ignored or despised. These aspects (exploitation and cultural expression) are not unrelated, for while "Bagazo" exposes the depths of suffering among blacks peasants, specifically the black ones as symbolized by the experience of Domingo, the main character, "El cuento del baquiné" highlights one of the important coping mechanisms to which they could resort in order to mitigate the effect of their oppression. Together, these narratives are seen to demonstrate the author's concern for the black condition and represent a scathing denunciation of a fundamental aspect of the social reality of the time.

The stories in this volume are set in the tobacco and sugarcane fields and factories of rural Puerto Rico. The atmosphere portrayed is one of a peasantry living, or eking out a living, at the mercy of harsh foremen or unscrupulous creditors; of nature (storms, drought, rain); overwhelmed by oppressive work, poor compensation and a general life of pain, sadness, suffering and exploitation. The people living in this environment suffer from poverty, hunger, sickness, lack of education—conditions that are very reminiscent of those existing during the period of slavery. Díaz Alfaro has been able, therefore, to integrate effectively the element of protest with the rural, "costumbrista" orientation of the narratives. It is of no small significance that seventy years after the abolition of slavery there would still be some people, descendents of slaves and others, existing in conditions so markedly similar to those that existed in the earlier era. Díaz Alfaro sums up these conditions quite alarmingly, making effective use of the device of repetition in focusing on the decrepit physical condition of men, women and children and the malnutrition which contributes to it:

> ¡Pobres mujeres, pobres hombres y pobres niños. Hombres de míseros jornales, curvados de sol a sol, macilentos, de cuerpos magros, comidos por la anemia, hurgados por el hambre. Caras casi verdosas, como la hoja amarga del tabaco. Mujeres gastadas por la maternidad y el trabajo excesivo. Niños prematuramente viejos, que no saben de los Reyes Magos y sí de la noche mala, y del "puya", cuando lo hay. Y después de toda esa labor ímproba, vi a estos pobres campesinos comer una "sopa larga" y rala. Maravilla de la dietética campesina. "Sopa larga", sopa filosófica, sopa de miserables. (41)

This rural setting may seem, at one levcl, to dilute the focus on the specific situation of Blacks as portrayed in the narratives chosen for analysis. But, at another level, it may serve to re-emphasize their extreme plight in that, however terrible are the conditions which the rural white peasant (jíbaro) must endure, these are made even more unbearable for Blacks simply because they are black. For the rural peasant, the problem is being poor and old, for the black rural peasant the problem is being poor, old *and* black.

Díaz Alfaro is one of the last Puerto Rican writers to use a rural setting as the background to his work. Subsequently, authors such as José Luis González were responsible for a change in the thematic orientation of Puerto Rican narrative from life in a rural setting to an urban setting, a shift which responded to the refocusing of the national development thrust from the land towards industrialization. At the same time, this collection helps to place him in the vanguard of the development of the short story in view of the attention he pays as a committed writer to the realities of black life in Puerto Rico as well as of the highly poetic language that characterizes his narratives.

Díaz Alfaro wrote during a watershed period in Puerto Rican history in which the island faced major social, political and economic problems and writers of his time felt compelled to address critically these issues in their works. At the same time, there was a stronger motivation to grapple with issues that were socially more controversial, including the black experience, in a way that earlier writers may not have felt constrained to do. The result of this is to be seen in the very critical attitude toward such conditions and, at the same time, a more liberal, open-minded and sympathetic attitude to Blacks and other victims of social, political and cultural exploitation. As commentator Josefina Rivera de Alvarez argues, "[e]n los relatos . . . el autor no juzga, sino que denuncia y examina la problemática insular del momento, manifestando su profundo compromiso moral con la trágica realidad que capta en el Puerto Rico de su época" (490). A significant element of this reality is the experience of exploitation which was the lot of many Blacks. Hence, Rafael Falcón's comment that "los cuentos de esta generación están marcados por un vehemente espíritu de denuncia social, elemento obviamente palpable en los relatos que abordan el tema negro" (38). This preoccupation is manifested quite markedly in the two pieces under discussion.

María Teresa Babín reflects also on this changing perspective on the part of some writers of this period, acknowledging what she sees as a systematic attempt to recognize and address in literature the problems of Blacks, as writers begin to understand (as apparently she did) that the legacy of slavery still weighs heavily on the shoulders of blacks:

> La visión poética del esclavo actual, del dolor de vivir después de un siglo de la abolición de aquella otra esclavitud es una constante en otros autores que se afanan por desentrañar las fuentes escondidas del prejuicio y de la miseria del hombre sometido a la penuria y a la explotación. (65)

In spite of his social, moral and ideological orientation as a social worker accustomed to personal involvement in the day to day struggles of his constituency, the author has succeeded in producing a work of high literary value. Even though the didactic element is clear, even though there is a strong note of protest and denunciation, this seems to be balanced by the effective use of adjectives, metaphors, similes, repetition and a number of symbols and images which together lend a strong poetic tone to the narratives, not least the two under consideration in this article. Díaz Alfaro acknowledges that his interest in painting has contributed to the creation of the vivid descriptions which characterize the volume. It is not difficult to agree with René Marqués when he asserts that:

> lo que seduce de inmediato al lector, no importa la categoría intelectual de éste, es la gracia alada de su adjectivación, la riqueza y originalidad de imágenes, la oportunidad tan precisa de la metáfora, elaborada estéticamente con elementos pintorescos del habla campesina. (Marqués 50)

In addressing the traditional treatment of blacks in Hispanic-Caribbean literature, Carol Beane argues that the approach mirrors social reality:

> Any discussion of black characters in literature must bear in mind that literary creation results from a complex interplay between historical and socio-economic factors and imagination.
>
> As literary subjects, Blacks and Mulattoes are charged with extraliterary associations. Slavery and oppression in the eighteenth century created stereotyped images, many of which appear in fiction. Early portrayals were ostensibly sympathetic; later ones are less so.

> Blacks and Mulattoes have become the Other in relation to the society, or society is the Other in relation to the Blacks. (Luis 181)

Writing relating to Blacks in Puerto Rico has traditionally accepted these stereotypes. They have been portrayed in the island's literature in a manner that is consistent with the way they have been viewed by the society. Antonio Nieves speaks of the false concept which whites have of blacks, pointing out that this perception—for example, sexual hyperactivity, inferiority, savagery, superstition— is based on "una combinación de mentiras, mitos, exageraciones, conceptos erróneos y prejuicios" (115). The status quo is accepted and upheld, directly and indirectly.

The subject of the black experience is addressed in every literary genre in Puerto Rico beginning in the nineteenth century, with certain recurrent themes which include the dispensability of the negro, exploitation of the race, (including sexual exploitation of the women), poor living conditions, cultural elements, the effort to hide the negro element in one's racial composition. However, this subject has not always received meaningful attention, since blacks continued to be seen as exotic and of little human value and their daily experience has not always been a matter of concern. As the black person was marginalized in society so too was serious treatment of his experience in the field of literature. Mayra Santos Febres expresses it this way:

> En la literatura puertorriqueña, desde los inicios del establecimiento de su canon, lo negro siempre ha representado lo irracional. Es el cuerpo, es lo sexual, es el origen antes de la palabra. A veces, con suerte, los personajes negros y negras que aparecen en las obras de la mayoría de nuestros escritores, cumplen un papel de víctimas, de depositarios de una posición ideológica, pero nada más. (152)

Hence, in José Luis González's "La galería", the main character, a white man, speaks of his father's attitude that suggests that the death of another black person would make no difference, while in "Santa Claus visita a Pirilio Sánchez", the young white protagonist remembers his elders' affirmation that "todos los negros son brutos".

Nieves further affirms that "[e]l hecho es que el negro que aparece en la literatura del país anterior a 1960 es la creación de los blancos, o por lo menos la visión que puede tener éste acerca de lo que es un negro y su versión literaria de ese ser humano" (116). This helps to explain why, traditionally, there have not been many black protagonists in Puerto Rican literature, even though black characters have been widely used in short stories, not to mention the body of negrista poetry by Luis Palés Matos. Even of José Luis González, the major exponent in his time of black themes, it cannot be said that most of the protagonists are black. However, the two stories chosen for discussion in this article offer, in one instance, a black protagonist and, in the other, one may speak of a collective protagonist, which is the group of blacks attending the wake for the dead child. Additionally, they depart strikingly from the negative and the stereotypical approaches. They challenge the readers to rethink their opinions and attitudes to the matter at hand—in this case, the experience of the black Puerto Rican. The author forces his readers to begin to question the racial prejudice and exploitation of which blacks are victims, and, by illustrating the spiritual and emotional—indeed, the practical—value of their cultural expression, he challenges them to rethink their negative attitude to black cultural manifestations.

As we shall see in "Bagazo", Díaz Alfaro clearly shows his commitment to expose and denounce social ills by strongly challenging the callous attitude to black workers on the sugar plantations. The traditional attitude of neglect and inconsideration is being exposed in the same way as would any other social ill. And, as Rafael Falcón points out, this represents a new and different response to the problem of racism and black exploitation, one which would be continued by others of this and subsequent eras:

> Este relato es de significativo valor, pues es el primero que presenta el tema con una contundente nota denunciatoria de la situación del negro puertorriqueño. Así que Díaz Alfaro introduce una actitud desconocida hasta ese momento y la cual van a abordar la gran mayoría de los escritores isleños que tratan el tema en años posteriores. (39)

"Bagazo" is the story of a poor, black man, Domingo, who, after working for many years in the cane fields, is overlooked because he is considered by the foreman to be too old to work productively. His pleas on behalf of his poor family, including his sick wife, are ignored and he has to return home empty-handed.

The next day, he sets out again in the hope of finding work and when the foreman refuses again to hire him, Domingo unsuccessfully attacks him with his cutlass and is fatally shot. This is a fascinating short story, excellently written and teeming with poetic images. In fact, some parts of it—verbless sentences, very short sentences, numerous descriptive adjectives, multiple metaphors and a variety of images—read more like poetry than prose. The tone of the story is sad. From the beginning, the atmosphere of desolation and hopelessness is evident in the description of the protagonist's emotional and mental state. This atmosphere is created by the use of a series of similes, buttressed by an effective selection of adjectives and verbs which describe Domingo's feelings, some of which are completely new to him:

> Un nudo tirante como de coyunda le ahoga. Y por vez primera en su vida mansa de buey viejo siente el rencor crecerle en el pecho como mala yerba. Y a él, negro impasible, resistente como el ausubo, le entran ganas de llorar, no sabe si de tristeza o de rabia. (25)

The atmosphere is reinforced by Domingo's memory of the disastrous accident that caused the death of another black worker in the factory, an accident which one is inclined to believe was not considered to be significant by a management which views poor people as of little worth and poor black people as worthless, if one is to judge by the comments of the dead man. The memory of the accident is noteworthy also because it brings to the fore an awareness of the hazardous conditions under which labourers such as Domingo work. One can imagine that little attention is paid to workers' safety and indeed to workers' compensation in conditions that for some are not far removed from slavery. All this anticipates the seemingly inevitable outcome.

The author uses the device of antithesis to stress the significance of the racial element is in this story. Race is projected as a critical factor in the conflict by the repeated reference to the foreman as "blanco", and to Domingo as "negro", suggesting that the two are on a collision course. Domingo, the black person, labours all his life for the enrichment of the Whites. Mr Power, the administrator, is white and Domingo is black; therefore, he cannot be approached for assistance. He is rich, therefore he cannot understand the plight of poor. Early in the story, Domingo recalls the comment of his dead friend regarding the attitude of Whites toward Blacks, who are seen not as people, but as Blacks, "'Mi jijo, malo es sel probe y negro, nunca semos niños, se nos ñama negritos'" (25). Indeed, Domingo believes that his race is an important factor that has condemned him to this situation and he finds it very difficult to accept. His anxious cogitations in this regard are reported by the author:

> No lo querrán por viejo, por pobre, por negro. Esa es la paga que recibe después de haber dejado su vida trunca en los cañaverales, para lucrar a los blancos. Ahora le lanzan al camino como perro sarnoso. (Díaz Alfaro 28)

The harsh, unyielding attitude of the foreman is contrasted with the strong and repeatedly expressed concern of Domingo for his wife and children. The reason he wants to work is to be able to provide for his family. He is willing to beg and be humiliated; he is willing to overlook the attitude of the foreman, hoping that the latter would show him some favour in view of his plight and that of his sick wife. One of the great ironies of this story is that Domingo did not have any intention to use violence against the foreman. He left home with his machete, hoping that he would be given the opportunity to work. It is only after the foreman callously ignores his desperate pleas that, overwhelmed by anger, hopelessness and pain, he reacts violently. And the outcome is even more tragic as, in the context, it suggests that the black man has no chance against the white man. It is as if, however innocent or guilty he may be, he is destined always to suffer the worse fate in any confrontation, a situation that aptly reflects the fate of Blacks in a society that is yet to accept them as equals with their white counterparts.

Blacks have been a part of Puerto Rican society since the early years of the conquest. The experience of slavery, however, was the defining element in determining their position at the bottom of the social ladder. Rafael Falcón affirms that "desde los tiempos de la esclavitud se le han asignado concepciones negativas y estereotipos prejuiciados" to the black person (16). The gross exploitation and mis-treatment which characterized the institution of slavery not only reflected the perception that whites had of Blacks during those centuries, but also informed attitudes towards Blacks even after slavery had been abolished. This helps to explain the attitude of the foreman towards Domingo and the lack of consideration for the latter's desperate circumstances.

Racial prejudice and racial discrimination have been ongoing features of Puerto Rican society, as they have been, and indeed remain, in every society where slavery existed. Many who have written on this subject in Puerto Rico seemed committed to proving either that it did not exist or that it was so mild as not to represent a real problem. Tomás Blanco, in his important work, *El prejuicio racial*, minimizes the problem by comparing the Puerto Rican situation with the institutionalized racism that was the norm in the southern states of America. Luis Díaz Soler quotes a 1920 article written by José Celso Barbosa which denies the existence of racial prejudice:

> el hombre de color en Puerto Rico no es, bajo concepto alguno, inferior al hombre blanco de Puerto Rico, y ha contribuído y contribuye con él a dar prestigio a la raza a que pertenece y al pueblo de nuestra cuna . . . Hoy la superioridad se manifiesta, no en la raza, no en la mayor o menor cantidad de materia colorante en la piel . . . (Díaz Soler 18)

Díaz Alfaro's perspective in presenting this story demonstrates clearly that he does not subscribe to the notion that Puerto Rico is free of racial prejudice or that any such prejudice is only mild. The experience of Domingo and many others like him discredits this idea. It challenges the reader to recognize the reality of a major social ill—the effective continuing enslavement of Blacks and other poor. For, while some may conveniently deny the existence of racial prejudice, others, including many with whom one may speak even today, affirm that, while there is no formal institutionalization of racial discrimination, the subtle variety is a definite reality in Puerto Rican society. "Bagazo" clearly illustrates the continued presence of racial prejudice. It demonstrates also that the black person is aware of his position at the bottom of the social ladder and of the epithets applied to him, which reflect the contempt in which he is held in the society—the poor, defenceless agricultural worker no doubt bearing the brunt of this rejection. This fact is reflected in the literature of the island and has inspired two of the best known works which address the issue of blacks—the poem "Y tu agüela, a'onde ejtá?" by Fortunato Vizcarrondo and the drama *Vejigantes* by Francisco Arriví.

The title of the story "Bagazo" provides another important image as it helps to create the atmosphere of hopelessness and frustration which is the lot of the black sugar cane worker and contributes to the depressing and demoralizing tone of the story. Just as after the sugar cane is ground and the "bagazo" that is left is fit only to be thrown away, so Díaz Alfaro presents the image of the hardworking labourer being used and then dismissed with no consideration being given to the huge contribution he has made over the years. The image is poignantly dramatized when Domingo, running away from the destructive monster that is the factory, falls on some heaps of bagasse. It is the seemingly heartless dismissal of old labourers as worthless that is the object of the author's denunciation of the system under which the poor are forced to live. This is part of the legacy of slavery that sees a black man as of no value beyond the hard labour that he can contribute to the development of the wealth that the white man enjoys, a reality of which Domingo is acutely aware. It is to be remembered also that, with the abolition of slavery, ex-slaves were required to enter into contracts to continue providing labour for their former masters or others, officially for a short period, but in reality often for longer periods. The point is that the slave (and ex-slave) was valued for his labour. Domingo is in a situation where he is seen as unable to provide the only contribution that gives him some value as a person in the eyes of the ruling class; hence the complete abandonment to which he is now subjected.

The story, and specifically the trauma being suffered by Domingo, is further dramatized by the portentous dream which he has on the night before the tragedy. In this dream, he is confronted by the foreman transformed first into a wild dog which sinks it sharp fangs into his body, and then into a gigantic being which attacks and severely wounds him with a huge spear, leaving him to be crushed, as one of his friends was, by a falling bundle of cane, from which he is saved only by awaking from his dream. The use of this widely exploited literary device is effective in reinforcing in the reader's mind the extent of Domingo's preoccupation with his seemingly hopeless situation and at the same time, it has the effect of foreshadowing the eventual tragedy. This is a fundamentally tragic story with a tragic ending. The tragedy lies in various elements of the action—the fact that it occurs after Domingo has finally summoned up the humility to go pleading to the foreman; that Domingo's attack was not premeditated (in fact, the tone of his words to the *mayordomo* was very plaintive); that it was destined to fail since the contest was so uneven. There is also the great irony that a man who goes desperately searching for a means of livelihood for himself and his family should end up dead at the hands of the very person who could have provided him with that opportunity.

This story is no mythification or folklorization of the black peasant. It is a chilling denunciation of the heartless exploitation of blacks, exemplified by the experience of the sugar cane worker, like Domingo, condemned to live in poverty, and at the mercy of white managers and overseers who do not understand and do not care about the plight of their struggling workers. As Domingo himself thinks regarding the manager of the factory, "Ese rubio no sabe lo que es la jambre de un pobre" (28). The black man cannot avoid the dehumanizing effects of slavery. Here, one is confronted with the marginalization and exploitation which make a mockery of the idea of freedom. In terms of the attitude of the dominant class, there has been little change and, in terms of the lived reality, the same may be said of the experience of the black worker.

One of the outstanding characteristics of the story is the vivid portrayal of the various psychological and emotional states of the protagonist as they vary from one situation to another, provoked by the desperate circumstances in which he finds himself. When he is rejected as a worker and his pleadings fail, he ambles off towards his home, totally disoriented, unable to walk normally. He moves around as if in a daze, too preoccupied to greet his neighbours and failing to recognize their greetings. He is assailed by deep preoccupations for the fate of his wife and children if he is not given the opportunity to work. He is emotionally and mentally disturbed to the point where he loses his appetite for eating. He does the unusual—goes to the bar to take an alcoholic drink. Yet he is determined to work for the survival of his family; hence he returns to the factory. At the same time, there is a convulsive emotional and mental upheaval churning in his innermost being, even manifesting itself in his physical body. On several occasions, the reader is given descriptions such as "una racha violenta de sangre le cruza los ojos" or "oleadas de sangre caliente le llegan violentas al cerebro" or "Una oleada de sangre le subió violenta a la cabeza" to reflect the intense concerns that continue to overwhelm him. He struggles with feelings of anger and thoughts of revenge. One gets the sense of an effort on his part to resist these powerful incitements to violence. At the same time, there seems to be an element of fatalistic inevitability regarding his inability to resist them. The structure of the story, with the repeated references to these seemingly irresistible feelings, seems to prepare the reader for Domingo's ultimately rash action which leads to his demise.

An important structural element of the story is the author's effectiveness in integrating into the action the presence of the sugar factory and the activity constantly taking place there: "la silueta ingente de la Central se recorta contra un horizonte en llamas rojas de crepúsculo" (26). The factory is ever present. Domingo can hear the rumbling of the engines—the only noise that disturbs the nocturnal silence; he can hear the whistle which marks the beginning of the work day; he can see the canes being lifted from one place to another—the movement of the canes in the factory forms part of his portentous dream—he can smell the sugarcane liquor; he can hear the creaking of the hinges of the crane. The factory forms an ever-present backdrop for all that is taking place in Domingo's life, and by extension, the lives of his neighbours; and, indeed, it is on the premises of the factory itself that he experiences the rejection which is the catalyst for the climactic ending of the story. It seems to take on a life of its own while it takes away the lives of the poor who struggle to survive in its shadow. In this context, it is a "monstruo que quema en sus caldeadas entrañas, carne de peonaje, sangre y sucrosa" (30).

But one can see also a much deeper symbolic significance in the omni-present sugar factory ("La Fábrica de la Central que se yergue amenazante sobre el pueblo negro"). It was around the factory, and the plantation as a whole, that the lives of one generation after another of black slaves were built (or destroyed). Here, it can be seen as symbolic of the systematic oppression of which Blacks for centuries have been victims; symbolic of the poverty and virtual destitution of Domingo and his family; symbolic of the desperately poor health of his wife; of the starvation his family faces if he is not given the opportunity to work which he so insistently seeks; and symbolic of the fact that, as a black man, his fate is even worse than that of his white neighbours, as he himself recognizes: "No lo querrán por viejo, por pobre, por negro" (28). When he is killed, the factory whistle blows as usual and life continues; the factory remains, active as ever destroying people's lives, turning them into "garbazo", "garbazo", "garbazo".

Some have written on the subject of religion as reflected in the work of Díaz Alfaro, and specifically in *Terrazo*. It has been asserted that his religious upbringing is evident throughout his work in the form of direct and indirect biblical references. His evident solidarity with the poor and his denunciation of their exploited status are seen to reflect attitudes of Jesus as demonstrated in the New Testament gospels (Collazo). Certainly, in some of the narratives in this collection and elsewhere, the author acknowledges the personal effect on himself of the condition of the rural peasant. In the stories under consideration, there is only one direct biblical reference, that of Domingo's wife's expression of faith in God when he returns home after being told by the foreman that there was no work for him since he is no longer productive. There is a certain sad irony in this expression of faith on the woman's part in that it is to the "God" of the white man, her oppressor who considers the god of her ancestors to be inferior, (if not non-existent) that she looks for deliverance. For some, the outcome of the story would suggest that her confidence was misplaced.

"El cuento del baquiné", which technically is not a "cuento", partly because the author gives a number of explanations and injects various personal comments which, according to his own theory of the short story, would be considered superfluous. It may rather be called an "estampa costumbrista", focusing as it does on an aspect of life of the black peasantry as it recounts the story of a wake held at the death of a black child. This ritual is believed to have been brought to the island by the slaves of French immigrants. Indeed, the term "baquiné" has its origin in creole French. Its importance can be gleaned from the fact that it was considered a ritual that would aid the dead child on its way to heaven. When one considers the presumed origin of the term "Gran Ciempiés", mentioned in Palés Matos's narrative piece "Baquiné" in reference to the "high priest" of the ceremony, this seems to reinforce the possibility of a relationship between the *baquiné* and other practices common among slaves in the French Antilles.

The author focuses on the cultural aspect of the black experience in Puerto Rico, highlighting a variety of situations in his life. Crucial to the understanding of the story is the fact that the description places the ritual in a context of a suffering race, as if to suggest that rituals such as these, which evoke ancestral memories, are at once an expression of the struggles of the people and an aid in mitigating the pain of suffering and oppression: "Era el lamento de una raza explotada . . . se expresa la vida de unos hombres, sus luchas, sus penas; queja amarga de una humanidad hecha a golpes de caña y a jaleo negrero de capataz" 44). Hence, Díaz Alfaro uses a structure that intersperses the account of the *baquiné* with references to the struggles of the people. And even though the whole ritual is a lament, it seems also to bring a form of relief from the harsh realities of everyday life. Indeed, the dramatizations directly relate to the people's everyday experiences and one particular example in which a character refuses to fulfil his commitment to another is portrayed by the author as being symbolic of the black peasants' rebellion against the oppression of his everyday experience. The satisfaction that cannot be gained from actual rebellion, which they fear to attempt, is symbolically experienced by a light-hearted dramatization of the same:

> Es la rebeldía del negro, hecho a golpes de caña y a jaleo de capataz. El negro ha sido buey de carga, y sobre su lomo de ébano tiene cicatrices de encono. Es la voz de Ogé y Toussaint L'Ouverture. Es el grito atávico de la libertad en la selva. Es la voz que se trueca en ansia de justicia. Es grito de hastío, de protesta, en el que se resume el dolor de los que por razón de pigmento sufren todos los oprobios y todos los vejámenes. (46)

The reference to early leaders of anti-colonial rebellions in Haiti connects the story to significant historical events. It is important in reaffirming the connection between the present and the past (slavery). The present condition of blacks demands liberation from oppression and suffering in the same way that Ogé and Toussaint sought freedom and equality for those whom they represented. Jacques Vincent Ogé, leader of a short-lived 1790 rebellion against the French of Sante Dominge (Haiti), did not aim for a comprehensive liberation of exploited slaves; yet his action was historic in that it helped to establish resistance to the prevailing system. The goals of Toussaint L"Ouverture were more comprehensive—the elimination of slavery from both the French and Spanish parts of the island of Hispaniola. Díaz Alfaro thus identifies with the plight of the black peasant and insists that the conditions under which he exists must be changed drastically. It is in this stance that his pioneering commitment is reflected. There is more; the repeated references to the past are important in infusing into the treatment of the black experience in Puerto Rican literature the element of history which is considered to have been largely lacking in the past. As Mayra Santos Febres has argued, Blacks tended to be presented ahistorically, as if they had no roots, and often for the purpose of adding an element of the exotic to the scene. In this narrative, Díaz Alfaro, unlike those who came before him, seems to acknowledge that black people in Puerto Rico have a history and that if they are to be understood and appreciated, that history, as well as the impact it has had on present circumstances, must be recognized.

In this sense, the *baquiné* may also be seen as one of the "rituals of conflict", some of which were born in slavery but which still exist today. These rituals, according to Robert Dirks, "contain such things as joking insults, playful threats, mock fighting, and other ludic displays of a similar nature" (173–74), elements that all form part of the *baquiné* ritual in the story. Dirks speaks also of the "copeira"—a "fight dance" in Brazil used by slaves as a means of resisting oppression. Again, the focus on the *baquiné* ritual serves as a means of underlining how much the conditions under which the peasants now function are reminiscent of those that prevailed in the days of slavery.

The story begins with a poetic evocation of the harshness of life as the natural elements overwhelm men who, like beasts of burden, cannot escape the hard labour demanded by the sugar plantation, where thc canc that is naturally sweet has become bitter because of the toll it takes on the lives of those who work with it: "Bueyes y hombres uncidos al mismo yugo y a la misma mansedumbre. Caña amarga, surcada por limosos zanjones de riego." (43). The reader is deeply moved by the impact of words and expressions such as "humanidad doliente" "gime penas" and "canto del hambre en las caras" as the author sets the scene, painting briefly a picture of the harsh life of the black labourer in the cane fields. And, as in "Bagazo", the author establishes and maintains the close connection between the "cañaveral" and the grief and degradation of these peasants:

> A la sombra del "jumazo" de la central una humanidad doliente, quemada por el sol canicular, gime penas de esclavo . En ese mi inolvidable barrio Yaurel, me inicié en el trajín amargo de la vida, y aprendí lo que en los libros nunca pude: escuela de dolor. Y supe de la malaria, y de la anemia y de la consunción de los cuerpecitos adiposos de los niños que miran con ojos melancólicos, y del canto del hambre en las caras sin sueño. (43)

This is an environment in which Sunday brings welcome relief from the crushing labours of the week. As the author writes, it is a way to "olvidar penas hondas de cañaveral" (43). In effect, this comment, and indeed all those sections of the narrative which relate to the suffering of the people, serves to establish a strong connection between "El cuento del baquiné" and "Bagazo". It is the sufferings such as those experienced in the latter which give particular meaning to the activities that constitute the former. This reference harks back to the days of slavery when slaves were allowed Sunday as well as other seasonal days of rest and recreation. The author's comment regarding the workers' use of Sunday has the effect of indirectly indicating the nature of the conditions under which they labour. There is an implicit comparison with slavery, such are the hardships they are compelled to endure. The *baquiné* is a ritual of solidarity, but it is not limited to a lament for the dead. It is also a journey into the past of the black person as well as an opportunity to re-enact recent experiences—sickness, work, death and even to trivialize current situations as is evidenced by the scene involving the killer who is being sought by the police.

This ritual is a tribute to the spirit of an oppressed people, a people with a seemingly innate capacity to survive the harshest battering from the hands of fate. It is a reflection of the spirit of the people that they can dramatize their struggles. It is as if they gain special strength from these rituals so that the experience of death is not a hopeless, debilitating lament, but an opportunity to draw strength from their ancestral rituals. This story finds a place of importance in the development of literature in Puerto Rico in that it is among the first to grapple at close range with elements of African culture as manifested in the descendents of slaves on the island. This is no distant, xenophobic representation of an exotic, unintelligible, empty and meaningless ritual born of superstition and ignorance. There is, instead, a clear effort to find meaning, to recognize value and to appreciate a practice that is an integral part of the life of a group of people and which gives meaning and value to their existence—and more so in view of their condition as an oppressed people.

"El cuento del baquiné", which portrays the blacks dancing freely and spontaneously expressing themselves in their cultural milieu, is reminiscent of the short story by the young *modernista* author Alfredo Collado Martell, "Un corazón de pura sangre", in which the slaves are forbidden to dance the *bomba*. The champion dancer is mercilessly beaten because he refuses to race his master's horse in protest against the ban. To him, dancing is the ultimate expression of what he is. If he cannot dance, freedom is of no significance: "Libertad, libertad, para qué te quiero si has de matar todos los sentimientos de mi corazón, todas las manifestaciones de mi sangre; no, no quiero libertades, prefiero el látigo" (Collado Martell 115). True liberty must include the freedom to be oneself, to practise one's culture. It is a liberation of the soul, of the mind and not just of the body. This reflects the importance of music and dance in the times of slavery, activities which the *baquiné* (as well as traditional Sunday and holiday activities) seems to perpetuate among the descendents of slaves. As Edward Brathwaite expresses it: "Music and dance, though recreational, was functional as well. Slaves, as in Africa, danced and sang at work, at play, at worship, from fear, from sorrow, from joy. Here was the characteristic form of their social and artistic expression. It was secular and religious" (220).

A comparison between this approach by Díaz Alfaro and that manifested in another narrative by Luis Palés Matos that focuses on the ceremony of the *baquiné* may prove insightful at this point. The difference between the two authors in the approach to the ceremony is most striking. Palés's approach is somewhat distant. Even though his characters are present at the ceremony, there is a clear emphasis on it being "something different", alien, strange, associated with magic or witchcraft, and belonging, as one of the characters in the story says, to "otro mundo: el mundo de los negros". The idea of "otherness" is very strong even though, arguably, the approach is not negative. If one considers also Palés's poem "Falsa canción del baquiné", again the sense of distance is evident and indeed heightened in the implication that the supposed *baquiné* chant for a child offered to Ogún, the god of war, turns out to be a prelude to an act of cannibalism against white people. Díaz Alfaro's approach is quite different; he takes a positive approach to this phenomenon. He seems prepared to examine it at close range and to understand its significance. He does not see it as some alien, exotic manifestation. To him, it is not meaningless mumbo-jumbo, far removed from accepted Puerto Rican expression (as seems to be the reaction of the observers in Palés's story), but rather an integral part of the everyday life of its practitioners. He thereby validates it as an authentic aspect of Puerto Rican culture.

As indicated earlier in this article, Díaz Alfaro was among the first writers to take a positive approach to the presentation of Blacks in Puerto Rican literature. His effort was part of a broader endeavour to correct the anomaly of ignoring or undervaluing the experience and contribution of the black population. The narratives discussed in this article continue to hold a place of importance in the annals of Puerto Rican literature and they represent alternately an interrogation of the anti-black status quo and a tribute to the value of the culture of the black population of the island.

References

Arce de Vásquez, Margo. *Luis Palés Matos: Obras (1914–1959), Tomo II: Prosa.* Río Piedras: Editorial de la UPR, 1984.

Babín, María Teresa. "Aristas de la esclavitud negra en la literatura puertorriqueña". *Sin Nombre* 4:2 (1973): 57–65.

Beane, Carol. "Black Character: Toward a Dialectical Presentation in Three South American Novels". *Voices from Under: Black Narrative in Latin America and the Caribbean.* Ed. William Luis. Westport, Connecticut: Greenwood Press, 1984.

Brathwaite, Edward. *The Development of Creole Society in Jamaica (1770–1820).* Oxford: Oxford University Press, 1971.

Collado Martell, Alfredo. *Cuentos absurdos y otros cuentos.* San Juan: Instituto de Cultura Puertorriquena, 1999.

Collazo, Luis G. "Teología en Abelardo Díaz Alfaro: Cristología y opción preferencial por el pobre". Universidad Interamericana de Puerto Rico—Recinto Arecibo. 10 July 2007 http://www.arecibo.inter.edu/biblioteca/abelardo/cristología.html.

Dirks, Robert. *The Black Saturnalia.* Gainsville: University of Florida Press, 1987.

Díaz Alfaro, Abelardo. *Terrazo.* Bilbao, Spain: Editorial Vasco Americana, 1948.

Díaz Soler, Luis M. *La esclavitud negra en Puerto Rico.* San Juan: Instituto de Cultura Puertorriqueña, 1975.

Falcón, Rafael. *El afronegroide en el cuento puertorriqueño.* Miami: Ediciones Universal, 1993.

Marqués René Ed. *Cuentos puertorriqueños de hoy.* Río Piedras: Editorial Cultural, 1985

Nieves, Antonio. "La marginación del negro en la literatura puertorriqueña". *Revista Iberoamericana* 18:1–2 (1988):112–17.

Palés Matos, Luis. *Poesía (1915–1956).* Ed. Federico de Onís. Río Piedras: Editorial de la UPR, 1974

Rivera de Alvarez, Josefina. *Literatura puertorriqueña: su proceso en el tiempo.* Madrid: Ediciones Partenón, 1983.

Santos Febres, Mayra. *Sobre piel y papel.* San Juan: Ediciones Callejón, 2005.

Chapter 10

Toward Deciphering Afro-Colombian Poetry: The Case of Helcías Martán Góngora and Guillermo Payán-Archer

Alain Lawo-Sukam

Afro-Colombian literature came to light with Candelario Obeso, considered by many, the first Afro-Hispanic writer. His book of poetry *Cantos populares de mi tierra* (1877) helped to uncover little known aspects of Afro-Colombian identity. Following Candelario Obeso, writers such as Jorge Artel, Arnaldo Palacios, Helcías Martán Góngora, Hugo Salazar Valdés, Carlos Arturo Truque, Juan Zapata Olivella, Manuel Zapata Olivella, Guillermo Payán Archer and Miguel Caicedo, gradually emerged. These writers however, remain relatively unknown. Gustavo Cobo Borda, a well known Colombian critic, makes no mention of their names in his *Historia portátil de la poesía colombiana* (1880-1995). However journals such as the *Afro-Hispanic Review*, *PALARA* and critics like Richard Jackson, Marvin Lewis, Laurence Prescott and Hector Orjuela, are helping Afro-Colombian literature gain exposure.[i]

Though there are novelists among Afro-Colombian writers, poetry remains their medium of choice, a medium allowing connection to the soul and heart of their community. As Aimé Cesaire is for Martinique, Afro-Colombians writers become the voice of those who cannot speak for themselves, the voice of the silent (26 percent of Colombia's current population is made up of people from African descent).

Afro-Colombian poetry can be defined as one of both representation and resistance. Mainly it constitutes the representation of the modus Vivendi through secular and sacred contexts and resistance to the dominant Eurocentric culture. This form of contestatory/oppositional attitude is a postcolonial concept deriving from a "preexisting" and ongoing "subaltern condition"(Klor de Alba 7-8). Afro-Colombians have been marginalized for centuries, at political, economic, social and cultural levels. To date, poverty is widespread among people whose cultures have been vilified for a long time, and who have been described as primitive or savage in both colonial and modern Eurocentric circles. José María Samper, a leading contemporary critic of Afro-Colombian culture, writes the following about the Curralao (a well known Afro-Colombian dance):

> El *currulao* es la danza típica que resume al boga y su familia, que revela la energía brutal del negro y zambo ... con una voluptuosidad, de una lubricidad cínica, cuya descripción ni quiero ni debo hacer ... la civilización no reinará en esas comarcas sino el día que haya desaparecido el *currulao*, que es la horrible síntesis de la barbarie actual (93-94).
>
> [The *currulao* is the typical dance of the fisherman and his family. It reveals the brutal energy of blacks and zambos...with a voluptuousness, a cynical lewdness which I cannot nor ought to attempt to describe...civilization will not prevail in these areas until the *currulao*, which is today's horrible synthesis of barbarism, disappears.]

Samper's view is symmetrical to the concept of civilization and barbarism of Sarmiento's *Facundo*. In this case, Afro-Colombian culture substitutes the indigenous Argentine culture. Widespread animosity towards Afro-Colombian culture remains prevalent in Colombia today; this is a sad state of affairs generating a destructive inferiority complex among Afro-Colombians, and the continuation of western culture's supremacy. This negative, inaccurate and distorted perception of Afro-Colombian culture is being challenged by the work of poets such as Candelario Obeso, Helcías Martán Góngora, Salazar Valdés, Manuel Zapata Olivella and Guillermo Payán Archer.[ii] Their poetry affirms Afro-Colombian identity, and culture, and calls for an improvement of the social, economic, political and environmental situation of Afro-Colombians. This essay focuses on the work of Helcías Martán Góngora and Guillermo Payán Archer, two of the principal voices of Afro-Colombian poetry.

Helcías Martán Góngora was born in 1920 in the village of Guapí. He overcame poverty, and was able to graduate from law school. He never practised law, but instead, turned his passion for literature into a career. He published his first collection of poems "Mazorca de ensueños" in 1939 in *Vanguardia*. Many others have since followed, with over a dozen of poetry books translated in

German, French, Italian and Basque. Among the most important are *Humano litoral* (1954), *Socavón* (1964), *Mester de negrería y habla negra* (1966), *Música de percusión* (1974), *Retablo de navidad* (1979), *Índice poético de Buenaventura* (1979), *Oratorio de San Pedro Claver* (1980) and *Los coloquios en la universidad* (1980).

Guillermo Payán Archer was born in 1921 in the city of Tumaco. Like Martán Góngora he also studied law and graduated from the University of Javeriana. He worked for many literary journals such as “El Liberal”, “El Tiempo” and “El Espectador” of Bogotá. His oeuvre includes the following books and essays: *La bahía iluminada* (1944), *Noche que sufre* (1948), *Solitario en Manhatta* (1953), *Cinco estampas: apuntes para un mapa político de Nariño* (1957), *La palabra del hombre (*1958), *Los cuerpos amados* (1962), *Poemas del éxodo* (1972), *Trópico de carne y hueso* (1974), *Los soles negros* (1980), *El mar de siempre*(1983), *La cábala y el signo* (1987), *Selección de poemas* (1988) and *Ceniza viva* (1992) (unpublished).

Even though Helcías Martán Góngora's poetic production explores national and international topics, it tends to focus on the cultural aspects of Afro-Colombian identity.[iii] Payán Archer is more interested in the physical environment in which the Afro-Colombian community lives.

In the work of both poets, the connection to Africa is omnipresent, as a (mythical) source of pride and inspiration. In “Mapa de Africa” for example, Martán Góngora retraces the glorious past of African kingdoms such as Ghana, Songoi, Hamasa, Fulki and Bambara (14). This celebration of Africa constitutes a source of empowerment for Afro-Colombians, and gives them a vision of change, renewal and hope. They need not feel defeated culturally but instead, should muster enough courage to rise, stand tall and forge a better future for themselves.

Martán Góngora' poetry addresses two important contexts of Afro-Colombian culture: the secular and the sacred. Norman Whitten, an anthropologist, characterises a context as secular “if no saints, spirits, or non-worldly beings are seen by cultural participants as part of the social interaction. But even in secular contexts information is communicated about other non-human actors" (97). The secular context is dominated by the Afro-Colombian music/dance, the *currulao*.

Instruments used in the *currulao* context are drums (*cununos* and *bombos*), the *guasá* and the *marimba*. The leading singer (*glosador*) starts the song and calls for the responders to answer. The *marimberos* then begin to play joined by the *bomberos* and *cununeros*. Then begins the dance. The *currulao* is not just a social gathering but also a space of entertainment where the community comes together to spend time socializing, discussing personal as well as community challenges. The *curralao* helps repair, maintain and consolidate social relations. The *currulao* is evident in poems such as "Currulao", "Antonio Morongo" and "Negro" among others. In "Antonio Morongo" the poet transcribe the song of currulao:

> *Antonio Morrongo*
> *Mató a su mujer*
> *Con un cuchillito*
> *Tamaño como él.*
> (1)Cuentan que Antonio Morrongo
> Mató a su mujer infiel.
> Con un cuchillito oblongo
> Desgarró su negra piel
> Cortó su cuerpo en el bongo
> Igual que pargo y jurel
> Y el tongo Antonio Morrongo
> Vísceras quiso vender....
> (2)Después se fugó en su bongo
> Ayudado por Luzbel
> Y a su aliado el monicongo
> Y jamás se supo de él.
>
> (3)Antonio Morrongo, pongo
> Tu nombre al hombre más cruel!
> La flor del zapotolongo
> Brotó de la sangre infiel
> Que segó Antonio Morrongo
> Con un cuchillo como él (131).

[Antonio Morongo/killed his wife/with a knife/the size of himself.(1)It is said that Antonio Morongo/killed his unfaithful wife/with a long knife/He ripped her black skin/cut up her body in the bongo/Just as he would cut up snapper and jurel/and the tongo Antonio Morongo/wanted to sell her body parts/(2)Later he ran away in his bongo/helped by

Luzbel/and nobody knew/ about his accomplice/el monicongo.(3)Antonio Morongo/I name you/as the cruellest man/the flower of the zapatolongo/grew from the blood of the unfaithful/that Antonio ripped to pieces/with a knife just like himself]

This song is a story about a man who murders his spouse because of infidelity and then runs away. The horror of the tragic death is represented by the decapitation of the body and the comparison between the size of the murderer's genitalia to the knife he uses to kill his wife. Even though the song evokes cruel death, it is thematically a significant part of the *currulao*. The *glosador* recounts in detail the story and the *responderas* repeat the refrain at the song of the *cununo*, *bombo* and *guasá*. The *jitanjafora* is also typical of Afro-Colombian poetry and translate the linguistic African heritage of the community.

Beside the secular aspect of the Afro-Colombian culture, Martán Góngora reveals also the sacred rituals such as the *alabao* and the *chigualo*. The *alabao* is a musical event which takes place at the death of an adult, within a week to nine days later, when a second wake is held (alabao-novenario). Unlike the *curralao*, no musical instruments are used. The presence of all the relatives of the deceased, expresses closeness and solidarity. Flowers are used to say farewell to the dead. Because of the praise nature of the *alabao*, the *cantadora* urges people not to cry. In the poem "Mamitica linda" Martán Góngora transcribes one such *alabao*:

Mamitica linda, murámonoj juntos
pa que noj entierren en la mejma caja
y nos digan junto misa de difunto
y pa que noj vijtan con iguar mortaja
que toaj laj campana
repiquen en güelo
cuar si juera un día
de jiejta en er pueblo
que ningún pariente
lujca traje negro
ni er llanto de nadie
enjuague er pañuelo.

Que corten laj flore
y dejen er huerto
sin una solita
y cubran tu cuerpo

toitico con ellas
antej der entierro (50).

[Beautiful Mamitica, let's die together/so that they bury us in the same coffin/say the same requiem mass for us/and bury us in the same shroud/Let them ring bells/as if it were a day/ of celebration in the village/May no one dress in black nor wet their handkerchiefs with tears/let them cut all the flowers/leave the garden/with none without a single one/and cover all your body with them/before they bury you.]

The orality of the poem is evident from the syntax constituting a mix of Spanish and African accents. It also reveals some of the characteristics of the *alabao*: the presence of flowers, bells ringing, absence of tears, and above all, an atmosphere of praise. As Norman Whitten describes "After the death of an adult, people from the community gather who regard themselves as related to one another through the deceased. Men make the casket, while women cover the corpse with a sheet and lay it out on a table, with candles around the table. Flowers are laid on his chest and sometimes by his head. That night the *alabaos* are sung." If the *currulao* is performed during the death of an adult, in the case of a child, the *chigualo* takes place.

The *chigualo* is performed for infants who are two years old or younger. The poem "Negro" captures the *chigualo* song:

Negro amigo,
Ven conmigo
-je....jé
Vamos de la mano
Negro hermano
-Tá bien

A orilla del mar
Vamos a cantar

Negro amigo
Ven conmigo
-Je...je (14).

[Black friend/come with me/-je...je/let's go hand in hand/black brother it's okay/to go to the edge of the sea/let's sing/black friend/come with me-je...je.]

The *cantadora* reassures the dead child that he will be fine in heaven since children, because of their presumed innocence, go straight to heaven after death. The corpse is washed by godparents and close female relatives, wrapped in white and laid on a table. Flowers and candles surround the table. During the ceremony, the song of the *bombo* scares the *Tunda* who runs away from the dead child and also from other children. The *tunda* is a bad spirit, very fierce and cunning. It is renowned for killing children. During the ceremony of the *chigualo*, the *cantadoras* shakes maracas and sing choruses or *arrullos*, prayer to the saints.

Arrullos are used for different purposes: the death of an adult, the death of a child, fishing expeditions, or prayer requests. In the poetry of Martán Góngora, the *arrullo* is mostly directed to San Antonio, San José y San Miguel, San Martín de Porres, San Miguel, San Rafael, Santa Bárbara y a la Virgen. The poem "Santoral" is an example:

> En el negro santoral
> en Antonio y en José
> tienes puesta la esperanza
> la caridad y la fe.
> Aoya é
> mi san José
> Aoya é
> A José y Antonio
> clamas, sin cesar
> cuando en tu canoa
> sales a pescar
> Aoya é
> San Antonio
> Aoya é.
> Bárbara bendita
> en la oscuridad
> líbrame del rayo
> y la soledad ("Santoral" 101-102).

> [in the black saint/in Antonio and José/you put your hope/Aoya é/My saint José/Aoya é/To José and Antonio/you pray without ceasing/when in your canoe/ you go fishing/Aoye é/Saint Antonio/Aoye é/Blessed Bárbara/In the darkness/Deliver me from the lightning/And from solitude.]

Each saint evoked during the arroyo has a specific function. Antonio and José strengthen faith, hope, and charity while also protecting fishing activities. Bárbara protects again lightening.

Thomas James Price reveal that prayers "offered to Santa Barbara, assures protection against *centellas* ... this prayer is effective in alleviating the violence of a thunderstorm, by making a cross on the ground with a handful of ashes in the back yard" (Price 142). Even the only Afro-Hispanic saint San Martín de Porres canonized in 1962 is mentioned:

> San Martín de Porres
> Santo trashumé
> libra del maldeojo
> al negro bebé (102)
> [Saint Martín Porres/migrant saint/save the black child/from the evil eye.].

The Afro-Colombian secular context is a product of syncretism. All these saints are explicitly part of the catholic pantheon. There is no open mention of Changó, Yemajá or other African deities but this does not mean that they are forgotten. These saints are transposed versions of African deities. For example Santa Bárbara is the catholic/western version of Changó for Afro-Hispanics and San Miguel is belcan (Ocampo López 171). Saints are a very important part of Afro-Colombian culture and identity; they define their lives and universe.

Like other Afro-Hispanic writers and poets, Martán Góngora is also aware of the difficult socio-economic condition of his peers. He denounces this in poems such as "Socavón", "Cristo negro", "Bisabuela negra", "Decires" and "Hughes" among others. These poems portray the dire straits, limbo, despair, harsh and degrading socio-economic conditions of the lives of Afro-Colombian people, from the colonial era to the present. They are depicted as working hard and making little, carrying heavy burdens, swimming in a sea of violence, discrimination, injustice, oppression and subjugation. In "Cristo negro" the poetic voice summarizes this suffering:

> Cristo de los socavones
> peón de zafra y soldado,
> galeote de las canoas
> madero del pantano
> bracero en Buenaventura
> y pescador a Tumaco (*Poesía* 138).

> [Christ of the gallery/labourer of zafra, soldier,/galley slave of the canoe/beam of the swamp/farmhand in Buenaventura/ and fisherman in Tumaco.]

By comparing the Afro-Colombian worker to Christ, the poet portrays their sacrifice in the mines, agricultural fields, industries and the army. By describing their condition, the poet hopes to stimulate awareness, change, and the need for restitution, especially among the elites in the government.

If the Afro-Colombian identity is revealed and valued by Martán Góngora through their cultural aspects, Payan Archer focuses more on the geographical dimension of the culture: the sea and ports. Afro-Colombians define themselves as people of the sea. Water is a very important element of their identity. By the sea they came from Africa to América. The sea is also a major source of their survival. *Mar de siempre* and *Bahía iluminada* are dedicated to the sea and life in the ports. The following poems highlight the value of the sea/scape: "El mar cambiante y eterno", "Llueve en la noche sobre el mar", "Una botella al mar", "Ventanas que miran al mar", "El marinero fue sepultado en el mar", "El mar en el olvido", "El mar en la sangre", "Croquis marino."

The sea is powerful, fearless, good and evil at the same time. This contrast is revealed in "El mar cambiante y eterno":

> Siempre,
> he mirado el mar, con amor y con miedo
> medio en fiebre y en éxtasis,
> asombrado con su misterio,
> ciego ante su horizonte sin límites
> atento a su silencio evocador y sugerente (114).

> [Always,/I have looked at the sea with love and fear/in its fever and ecstasy,/amazed by its mystery,/blinded by its limitless horizon/attentive to its evocative and fascinating silence.]

By using the first person singular "yo" (I), the poetic voice tries to authenticate and give more veracity to the reality and the double nature of the sea. The sea provides fish, marine food for the population and for the survival of the local economy as well as cemetery for fisherman. The life of the people is tied to the sea. Because many fishermen and people perish in the sea each year, the women perform the *arrollo* ritual before they leave for the sea:

la hora de partir hacia el mar
Oh! los adioses
de las mujeres suplicantes y el recuerdo
de los besos tempranos,
y el mar
el mar de siempre! (*El mar de siempre* 17)

[At the hour of departure to sea/Oh! The goodbyes/of women pleading/and the memories/of early kisses/and the sea/the ever-present sea.]

Before the departure, the atmosphere is tense because nobody knows if the fishermen will come back alive. The prayers, kisses and goodbyes are desperate attempts to boost the morale of the fishermen. The uncertainty of the sea is accentuated in the following verses:

"¿Volverán?
Nadie sabe. Nadie lo sabe" (*La bahía iluminada* 83).
[Will they return?/Nobody knows. Nobody knows.]

The sea is a mystery, a living being; a god who decides the future of people. The sea is a pivotal part of Afro-Colombian identity. Its importance is not just in this life but remains crucial after death and becomes a way to reconnect and return black Colombians to Africa.

Close to the sea, ports constitute a physical space where Afro-Colombians survive. Many work there as employees of the government and also live there. At night the port constitutes a place for social gathering and interaction where people tell stories about their existence, and discuss issues related to the sea. In "Hablan de la vida del puerto" the poet listens to the story of sailors on the boat named "El Faro del Carmen", who recount the misfortune of the cruise ship "El Invencible":

Yo escucho alucinado
sus voces, sus palabras locas y hondas
en las que vivo y muero y vuelvo a vivir
la vida del puerto (*El mar de siempre* 31).

[I listen with amazement/ their voices, their words, crazy and deep/In which I live, die and live again/The life of the seaport.]

The port is also a romantic place where people search and meet for love and matters of the heart. In “Las luces del puerto y tus labios” the poet talks about his female conquests and never ending broken relationships. Ports can also turn into a space of debauchery, drugs and other crimes.

In conclusion, Afro-Colombian poetry reveals, exalts and appreciates the identity and culture of people of African decent. By describing the secular and sacred rituals of the community, the Afro-Colombian poets aim to deconstruct the distorted images that some people including cultural critics like Samper have circulated about the Afro-Colombian people and their culture. Martán Góngora and Payán Archer achieve these goals through different channels. The first uses the cultural aspect of Afro-Colombian identity, while the other focuses on the physical environment, especially the realm of sea, shore and ports. This study is a step towards furthering our understanding of the depth, scope and range in the interaction between Afro-Colombian writers, and the people they speak of and for.

References

Klor de Alba, Jorge. “Postcolonialization of the (Latin) American Experience: A Reconsideration of ‘Colonialism’ and ‘Mestizaje’.” *After Colonialism: Imperial Histories and Postcolonial Displacements.* Ed. Gyan Prakash. Princeton: U P, 1995.

Lewis, Marvin. *Afro-Hispanic Poetry, 1940-1980: From Slavery to Negritude in South American Verse.* Columbia: University of Misouri Press, 1983.

Martán Góngora, Helcías. *Breviario negro.* Santiago de Cali: Esparavel 106,1978.

- - -. *Cauce.* Popayán: Talleres Editoriales del Departamento del Cauca, 1953.

- - -. *Mester de negrería y habla negra.* Bogotá: n.p., 1966.

- - -. *Música de percusión.* Cali: Imprenta Departamental del valle de Cauca, 1974.

- - -. *Océano.* Popayán: Universidad del Cauca, 1950.

- - -. *Suma poética, 1963-1968*: Bogotá, Editorial Kelly, 1969.

Payán-Archer, Guillermo. *El mar de siempre*. Bogotá: Ediciones Minoría, 1983.

- - -. *La bahía iluminada*. Bogotá: Edición Espiral, 1944.

Prescott, Laurence. "Voces del litoral recóndito: Tres voces de la costa colombiana del Pacífico." *Revista de estudios colombianos* 29 (2006): 24-36.

Price, Thomas James. *Saints and Spirits: A Study of Differential Acculturation in Colombian Negro Communities*. Diss. Norwestern U, 1955.

Whitten, Norman E. *Black Frontiersmen: AfroHispanic Culture of Ecuador and Colombia*. Prospect Height: Waveland Press, 1974.

---

[i]Marvin Lewis. Afro-*Hispanic Poetry, 1940-1980: From Slavery to Negritude in South American Verse* (1983). Laurence Prescott. "Voces del litoral recóndito: Tres voces de la costa colombiana del Pacífico" (2006). Héctor Orjuela. *Bibliografía de la poesía colombiana* (1971). Richard Jackson. *The Black Image in Latin American Literature* (1976).

[ii]We also have to recognize the contributions of the anthropologist Norman Whitten (*Black Frontiersmen*) whose studies have been important in the understanding of the afro-colombian people and way of live.

[iii] Marvin A . Lewis (*Afro-Hispanic Poetry*) and Laurence Prescott ("Voces del litoral recondito") who have studied the work of Martán Góngora have also noticed the thematic diversity of the afro-colombian poet and his attachment of to his native land (Guapí): "[...] la vision de Martán Góngora, como su producción,es más amplia, abarcando figures y territorios nacionales e internacionales pero siempre manteniendo un espacio predilecto para su querida costa" (34).

Chapter 11

The Africanness of Mexican Traditional Medicine

Marco Polo Hernández Cuevas

One of the most important
of the shared religious elements
[of African heritage] is the circle dance.
The Spiritual's Project

A la rueda, rueda de San Miguel
Todos piden su caja de miel.
Children's popular play song

"Santeria Invades Mexico"[i] read the headline of an article that appeared in *El Nuevo Herald* of Miami, USA on 29 September 2000 ("Santería"). Anthropologist Yólolt González, president of the Mexican Association for the Study of Religions, is quoted as saying, "Just as in Mexico the Catholic forms of expression have an influence from the pre-Hispanic cultures, in Cuba the presence of African religions has been very strong [...]." According to the report, these statements were made during the II Congress of Mexico-Cuba Popular Religiosity at the Institute of Anthropological Research of the *Universidad Nacional Autónoma de México* (National Autonomous University of Mexico).

González's perspective reveals the effects of Mexican official discourse on nation that obscures the fundamental investment of African cultural capital in the making of the Mexican nation and national identity.[ii] Beginning in a period I have dubbed elsewhere "the cultural phase of the Mexican Revolution, 1920-1968," views such as González's, deny agency to the Africans and their American offspring, who, in spite of the official denial, are the majority of the Mexican population today. This disappearance discourse was forged by the "*criollos*"[iii] (who proudly exalted their "pure" Spanish heritage) to appropriate patrimonies that did not belong to them. The Mexican *criollo* elite, the Spanish counterparts of the British "pals," have in this manner embezzled the cultural capital that the Africans and their descendants have been investing throughout the centuries in the production and development of Mexican Traditional Medicine, whose cures are made generally in the name of a given Saint (Torres 56, Rius 34).

Mexican Traditional Medicine possesses traits that distinguish it from other African American cosmologies such as *Candombe, Candomblé, Batuque/Nación, Africanismo, Santeria, Umbanda, Voodoo*, (Frigerio 2),[iv] *Macumba* (González 11), and the Spirituals, among others. However, it is irrefutable that given to part of its fundamental characteristics, Mexican Traditional Medicine is a relative of the religions that flourished in places where Europeans and their lackeys transported enslaved Africans. The Spiritual's Project of the University of Denver, Colorado, USA sheds further light:

Throughout the Americas, from Boston in New England to Montevideo in the Viceroyalty of La Plata, in every place where African women, men and children were enslaved, there emerged cultural and religious forms reflecting the particular complexities, terrors and exigencies of each situation. (II)

The present work exhibits the African presence and persistence in Mexican Traditional Medicine in New Spain and in Mexico since the first half of the 16th century to the present. This task is carried out relying on the list of cases appended to Gonzalo Aguirre Beltrán's *Medicina y magia: el proceso de aculturación en la estructura colonial* (1992). Part of the data in these cases (litigated before the Saint Inquisition in the 16th and 17th centuries) is analyzed from an Afrocentric perspective.[v] This approach's primary objective is to restitute the place that Africa, black Africans and African Americans of multiple phenotypes have built against the current; it observes and explains black phenomena departing from yesterday's and today's know-how of the Africans and their American descendants.

This essay documents the presence of African-influenced know-how practiced by Africans and their American offspring beginning 1536 in urban centers as well as in the remotest places of New Spain. It shows that the Mexican belief system is analogous to Cuban Santeria. The work adopts the perspective that the incalculable African contributions throb[vi] as fundamental entities of the ancestral know-how practiced and known together as "traditional medicine" in Mexico as well as in other places of the Americas. It is also established that Mexican healing practices and know-how are not a "recent invasion"[vii] but rather are a segment of an African and African diaspora ancestral whole disfigured and dismembered through a European discourse that seeks to make it unrecognizable and invalid. Spaniards persecuted this know-how that bonded subjected communities, as it countered the Spaniards divisive discourse. Through words laden with ethnocentrism, African and African-American know-how was defamed, degraded, repudiated and criminalized.[viii] In addition, it is exposed that African-based philosophies and theologies in Mexico did not "disappear;" and that notions such as "syncretism" and "acculturation" (in the sense of vanishing through absorption), among others, are inoperable perspectives for a holistic[ix] study of the African presence and persistence in the Americas.

The First Nations,[x] Asian, and European contributions to the formation of the present Mexican cultural sites are hereby acknowledged at this point. Regarding the African contributions, there is a two-pronged concurrent objective to this study. On the one hand, to continue disarticulating the myth of European supremacy that deliberately ignores the African contributions to the development of Mexicaness. On the other, to review the universal collective memory with an approach that allows one to better evaluate the fundamental investment of the diverse ancient African know-how in the formation of Mexican Traditional Medicine that is part of the American experience of Africans from Senegambia, Sierra Leone, Congo, and Guinea, among others.[xi]

Aguirre Beltrán extracts from the Mexican National General Archives data from 523 entries of cases (many concerning the same people) to inform his persuasive book-length essay *Medicina y magia*. From the data he presents, the following is highlighted in support of our aims: the years in which the cases took place; *calidades* (caste or race) of the accused; gender; charges; and places where the accused lived.

Based on the data, the characteristics of Mexican Traditional Medicine, of part of its practitioners, and of the patients, are presented to show the overwhelming presence of African religions in Mexico; and to expand the understanding of this Mexican know-how within the so-called popular cultures. Also, *criollo*-European ethnocentrism is exhibited as having distorted this know-how through negative labels such as *jitanjáfora, mumbo jumbo, hocus pocus*, among many other labels.

The cases are dated from 1536 to 1784 (16th-18th centuries). Three hundred and seventeen (317) cases, or 63%, are against Africans and Afrodescendants born to mixes with First Nations, Asians and Spanish. The rest of the cases do not mention *calidad* or are against "mestizos"[xii] and Spaniards. From the 317 cases against Africans and Afrodescendants, over 50% are against women.

Some of the *calidades* of the accused individuals include: negra, negro, esclava, negra ladina, mulato zapatero, negro esclavo, negra esclava, mulatas, negro de Gabriel de Castro, mulata, mulato, mulato esclavo, morisco, multa libre, moreno, mulata blanca herrada, moresquilla, zambillo, negra libre, multa de Toluca, negro cimarrón, chino, negro ladino de nación conga, negra mandinga, mulata gachupina, negro bozal, casta loba, mulatilla, negro francés, parda libre, coyote, coyota, negro amoriscado, y mulato achinado . It should be mentioned that there are two actions against dead people. Also, one of the cases includes the age of the accuser (a 16 year old single male mulatto) and of the accused (a 13 year old "half crazy *mulatilla* named María de Guadalupe").

The data documents the African and African American presence in New Spain from the 16th to 18th centuries in towns, plantations, mine-townships, and urban centers. Among the sites where the accused women and men practiced medicine are: Acapulco, Atoyac, Acámbaro, Acayucan, Actopan, Aguascalientes, Antequera, Atlixco, Campeche, Caracas, Chalco, Chiapas, Cholula, Chihuahua, Ciudad de México, Colima, Córdoba, Cuautla, Cuernavaca, Culiacán, Durango, Guadalajara, Guastepec, Guanajuato, Guatemala, Guayangareo, Hauchinango, Huejotzingo, Izúcar, Manila, Mérida, Michoacán, Minas de Pachuca, Naolingo, Nueva Galicia, Nueva Segovia, Tixtla, Nuevo México, Oaxaca, Orizaba, Pachuca, Pátzcuaro, Pénjamo, Puebla, Querétaro, Real de Guadalcázar, Real y Minas de Ramos, Salamanca, San Luis Potosí, San Lorenzo de los Negros, Santa Fe, Sayula, Sichú, Sinaloa, Tabasco, Tarímbaro, Taxco, Tepatlán,
Tepeapulco, Tepeaca, Tequixquiapan, Tlaxcala, Toluca,
Tulancingo, Valladolid, Veracruz, Villa de León, Villa de Lagos,

Xalapa, Yucatán, and Zacatecas. The following four paragraphs list some of the allegations.

The accusations include: reading *fava* beans; curing with goat black heads and other spells; simple fornication; eating the food that the First Nations people offered to their gods in their idolatry; superstitions; incantations; charlatanry; blasphemy; witchcraft and trickery; using powders of the heads of *aura* birds, jackass brains, heads of turtledove, lice and dung worms to make one loveable; making a pact with the devil; taking good-love powder; bigamy and *vaqueria*; match-making; stealing two sticks that had the virtue of allowing a couple to live in peace; divination; peyote ingestion; saying that a little stick would get the desired women; disinterring the dead and stealing bones for making incantations; possession of a bag with hair; prayers; prayers to stop hemorrhaging; prayers against sudden death and against all evil; copying incantations from the book *Clavículas de Salomón*; making magical rings to cure illnesses; possession of an idol; washing the lower parts of the body and giving the water to drink so that the lovers would desire them; filth.

In the same vein they were accused of the following: using the finger of a hanged person and putting menstruation blood in a chocolate drink; taking *nanacates* (hallucinogenic mushrooms); giving powders, mushrooms and herbs; taking *ololiuhqui*[xiii] seeds; extracting three dead men's bones introduced in a person by a warlock through spells; having a stone that gives one whatever is requested; invoking the devil; having the devil's figure painted on the bottom of the foot; having stones to win while gambling and in marriages; having a monkey's hand, a deer's tail, a cock's nail, an egg and wooden statue; feeding turkey snot to a man so that his wife would not mistreat him; giving nail powder to men to make them loveable.

Additionally accusations included: giving earthworms to a man to make him infertile; possessing books of devil drawings and making documents that offer the soul; praying to the moon; selling the soul to the devil; cutting olive branches to discover silver deposits with them; consulting a black diviner who speaks through the chest to discover a mine; having a black mound ornamented with coins among images of saints; having a serpent that tells her how to steal and counsels her, and having a stick that eats, sleeps, speaks and drinks as a person, using magic sticks to find money; practicing necromancy; initiation of evil deeds; using ray powders; calling the devil; having devil figures painted in two parts of the body; divining and apostasy; using the herb called *Rosa Maria*; performing trickery; giving poison; drinking a beverage and having a devil painted on the back.

Finally the list mentions: giving jackass brains, red ants and crocodile penis to render one simple; whipping a Christ statue; faking apparitions; disinterring the body of a black child; distributing little birds and powders; possession of human bones; evil deeds via a toad's saliva; leaving home on Mondays with grease candle butts to go to a grotto and light and leave them under a pot; saying that there is a bird called hummingbird for attracting and trapping women; giving a human bone so that any woman would desire him; using a human bone to keep watch on his woman; passing prayers to the *duende*, *Juez Justo*, and Holy Trinity to help capture wild herds; and catching a little girl's shadow.

Aguirre Beltrán makes eight groupings from the charges that occur more often in his citations of Inquisition cases against healers in New Spain: 1) Witchcraft, superstition and trickery; 2) healing, herbs, filth and matchmaking; 3) fortune telling, sorcery, divination; 4) spell, spellbinding; 5) witchcraft, associations and commerce with the devil; 6) blasphemy, reneging, apostasy, and idolatry; 7) heretic words and propositions; and 8) simple fornication and bigamy. All these acts were considered acts of heresy and profane contrary to the Catholic mores that permeated the European worldviews of the times.

An additional piece of information that surfaces from the data is that the practice of traditional medicine shows a growing number of African and Afrodescendant women and men healers who covered greater territory with the passing of time notwithstanding the *Santo Oficio's* hounding. Along with African Mexican profane songs and dances, the healing practices in New Spain may be placed at the center of the popular anti-Spanish discourse that in 1810 acquired sufficient political force to dethrone the oppressors and initiate the armed phase of the Mexican War of Manumission[xiv] that laid the foundation for independence from Spain and the birth of the Mexican nation.[xv]

Joseph M. Murphy explains:

> One of the highest hurdles to overcome in interpreting diasporan traditions is the deep-seated popular image of them as "voodoo," malign "black magic." Hundreds of books and scores of films have portrayed the spirituality of millions of people of African descent as crazed, depraved, or demonic manipulations of gullible and irrational people. These images have their origins in the French colonial reaction to the revolt of Haitian slaves whose motive in liberating themselves from grinding and brutal enslavement was thought to rest in *vaudoux*. The success of the Haitian Revolution sent shock waves through the white world that are still being felt today. I think that the relegation of "voodoo" to the horror genre reflects mass America's real horror of independent black power. If voodoo was powerful enough to free the slaves, might it not free their descendants? (Preface x)

The labels of "healing," "folk medicine," "magic," "divination," "spiritualism," "Santeria," "bewitching," "witchcraft," "charlatanry," among a host of others, were contrived to negatively mark everything that contradicts the official imperial discourse. Thus, legitimacy was eradicated from the ancestral medicine and the road for an ideological substitution paved. These actions also exhibit the knowledge that the colonizers have had about the "magical" or persuasive powers intrinsic to words. Also, that they have been using words via various means for mass persuasion, as spells, to do damage and plagiarize know-how.

It should be mentioned that New Spain was the main receptor of enslaved Africans, from Senegambia and Sierra Leone in the16th century (Thornton 89) and mainly Congo and Guinea (Aguirre Beltrán, *Medicina* 60) during the 17th centuries; and that although the number of arrivals decreased from that time on, and its proportion became reduced in comparison with other continental regions where the Transatlantic Trade exploded, it is known that "bozales" (the name for "black" people brought directly from Africa) continued to be brought to New Spain until the 19th century. In fact, enslavement of black bozales, American blacks, and the infinite rainbow of their offspring (born to their relations with First Nations, Asians and Spaniards)[xvi] was legal in New Spain until 1829. This does not mean that the "legal" trade, and in particular the illegal trade, ceased immediately.

By the 19th century, blacks and their offspring became the majority of the Mexican "mestizo" population (Aguirre Beltrán, *La población* 243). According to Aguirre Beltrán, New Spain's population "at the end of the day was integrated through the mixture, in various degrees, of the three great races that converged in our country: the indigenous, white, and black" (*La población* 276). He elucidates as well,

the integration of black population to the society is, in fact, a process that started when blacks were transferred to the American colonies that gave support to the European expansion; an operation that was sustained during the three centuries of foreign control, that continued into the formative century of the nationality [...]. (278)

Black Africans and their children in New Spain, the same as in other places far and wide throughout the Americas, constituted the driving force behind mines, plantations, ranches, *obrajes* (prison-like sweat shops), transport (including trafficking), domestic service, and trades, among other physical activities. Spaniards that arrived to the Americas, of which the majority came from the lower classes, overnight turned into fervent defenders of *hidalgia* (chivalry) and *pundonor* (self love).[xvii] The Spanish belief system dictated that the labor, in particular physical work, was for the colored commoners and not for the "white conquistadors" (a worldview that lingers as a sign of whiteness and therefore "supremacy").

The First Nations populations, as a consequence of the European invasion, decreased from tens of millions to one million two hundred thousand within the first seventy years of colonization. Their recovery occurred through the mixture with mestizos and mulattos, both Afrodecedents according to Aguirre Beltrán (*La población 243*). In *Medicina*, Aguirre Beltrán informs through a letter to Fry Ambrosio Carrillo, that "the mestizos and mulattos being born of Indian women and raised with them, among Indians, follow in every way the nature of the mothers, speaking their indigenous tongue, dressing as Indians and looking like them in every way" (76). This he coins as a process of "*endoculturation.*" Aguirre Beltrán avoids analyzing the "outside" relations that produced these births and the emergence of the new Amerindian lineage of African decent or Mexican Black Indians.

Alejandra Cárdenas, after explaining the ancestral relation between women and the cultivation of plants and how women became botanists by working with the land and in "the search for greens and edible roots" throughout millennia, points out:

> starting with rationalism, all of the [ancestral] know-how is expropriated, classified and included in the official know-how [...] [U]niversities organized the groupings of know-how that allowed the homogenization of knowledge. [...] Universities granted permits that allowed the exercise of know-how to selective groups. [...] Thus, there is a corpus of ideas considered scientific, rationally proven, with a written permit to be practiced and all the rest that remains outside is considered trickery, witchcraft, a thing of the devil. (68-69)

Ancestral medicine is the source of Carnival. From time immemorial, this liturgy of ceremonies was displayed to revitalize the communal and productive spirit. At the onset of reflexive thinking, the community learned to keep in cadence with creation, the divine. Lilian Scheffler identifies Mexican specialists who "frequently are in charge of directing rituals and ceremonies [...] for the group's benefit" (35). She elucidates, "The *Huichol* shamans, called *maracáme*,[xviii] are singers, healers, and they are in charge of directing the fiestas, and the magical-religious rituals of their group" (35). Cardenas meanwhile, after reviewing the Latin etymology of "*mirar*" [*mirari, miraclo, milagro* (admirable fact)], reveals, "Christianity assimilated the marvelous, constraining it to the supernatural. Magic from this perspective is the evil supernatural while the Christian marvelous is the miracle" (57).

Aguirre Beltrán states that , "while Western cultural changes from the Renaissance to the present have occurred at a breakneck speed, in the cultures called primitive, where black cultures are customarily placed, the speed of change has been so slow that it gives the sensation of stagnation" (*Medicina* 60). From his perspective, given what he perceives as "cultural conservative-ism" black medicine "is basically unchanged." He declares, "Today's concepts, present practices and even the cultural climate where they unfold, do not differ, in essence, from the concepts, practices and environments of four hundred years ago" (*Medicina* 60).

Aguirre Beltrán places the origins of Western Medicine in Greece. Thus, he reinforces the disjunctive, Europe versus the rest of the world. This worldview generates a way of thinking "which foreshadows modern racism" (Anderson 59); a phenomenon Benedict Anderson explains in light of the dawn of the religious communities, Classical Latin decadence, the rise of vernacular languages, the appearance of the printing press, the invention of maps and Western chronometry, the logos and thus the emergence of print capitalism. The Catholic faith that maintained that the world was flat begins to crumble with Christopher Columbus' main discovery.

Columbus "discovers" for those sponsoring his trip that the Earth is not flat. And European financiers realize, toward the end of the 15th and the beginning of the 16th century, how to forge a discursive New World where they imagine and position themselves at the center of the universe by means of their own stratagems and rules. Europeans develop their own disciplines for self-legitimating and inventing the Other; they deploy fragmentary methods such as Western chronometry, census, maps and museums (Anderson 163-85), among other strategies that will allow them to shape and reshape at will the collective memory of their subjects and their own. Europe will emerge from the Mediterranean world as an entity that denies its African lineage and does not recognize Africa as the oldest of the continents and the crib of human civilization.

In "Keeping It Real," Ian Isidore Smart cites Michael White regarding how life was at the time in the lands where Columbus set sail:

> The average life expectancy was twenty-four years for a woman and perhaps twenty-seven years for a man. The majority of people were hungry and ill most of the time and the rich suffered most of the same horrors as the poor; plague, war, and pestilence were supremely democratic. All but a few were illiterate, innumerate and spent much of their time inebriated. Most people traveled no further than ten miles from their own homes during their entire lives and were pathologically suspicious of strangers; few had any inkling of the year in which they lived, nor any knowledge of the world beyond their village or town. (*New Orleans* 24)

Centuries later, regarding Western Medicine, in an account of the Piedmont Plantation of North Carolina, the following is stated:

> Medical practitioners in the eighteenth and nineteenth centuries, besides the copious use of drugs, resorted almost entirely to bleeding and blistering, measures which weakened the patient or aggravated his suffering. Emetics, purgatives, opiates, and barks formed the *materia*

> *medica* and could be dispensed by anyone, along with home remedies of herbs and tonics, whisky and brandy. (Bradley 106)

Aguirre Beltrán deliberately ignores the Egyptian African Imhotep, defined as the father of medicine and deified 2650 years before Christ (Ashanti 2). In fact, Imhotep, called "God of Medicine," "Prince of Peace," and a "Type of Christ" [...] was worshipped as a god and healer from approximately 2850 B.C. to 525 B.C., and as a full deity from 525 B.C. to 550 A.D. Even kings and queens bowed at his throne. Imhotep lived during the Third Dynasty at the court of King Zoser. Imhotep was a known scribe, chief lector, priest, architect, astronomer and magician (medicine and magic were used together.) For 3000 years he was worshipped as a god in Greece and Rome. Early Christians worshipped him as the "Prince of Peace."

Imhotep was also a poet and philosopher. He urged contentment and preached cheerfulness. His proverbs contained a "philosophy of life." Imhotep coined the saying "Eat, drink and be merry for tomorrow we shall die."

When the Egyptians crossed the Mediterranean, becoming the foundation of the Greek culture, Imhotep's teachings were absorbed there. Yet, as the Greeks were determined to assert that they were the originators of everything, Imhotep was forgotten for thousands of years and a legendary figure, Hippocrates, who came 2000 years after him became known as the Father of Medicine. ("Imhotep")

Another fundamental piece of information that Aguirre Beltrán bypasses is that the Moors having inhabited parts of the Iberian Peninsula for nearly eight centuries (from 795-1492) brought and bequeathed to that region ample know-how in various fields. The Andalusian *duende*, or Spanish soul, is a prime example.

From Aguirre Beltrán's position, prevalent in Mexico and other places of the Americas, notions are forged such as "mestizaje" and "syncretism" among other ideological-words pillars of the Eurocentric structural violence[xix] that lingers to-date against the invented "Others" and their cultural practices. These concepts propose that the "superior" cultures, i.e. the European, have absorbed to disappearance the inferior ones: those that are not European. They conceive a set of values that assign the European or "white" as a synonym of the greatest human development, beauty and goodness, and the direct opposite to the African or "black." Within such a dimension, the ancestral African and African-Mexican know-how are catalogued as "mestizo medicine" (Aguirre Beltrán, *Medicina* 81).

"Mestizaje" and "acculturation" insist on the disappearance by "integration" of the characteristics understood as "primitive" or "inferior" and are vehicles to erase and denigrate the Africaness of the American Afrodescendants born of the relations among Africans, First Nations, Asians, and Europeans. As an antidote to that structural violence, postcolonial critical perspectives germinate; among these is the Afrocentric idea.

In her study of the Seven African Powers candle, Mary Ann Clark elucidates, "*these candles represent a case of religious appropriation. Religious appropriation is the use of one or more elements of an alien religious system in a way that does not fundamentally change the borrowing system*" (5). The fundamental form of the African cosmos with their veneration for the ancestors and the elements that allow communication with them in 17th century Acapulco is exhibited by Cárdenas: "The sound of the drums, the dance and the ingestion of divine plants provoked states of illumination where the ancestors descended over the heads of the chosen ones [...]" (62); and she continues, "The dances can also be part of a religious ceremony tied to divination, because dance helps to establish communication with the ancestors' spirits. Dance and prayer are often part of the oracular consultation" (63).

In reference to the ancient African medicinal know-how that pulses within a dimension beyond the Eurocentric limits of space and time, Smart enlightens:

> African philosophers and theologians from the dawn of time have understood that the supernatural forces, the gods, are basically energy sources and therefore they manifest as vibrations. The keepers of knowledge have taught that in order for humans to enter in intimate contact with the divine with the supernatural forces all one has to do is to start vibrating in accordance to the rhythm of the [god or mood invoked]. (*Literatura oral* 36)

Moods, the state of the soul, are understood as vibrations tied to deities or Orishas who vibrate within the Yoruba pantheon and in the pantheons of Afrodescendants in the Americas. The various rhythms deployed whose function is to touch the soul through vibrations and thus influence the mood (the state of the soul) are emitted, transmitted and received via various call-response means that are as ancient as the reflexive thinking capacity of the *Homosapiens Africano*, the spring of civilization (Zapata Olivella 8).[xx]

Aguirre Beltrán, in his discussion of "black medicine," exposes that "the drums play the rhythm of the given god" (*Medicina* 72); and that "dances do not have another goal other than serving the duty with the gods, their veneration and propitiation and in them the medical goal is a byproduct" (*Medicina* 71-72).

One of the central problems with the European fragmentation of the African healing know-how is that it is unable to perceive its holistic quality. Within the Carnaval perception, the being of yesterday, today, and tomorrow is one, the *Muntú*. The "individual" is part of a community of today, yesterday, and tomorrow. In the same manner, music, dance, song, food, and all other oral cultural texts are channels of communication with the ancestors. The affectations of the member of a community are related to the disgust, alteration or ire of a given ancestor that may have been offended with the injurious behavior of the ill person. The treatment for the ailments therefore is found outside the Western space and time limitations and is performed via an intermediary who will communicate with the offended ancestor to appease her or him with offerings.

Whomever has been touched, stimulated or "affected" by the rhythm of a dance; the melody of a song; the balsam of violet or jasmine; animated by the succulent aroma of *fritangas* (fried foods); or by tonalities; or entered into the frequency of a certain feeling through vibrations that produce melancholy (rhythm blues), nostalgia (*bolero*), vitality (*rumba, samba, candombe, mambo, charanga, guaracha, reggae, kaiso, calypso*), etc.; has entered into the frequency of a deity: he or she has communicated with a given Orisha. Through the vibration of a specific rhythm the person enters in contact with a certain aspect of his or her universal soul (an unknown dimension for the positivist whose spiritual non-know-how or "science" is rooted in the so-called reason).

The Spiritual's Project

> [l]ong defines religion as "orientation in the ultimate sense, that is, how one comes to terms with the ultimate significance of one's place in the world." For people of African descent in the Americas, both during slavery and in its long aftermath, religion thus becomes the means by which one remembers and cultivates an alternative understanding of one's humanity, in the face of constant affronts and denials. Not limited to the institutional church, rather spread across the breadth of culture, family, community, and language, this meaning of religion feeds *an-other* experience of reality that nurtures connection to the divine and sustains a truly human identity. (II)

The medicinal strength of the "word," the vibration that it contains or liberates, the rhythms of musical instruments, songs, dances, flavors, colors, aromas, and more, captured as mere "merrymaking" by the Western lens, in fact are "ceremonial liturgies" of ample healing powers for body and spirit. They are vehicles of access to the *momento pleno,* "that eternal moment of transcendence when the human being reconciles his accidental materiality with his essential spirituality" (Smart, "Carnaval" 31). This is when the individual enters in contact with the soul of his being. That this know-how is integral to the contemporary Mexican is verified by the character Chin-Chin of Armando Ramirez' *Chin-Chin el teporocho* (1981) Chilango novel. (The grammar and style of the work are respected):

Some couples dance with harmony of bodies to the rhythm of a *cumbia* or a *guaracha* or a *rumba* [...] and one starts to move with the rhythm when one hears "*Elegua*" of the *Matancera* [group] and I move the feet and the legs have music and I move the waist with cadence and the shoulders and the arms either you embrace the chick with whom you are dancing and give turns together, moving the body in accord with how you feel that the musical notes touch the fibers of your body and the rhythmical fury that you carry inside your body is unchained, and make you dance and dance without worrying about anything, it does not matter whether it is a blues or a *cha cha* or a rock [and roll] or a *mambo* or a *samba* or a twist or *watusi*, **what matters is that you communicate**, that you feel the music, let it possess your body, free it to the music, allow it to sink free it from that tension that you have it constantly subjected to throughout the day, allow it to wander, allow it to exhibit itself, let it do, let it be ... (30) (Emphasis added)

Mexican ancestral medicine, just as the medicine in other places of African heritage, is total, it treats the ailments of the body and the state of the soul or mood departing from the spirit or the spiritual. It uses sound-therapy, chromo-therapy, aroma-therapy, flavor and consistency-therapy to modulate the *amima's* cadence of the being that is out of tune with the cosmos, or ill. It touches the senses and sharpens them, it lifts the spirit through the trip to the *momento pleno*, where the individual ceases to "be" and abandons the body to become one with everything through the soul or anima that gravitates in the sounds, flavors, smells, textures, and colors. Ancestral traditional medicine changes the state of the anima; it comforts, revitalizes the being through music, food and drink, dance, and singing, among others.

Under this light, it is possible to explain the curative powers of the ancestral *fandangos* where Mexicans, the same way as their grandparents from diverse African nations, gathered to celebrate life and through their *pachangas*, black masses or liturgies, (accused of orgiastic) enter in contact with the ancestors, the guiding forces, through the "medicine" of music, dance, song, food, colors, and textures, among others. *The Spiritual's Project* explains,

> With a combination of resources from their homelands and their captivities, enslaved people in the Americas, found ways to negotiate, resist, and in some moments, even transform the afflictions they faced. African American spirituals arose out of response to enslavement in the United States, not only in terms of evocative, often coded, lyrics, but also in the very circumstance of the creation and development of the music. The songs, almost always accompanied by ritual movement and dance, melded Biblical language to African religious values and New World experiences of struggle. They provided the foundation for the emergence of a distinctive, African America Christianity marked by many elements common to other traditions of the diaspora such as Santeria, Vodou and Candomblé. (II. A.)

According to Scheffler, "the present panorama of magic or witchcraft in Mexico" subsists as the result of the fusion of cult traditions of pre-Hispanic indigenous people and the Spanish [...] in addition to those with the same type of elements bequeathed by black slaves" (16, 34). Central to the present study is that just as

Aguirre Beltrán, Scheffler documents that traditional medical practices, in-part fundamentally of African heritage, persist in present Mexico. The Mexican medicinal know-how are related to those of other places in the Americas such as Argentina, Uruguay, Brazil, Cuba, Puerto Rico, Haiti, Trinidad y Tobago, Jamaica, among a growing list where a "greater" African heritage is recognized, although their most vocal practitioners as is the case of Argentina or New Orleans, are "white."

Migene González-Wippler has written extensively on Cuban Santeria and its diaspora. Some of her works include: *Santería: magia africana en Latinoamérica(Santeria: African Magic in Latin America)*; *Santería: la religión (Santeria: The Religion); Santería: mis experiencias en la religión(Santeria: My Experiences in the Religion); y Leyendas de la Santería: pataki (Santeria Legends: Pataki)*. One of the themes that emerges constantly in the worldview that informs González-Wippler's work is the Yoruba cult of the ancestors. This paradigm is explained by Aguirre Beltrán as "the constellation disobedience-punishment, obedience-gratification [which] informs the principal etiology of black medicine; [where] sickness [is understood as the result of] the transgression and breaking of taboos" (Aguirre Beltrán, *Medicina* 63). Although González-Wippler speaks of religion, it is clear that the health of the community members, within the African perspective, depends on the respect and dignifying of the ancestors.

Aguirre Beltrán notes in his classic essay, *La poblacion negra en Mexico* (*The Black Population of Mexico*) that the Yoruba "entered our country with the name of Locumi" (133); and with various other names (133-34). According to González-Wippler, "in Cuba where Santeria started, the Yoruba became known as Locumi" (2). This data and the fact that parallel know-how exists in the land occupied by Mexico today beginning in 1536 allows one to conclude as incorrect anthropologist Yólolt González' statement that Santeria began to invade Mexico in 2000 and shows that the African influence is an integral part of the ancestral Mexican holistic "medical" know-how.

It is clear that "western medicine" and ancestral traditional medicine are different; and that African, American, Asian, and European religions have unique characteristics that make them dissimilar from one another. It is also understood that from the union, or clash of the parts of these world-views emerged other religions or medicines in the Americas; and that if one subtracts any of their elements they would cease to be the entity they are. To perceive with clarity the Mexican site of traditional medicine, it is a requirement to recognize all and each of its parts. When one subtracts the African diaspora from the Mexican experience, at best a distorted understanding of the phenomena is produced.

The diverse African perceptions that form part of the Mexican cultural dynamic pullulate as protons or neutrons of a new nucleus. They are a new sun that radiates light with the added energy of other energies that come from others that emerged from others and will feed others. One might ask, could water be "water" without one of its hydrogen or oxygen particles? Can the water be recognized through each one of its elements separately? African ancestral know-how with its very particular forces or vibrations provides sense, color, flavor, texture, aroma, sound, to this singular identity or ancestral form of knowing and being, sister to other identities that emerged in the Americas throughout the colonial period with the fundamental contribution of the African diaspora.

References

Aguirre Beltrán, Gonzalo. *Medicina y Magia: el proceso de aculturación en la estructura colonial.* México, D. F.: Fondo, 1992.

---. *La población negra de México. Estudio etnohistórico.* México, D.F.: Fondo, 1972 (1st ed. 1946).

Anderson, Benedict. *Imagined Communities: Reflections on the Origin and Spread of Nationalism.* New York: Verso, 2000 (1st ed. 1983).

Ashanti, Kwabena F. *Psychotechnology of Brainwashing: Crucifying Willie Lynch.* Durham: Tone, 2001 (1st ed. 1993).

Bradley Anderson, Jean. *Piedmont Plantation.* Durham: The Historic Preservation Society of Durham, 1985.

Cárdenas, Alejandra. *Hechicería, saber y trasgresión: afromestizas ante la Inquisición (Acapulco 1621-1622).* Chilpancingo, Guerrero: Self publication, 1997.

Clark, Mary Ann. "Material History of American Religion Project: Seven African Powers: Hybridity and Appropriation" http://www.materialreligion.org/journal
/candles.html 31 December 2006.

Davis, F. James. *Who is Black: One Nation's Definition*. University Park: Pennsylvania State University P, 1998 (1st ed. 1991).

Frigerio, Alejandro. "Outside the Nation, Outside the Diaspora: Accommodating Race and Religion in Argentina. (The 2001 Paul Hanly Furfey Lecture)."
http://www.highbeam.com/doc/1G1-92284222.html 31 December 2006.

González-Wippler, Migene. *Santería: la religión*. St. Paul: Llewellyn, 2004 (1st ed. 1999).

Hernández Cuevas, Marco Polo. *África en el Carnaval Mexicano*. México, D.F.: Plaza y Valdés, 2005.

"Imhotep 'Father of medicine' (2980 B.C.)". 16 January 2007. http://www.nbufront.org/
html/MastersMuseums/JHClarke/HistoricalPersonalities/hp2.html.

Murphy, Joseph M. *Working the Spirit: Ceremonies of the African Diaspora*. Boston: Beacon P, 2003 (1st ed. 1994).

Rius (Eduardo del río García). *El yerberito ilustrado*. México, D.F.: Posada, 1994 (30th ed.). "*Santería invade a México, La*". *El Nuevo Herald.* 29 September 2000.
http://www.latinamericanstudies.org/religion/santeria-mexico.htm

Scheffler, Lilian. *Magia y brujería en México*. México, D.F.: Panorama, XVII reprint, 2004 (1st ed. 1993).

Smart, Ian Isidore. "Carnival, the Ultimate Pan-African Festival". *Ah! Come Back Home: Perspectives on the Trinidad and Tobago Carnival*. Washington, D.C., Old World Press, 2000.

---. "*Literatura oral tradicional: el bunde y el bullerengue darienitas*". *Cosas jamás contadas*. Washington, DC: Forthcoming.

---. *New Orleans: Genocidal Negligence or Cosmic Reconciliation*. Washington, DC: Old World P, 2005.

"Spirituals Project at the University of Denver, The." 2004 Center for Teaching and Learning. 10 January 2007. <http://ctl.du.edu/spirituals/religion/>.

Thornton, Joseph, K. "Central Africa in the Era of the Slave Trade." *Slaves, Subjects and Subversives: Blacks in Colonial Latin America*. Albuquerque: U of New Mexico P, 2006.

Torres, Eliseo “Cheo”. *Mexican Folk: Medicine and Folk Beliefs: Curanderismo y yerbas medicinales.* <www.unm.edu/~cheo/Cheo’s folk healing page.htm>. 23 December 2006.

Wasson, Gordon R. “Notes on the Present Status of *Ololiuhqui* and the Other Hallucinogens of Mexico.” *Botanical Museum Leaflets, Harvard University.*
Vol. 20, No. 6, Nov. 22, 1963, pp. 161-212.

Zapata Olivella, Manuel. "*Omnipresencia africana en la civilización universal.*" *PALARA* (2000): 5-15.

---

[i] All translations from Spanish to English are mine unless otherwise specified.

[ii] For more information, see my prior works: *African Mexicans and the Discourse on Modern Nation*, Lanham: UP of America, 2004; *África en el Carnaval Mexicano*; México, D.F, Plaza y Valdés, 2005; and *África late en la mexicanidad*, Lewiston, E Mellen P, 2007.

[iii] *Criollos* are supposed to be the American offspring of peninsular Spanish parents. This however, often was not the case.

[iv] “Afro-(Latin)-American religions have spread beyond their original boundaries of race, class, and increasingly, nation, to attract an economically, ethnically and nationally diverse constituency. In the process, issues of race and nationality, which have always figured prominently in these religions' discourses -- as well as of those who wrote about them -- have now acquired even more relevance” (Frigerio 1).

[v] "Molefi Kete Asante coined the perspective as Afrocentrism in 1976. Afrocentrism, the same as all ideas, has a variety of tendencies, but for the present purpose, which is to give agency to the African voice of yesterday and today of Mexico that throbs in the shadows of silence and popular culture, means rediscovering African and African American achievements and restoring the place that Africa and Africans disserve in universal history the same as any other civilization [...]." (Hernández, *Africa en el carnaval*, 2).

[vi] For a closer look into the African presence and persistence in Mexico, see my work *África late en la mexicanidad*. Lewiston: E. Mellen P, 2007.

[vii] Although beyond the parameters of the present work, it should be noted that according to Ivan Van Sertima's theory articulated in *They Came Before Columbus*, the Olmec heads that are among other overwhelming evidence of the African presence in the Americas centuries before the Spanish presence in the 15th century de-myth-ify the Eurocentric account of history and exhibit the myth of the conquistador under a more appropriate light.

[viii] It should be mentioned that future works on the theme will include: “Los comics mexicanos *Hermelinda Linda* y *Aniceto Verduzco Platanares*: la

codificación de saberes ancestrales africanos", "Del Congo al congal: de yerberas a rameras", "El Nganga y la medicina de las fuerzas ancestrales en Veracruz", y "La moronga y otras medicinas preventivas mexicanas: comida de dioses".

[ix] Holistic comes from the Greek "*holos*:" all or whole. The holistic approach embraces simultaneously all of the characteristics that form an entity and the way in which all of its parts interact among themselves to produce the object, life, being, or such a particular or original idea that cannot be confused with any other (http://club.telepolis.com/agaigcu/conceptoholistico.htm).

[x] Many of the people of pre-Hispanic and pre-European origin in the Americas prefer to be called "First Nations."

[xi] John K. Thornton in "Central Africa in the Era of the Slave Trade" sheds new light by explaining that "the vast majority of the slaves delivered to the Spanish Indies during most of the 16th century came from Senegambia and Sierra Leone" (89).

[xii] Although officially denied it has been established that mestizos are Afrodescendants as well. This matter is further elucidated in the following pages of this work. See *African Mexicans and the Discourse on Modern Nation.* Langham: U P of America, 2004.

[xiii] According to Gordon R. Wasson: *picietl, peyotl, teonanactl,* and *ololuihqui,* were the four main hallucinogenics used by the First Nations people at the time of the Spanish [and African] arrival.

[xiv] Ted G. Vincent has called thus the Mexican War of Independence and the present work adopts this perspective.

[xv] For a greater insight on African Mexican oraliture, inclusive of the medicinal practices addressed here, see *África en el Carnaval Mexicano* (2005), Hernández Cuevas.

[xvi] F. James Davis points out that in Spanish America there were up to 64 classifications for the mixes (64).

[xvii] Aguirre Beltrán explains "these disinherited Spaniards that came running from the misery that they endured in the motherland, upon arrival to the colony were transformed into gentlemen, forced by the psychological climate of deep economical roots that made of the Peninsular man, whether a nobleman or plebeian, whether he was blond or dark skinned, a European, a staunch defender of a metropolis where he, oh paradox!, he was starving to death" (*La población* 214).

[xviii] The phonetic closeness to *Marcumbé* must be noticed. *Marcumbé* is a musical piece from *Tierra Caliente* whose words are: *Este es el Maracumbé/ El rey de todos los sones/ Querido de las mujeres/ Y apreciado de los hombres/ Este es el Maracumbé./ De tierras abajo vengo/ Pa' rezar una novena./ Ahora que vengo santito/ Ven abrázame morena./ De tierras abajo vengo./ Estaba el Maracumbé/ Tomándose una copita./ Por el amor que le tiene/ A una muchacha bonita/ Estaba el Maracumbé/Tariacuri soy, señores/ De la tierra Michoacana/ Y vengo cantando sones/ Al compás de mi jarana/ Tariacuri soy, señores.*

[xix] Johnny Webster's explanations of this subject allowed me to articulate this subtle form of violence that nevertheless permeates the European and Eurocentric discourses, languages and worldviews; and constitutes perhaps the greater barrier to be deconstructed to level the plain for everyone.
[xx] According to Manuel Zapata Olivella "The creative intelligence of the *Homosapiens Africano* was the original spring of culture" (7-8). He traces the origin of humanity to Northeast Africa two million years ago (8).

Notes on Contributors

Miguel Arnedo-Gómez holds a PhD from the University of London and is a Senior Lecturer in the Spanish Programme of the School of Languages and Cultures at Victoria University Wellington in New Zealand. His research focuses on the connections between Latin American literary works and the socio-cultural characteristics of the societies in which they are produced, with a particular focus on the representation of race and ethnicity and the literary incorporation of African or indigenous cultural elements. Dr Arnedo-Gómez is the author of *Writing Rumba: The AfroCubanista Movement in Poetry* (2006) and is currently working on a book project entitled *Cuban Blacks, National Identity and Afro-Cuban Culture in the Poetry of Nicolás Guillén.*

Mario Chandler is associate professor of Spanish at Oglethorpe University. He holds a B.A. from Iowa State University and a PhD from the University of Georgia. Professor Chandler's research and teaching interests are Medieval and Golden Age Spain with particular emphasis on their trans-Atlantic and Afro-Hispanic connections.

Lance Cowie is the founder and director of CENLAC at the University of the West Indies, St. Augustine, Trinidad and Tobago. Dr Cowie received his PhD from the University of the West Indies, Mona in 1976 and has since published numerous articles and books on a wide range of cultural issues in Latin America.

Dr. Marco Polo Hernandez Cuevas holds a Ph.D. in Hispanic and Italian Studies from the University of British Columbia, an MA. in Spanish Language and Peninsular and Latin American literatures and a BA. from Portland State University. He has written five books in English and Spanish: *African Mexicans and The Discourse on Modern Nation* (Lanham: UP of America, 2004); *Africa en el carnaval mexicano* (*Africa in Mexican Carnival*) (Mexico D.F.: Plaza y Valdes, 2005); *Africa en Mexico:una herencia repudiada* (*Africa in Mexico: A Repudiated Heritage*) (Lewiston: E Mellen P, 2007); *The Africanization of Mexico From the Sixteenth Century Onward: A Review of the Evidence*

(Lewiston: E Mellen P. 2010); and *Eternidad* (*Eternity*) a collection of his own poetry (Mexico D.F.: Plaza y Valdes. 2010). Dr. Hernandez has also produced and directed a series of short films.

Conrad James holds a PhD from the University of Cambridge. He teaches Caribbean literature, history and cinema at the University of Birmingham.

Dr. Alain Lawo-Sukam is an Assistant Professor of Hispanic and Africana Studies at Texas A&M University. He holds a Ph.D. in Spanish from the University of Illinois at Urbana-Champaign. His area of concentration is Latin American Literature and Culture with special interests in Afro-Latin American Literatures and Cultures, Afro-French Literature and Culture, Post-Colonial Cultural Studies and Ecocriticism. He is the author of several articles published in peer reviewed journals such as *Revista Iberoamericana, Revista Hispánica de Literatura y Cultura*, *Revista de Literatura Hispánica* and *Revista de Estudios Colombíanos*. He has also published his own poetry in the *Afro-Hispanic Review* and *Collar de la paloma*. He is currently completing a book-length project entitled *Hacia una poética afro-colombiana: El caso del Pacífico* and a collection of poetry entitled *Cantos a África*.

Emily Maguire is associate professor of modern Latin American literature and culture at Northwestern University. She is affiliated with the Latin American and Caribbean Studies Program and the Latino Studies Program. Her book, *Artist Ethnographers: Racial Experiments in Cuban National Narrative,* explores Cuban writers in the first half of the twentieth century who forged a literary space in which to write the nation by drawing from two forms of expression, ethnography and literature, in their re-valorization of Afro-Cuban culture as the source of Cuban-ness. She has published articles on Afro-Cuban poetry, the translation of Négritude, the place of poetic declamation in black internationalism, and Cuban cyberpunk writing. Her new project examines the uses of science fiction in Caribbean literature.

Lourdes Martínez-Echazábal is professor of Literature and provost at Merrill College, University of California at Santa Cruz. Born and raised on the island of Cuba she moved to the United States in 1970. She received a Master`s degree in History (nineteenth century African and Caribbean histories) in 1980, and a Ph.D. in Latin American literature in 1984, from the University of California San Diego. Her broad area of specialization is twentieth-century Caribbean and Latin American literatures and cultural studies. Central to her research on Caribbean and Latin American writings and other forms of cultural expressions are issues of national, racial, cultural, and gender identity formation (and transformations) in an area broadly termed "Afroamérica." Professor Martínez-Echazábal is the author of Para una semiótica de la mulatez (1990) and guest editor of a Special Issue of Afro Hispanic Review 22, dedicated to the late "Afro-Cuban" writer Manuel Granados. Spring 2005.

Claudette Rosegreen-Williams is Professor of Spanish, deputy dean of the Faculty of Humanities and Education and director of the Institute of Caribbean Studies at the University of the West Indies, Mona campus. Professor Williams holds a PhD from Stanford University and in addition to numerous articles on Latin American literature she is author of Charcoal and Cinnamon: The Politics of Colour in Spanish Caribbean Literature (2000).

Victor C. Simpson was born in Barbados and received his PhD in Spanish from The University of the West Indies. He has taught a number of courses in Peninsular Spanish, Hispanic Caribbean and Spanish American literatures. His area of specialization is the literature and culture of Puerto Rico. He is the author of *Colonialism and Narrative in Puerto Rico* (Peter Lang, 2004) and *Afro-Puerto Ricans in the Short Story* (Peter Lang, 2006), as well as a number of articles on Puerto Rican literature and culture. He also has a strong interest in translation and several of his academic translations have been published. Dr Simpson is senior lecturer in Spanish and deputy dean (outreach) at UWI (Cave Hill).

Antonio Tillis is Associate Professor and Chair of the African and African American Studies Program at Dartmouth College. Dr.

Tillis, studied at Vanderbilt University, Howard University and the University of Missouri Columbia where he received his PhD. His areas of expertise are, among others, Latin American, Afro-Hispanic, US Latino, African Diaspora and Comparative Literatures, Film Studies and Contemporary Critical Theory. Professor Tillis is author of *Manuel Zapata Olivella and the "Darkening" of Latin American Literature* (2005).

Index

www.ingramcontent.com/pod-product-compliance
Lightning Source LLC
Chambersburg PA
CBHW060529310726
48982CB00002B/477

9781906704889